The Psychology of Citizenship and Civic Engagement

The Psychology of Citizenship and Civic Engagement

S. MARK PANCER

UNIVERSITY PRESS

OXFORD
UNIVERSITY PRESS

Oxford University Press is a department of the University of Oxford.
It furthers the University's objective of excellence in research,
scholarship, and education by publishing worldwide.

Oxford New York
Auckland Cape Town Dar es Salaam Hong Kong Karachi
Kuala Lumpur Madrid Melbourne Mexico City Nairobi
New Delhi Shanghai Taipei Toronto

With offices in
Argentina Austria Brazil Chile Czech Republic France Greece
Guatemala Hungary Italy Japan Poland Portugal Singapore
South Korea Switzerland Thailand Turkey Ukraine Vietnam

Oxford is a registered trademark of Oxford University Press
in the UK and certain other countries.

Published in the United States of America by
Oxford University Press
198 Madison Avenue, New York, NY 10016

Library of Congress Cataloging-in-Publication Data
Pancer, S. Mark.
The psychology of citizenship and civic engagement / S. Mark Pancer.
pages cm
ISBN 978-0-19-975212-6 (hardback)
1. Citizenship—Psychological aspects. 2. Political participation—Psychological
aspects. 3. Community development—Psychological aspects. 4. Political psychology. I. Title.
JF801.P298 2015
323.6019—dc23
2014024194

For Ruth

While I was sitting at my computer, writing about civic engagement, Ruth was out in the community, doing it.

CONTENTS

ACKNOWLEDGMENTS

This book is about people's connections with community and how these connections can enrich their lives. I have been fortunate to be a member of several communities, each of which has enriched my life immeasurably. One of these is the community of researchers and students with whom I have worked since I first became interested in the topic of civic participation, more than two decades ago. Their names are on many of the publications described in the pages that follow. They include Geoff Nelson, Mike Pratt, Bruce Hunsberger, Steve Brown, Thanh Tieu, Trevor Taylor, Mark Baetz, Linda Rose-Krasnor, Gary Cameron, Karen Hayward, Susan Alisat, Ailsa Henderson, Leslea Peirson, Enoch Landau, Evelina Rog, Dianne Heise-Bennett, Michael Busseri, Lisa Loiselle, Julian Hasford, Ray Peters, and Colleen Loomis, among others. This community of researchers and scholars also includes those whose work has inspired me and many others to do research on this important topic—people like Connie Flanagan, the quintessential builder of scholarly communities; Jim Youniss, the intellectual grandparent of this field of study who enthusiastically supported my writing of this book from the time I first described it to him in idea form; and Shep Zeldin, whose ground-breaking work on youth participation in organizational decision making serves as a model of research and practice.

I have also been fortunate to be a part of a faith community—Reform Judaism—that has contributed considerably to my ideas about, and commitment to, civic engagement. My links with Temple Shalom—and with people like Charlie and Susie Rothschild, Laura Wolfson, Wendy Weinberg, Andrea Leis, Bob Chodos, Eli and Bluma Teram, and Carol McMullen—have helped instill in me a strong sense of social justice and a profound feeling of belonging that comes from being embedded in a loving and caring community.

One of my greatest joys in life has been making music with others, and I am grateful to the community of musicians with whom I have had the pleasure of playing and singing over the years. They, too, have taught me about the importance of community and the support it provides in times of both joy and sorrow. I am grateful to all the members of the Fair Wind, Single Malt, MT3, and Neshama and to my other musical friends—particularly Tom Wood, Trevor Friesen, Tom Kelly, Carole Pines, Bob Mino, Joanne McAuley, Ruth Shushan, Laura Wolfson, Wendy Weinberg, and Chuck Ander—for their musical talents but, more important, for their friendship and generosity of spirit.

I would also like to express my gratitude to Sarah Harrington and Andrea Zekus, of Oxford University Press, for their encouragement and their patience while waiting (a long time!) for me to finish this book.

The embryo of community is the family, and I have been blessed by the love and support of a wonderful family—my sons, Jordie and Matt Pancer; my step-daughter, Rachel Woods; and my wife, Ruth Shushan. It is to Ruth that this book is dedicated.

The Psychology of Citizenship and Civic Engagement

1

Citizenship and Civic Engagement

An Introduction

The 2008 federal election in the United States was seen as an historic event, not only in America but also all over the world. It was the first time that an African American had run in the general election for president, and many viewed the Democratic Party's candidate, Barack Obama, as a champion of those who had suffered under the harsh policies of the previous administration. One would think that such a watershed election would bring droves of people to the polls on election day. So how many people did turn out to vote? Only a little over 60% of eligible voters cast a ballot in the election. Other countries have fared even worse. In the Canadian federal election that same year, fewer than 59% of eligible individuals voted, the lowest turnout in Canadian history. Most alarming was the voting rate among the youngest Canadians; only about 1 in 5 of young first-time voters cast a ballot. Choosing political representatives through voting is one of the most important rights of citizens in a healthy democracy. What then, does such low voter turnout say about the health of the democratic process in countries such as the United States and Canada?

Voting is a complex behavior. Whether a person votes, and how that person votes, is influenced by many factors, including the person's gender, ethnic and cultural background, socioeconomic status, group memberships, and personal values, as well as how individuals have been influenced by their family and friends and by the barrage of campaign messages directed at voters through the media. It is exactly this kind of complex behavior that psychology, the science of behavior, was developed to understand. Research in several areas of psychology can do much to inform us about civic behaviors such as voting. In the area of political psychology, for example, several studies have attempted to identify some of the key factors that deter people from voting. One of the factors seems to be the prevalence of negative advertising in contemporary political campaigns. The broadcast media are rife with "attack ads" in which candidates seem to be more intent on maligning their opponents' character than criticizing their policies or political platform. Research in political psychology shows that negative advertising increases citizens' lack of trust in government, and it dampens people's inclination to go out and vote. Interestingly, it also indicates that negative ads tend to tarnish the image not only of the victim of the attack but of the perpetrator of the attack as well (Lau, Sigelman & Rovner, 2007; Allen & Burell, 2002; Pancer & Landau, 2009). Research in political psychology, it would seem, has important implications for our understanding of some of the key factors that may explain why some people might not participate in one of the most fundamental of civic activities—voting.

Citizenship and Civic Engagement

Voting is a key component of citizenship. It is seen as one of the most important rights and responsibilities that a citizen of a democratic country has. Indeed, it is considered so important that several countries, such as Australia and Argentina, make it compulsory under law for every citizen to vote in national elections. Failure to vote is against the law, and brings a penalty. But voting is only one aspect of citizenship. Dictionary definitions of citizenship typically describe two kinds of meaning associated with the term. One is a legalistic meaning, in which citizenship is a legal status that individuals in a country may enjoy, that has associated with it certain rights and privileges (such as the right to vote). The other has to do with "the qualities that a person is expected to have as a responsible member of a community" (Merriam-Webster, n.d.), or, in other words, how individuals *behave* as members of their community. It is a person's *behavior* as a citizen that determines what kind of citizen that individual is. Someone who is a good citizen would be expected to vote in an informed and responsible manner, certainly, but a good citizen would also be expected to do other things, as well. Such a person would take an active role in making decisions that affect the community, help others by doing volunteer work, keep informed about people and events in the community, participate in neighborhood organizations, or perform many other activities that have as their purpose the enhancement of life for all members of the community. Some have used the term "active" citizenship to describe this kind of citizenship. Bryony Hoskins and Massimiliano Mascherini (2009), of the European Commission's Joint Research Centre, define active citizenship as

> *participation in civil society, community and/or political life, characterized by mutual respect and non-violence and in accordance with human rights and democracy.* (p. 462)

Hoskins and Mascherini see active citizenship as encompassing four spheres of activity. The first of these spheres is "representative democracy." In this sphere, a person would practice active citizenship by voting, becoming involved with a political party, or working with elected representatives or government officials, for example. The second sphere is "community life." The person demonstrating active citizenship in community life would be someone who supports and enriches his or her community by donating money, for example, performing volunteer work, or participating in religious, cultural, business, educational, or sports organizations. The third sphere of activity that Hoskins and Mascherini discuss has to do with "protest and social change" (see also Watts & Flanagan, 2007). In this sphere, active citizens work toward community betterment and social justice by participating in activities such as protests, boycotts, demonstrations, and strikes. The fourth sphere of active citizenship has to do with "democratic values." Underlying all actions of the active citizen must be values that are consistent with bettering the condition of all members of the community. These include values such as democratic participation, human rights, and nondiscrimination.

Closely related to the notion of citizenship is the concept of civic engagement. One of the most commonly cited definitions of civic engagement is by Michael Delli Carpini, formerly of the Pew Trusts, who describes it as "individual and collective actions designed to identify and address issues of public concern" (Delli Carpini, 1996). The focus of Delli Carpini's definition is clearly on activities that are aimed at dealing with social problems. His notion of civic engagement encompasses activities such as "working in a soup kitchen, serving on a neighborhood association, writing a letter to an elected official or voting." Thomas Ehrlich, in his book, *Civic Responsibility and Higher Education* (Ehrlich, 2000), provides a somewhat broader definition of civic engagement:

> *Civic engagement means working to make a difference in the civic life of our communities and developing the combination of knowledge, skills, values and motivation to make that difference. It means promoting the quality of life in a community through both political and non-political processes.* (p. vi)

Ehrlich's definition of civic engagement would include all activities aimed at enhancing the quality of life in a community, not just those designed to address social problems. These activities would include things such as participation in arts or cultural activities and organizations, activities that certainly enhance a community's quality of life, but have nothing directly to do with "issues of public concern."

Perhaps the best way to gain an understanding of what is meant by citizenship and civic engagement is to look at how these constructs have been measured. One of the most comprehensive measures of civic engagement is the survey instrument developed under the auspices of the Center for Information and Research on Civic Learning and Engagement (CIRCLE). This survey was administered to a nationally representative sample of Americans in order to assess the "civic and political health" of American society (Keeter, Zukin, Andolina & Jenkins, 2002; Lopez, Levine, Both, Kiesa, Kirby & Marcelo, 2006). The CIRCLE survey contains 19 items, divided into three categories. One category has to do with "civic activities" that involve helping people and improving the local community. It includes behaviors such as doing volunteer work or working with a local group to solve a community problem. A second category focuses on "electoral activities" that revolve around the political process, and includes behaviors such as voting or persuading other people to vote for a certain candidate or party. The third category concerns "political voice" activities in which people express their viewpoints on significant social issues by doing things such as protesting or boycotting a particular product. Table 1.1 lists the 19 core indicators of civic engagement used in the CIRCLE survey and the questions used to tap civic engagement.

Much of my own research has focused on civic engagement in young people. In order to assess civic participation in youth, I and my colleagues have developed our own measure of civic engagement—the Youth Inventory of Involvement (YII) (Pancer, Pratt, Hunsberger & Alisat, 2007). This measure asks respondents to indicate on a five-point scale, ranging from "never did this" to "did this a lot," how often over the previous year they have engaged in each of 30 activities. These activities represent a broad range of behaviors that we considered to demonstrate different aspects of civic engagement. We ask respondents to indicate how often they have helped people in their community by visiting those who were ill or taking care of children (without pay). We ask them how often they have participated in sports, ethnic, cultural, or arts groups in their school or neighborhood. We also ask how often they have been involved in traditional political activities, such as working on a political campaign, and how often they have expressed their political "voice" by participating in protest marches, signing a petition, or other activities. Table 1.2 shows the full YII measure.

We and others have administered this measure to thousands of young people. In one of our studies (the "Futures Project"), we had nearly a thousand students from 16 Canadian high schools complete the YII when they were in their second-to-last year of high school. We calculated a total score for each respondent, as well as four subscale scores: a political involvement score (calculated by summing their responses on all items having to do with political activities), a community involvement score (the sum of the rated level of involvement in activities such as organizing a community event), a helping activity score (the sum of ratings on activities that involved providing care for others, such as taking care of children), and a "passive" involvement score (the sum of ratings on activities that usually involve responding to requests rather than actively initiating something, such as signing a petition or giving money to a cause). We then used these subscale scores in a cluster analysis, which placed students who had similar scores on each of the subscales into different groups or clusters. This analysis revealed four types of

Table 1.1 **Civic Engagement Questions from the Center for Information and Research on Civic Learning and Engagement (CIRCLE) Civic and Political Health Survey**

Indicator	*Survey Question*
Civic Activity Indicators	
Community problem solving	Have you ever worked together informally with someone or some group to solve a problem in the community where you live?
Regular volunteering for a non-electoral organization	Have you ever spent time participating in any community service or volunteer activity, or haven't you had time to do this? By volunteer activity, I mean actually working in some way to help others for no pay.
Active membership in a group or association	Do you belong to or donate money to any groups or associations, either locally or nationally? Are you an active member of this group/any of these groups, a member but not active, or have you given money only?
Participation on a fund raising run/walk/ride	Have you personally walked, ran, or bicycled for a charitable cause?
Other fund raising or charity	Have you ever done anything else to help raise money for a charitable cause?
Electoral Activity Indicators	
Regular voting	Can you tell me how often you vote in local and national elections? Always, sometimes, rarely, or never?
Persuading others	When there is an election taking place do you generally talk to any people and try to show them why they should vote for or against one of the parties or candidates, or not?
Displaying buttons, signs, stickers	Do you wear a campaign button, put a sticker on your car, or place a sign in front of your house, or aren't these things you do?
Campaign contributions	In the past 12 months, did you contribute money to a candidate, a political party, or any organization that supported candidates?

(continued)

Table 1.1 **(Continued)**

Indicator	*Survey Question*
Volunteering for candidates or political organizations	From volunteer sequence, respondent indicated having volunteered for "A political organization or candidates running for office"
Political Voice Indicators	
Contacting officials	Have you contacted or visited a public official—at any level of government—to ask for assistance or to express your opinion?
Contacting the print media	Have you contacted a newspaper or magazine to express your opinion on an issue?
Contacting the broadcast media	Have you called in to a radio or television talk show to express your opinion on a political issue, even if you did not get on the air?
Protesting	Have you taken part in a protest, march, or demonstration?
E-mail petitions	Have you signed an e-mail petition?
Written petitions	Have you ever signed a written petition about a political or social issue?
Boycotting	Have you NOT bought something because of conditions under which the product is made, or because you dislike the conduct of the company that produces it?
Buycotting	Have you bought a certain product or service because you like the social or political values of the company that produces or provides it?
Canvassing	Have you worked as a canvasser—having gone door-to-door for a political or social group or candidate?

students: Activists, who had high scores on every type of involvement; Helpers, who had high scores on the "helping activity" subscale but were not very politically involved; Responders, who helped or participated when asked to do so (as indicated by their relatively high scores on the passive involvement subscale) but were otherwise not very involved; and the Uninvolved, who had the lowest scores on every subscale. The cluster analysis we did allowed us to determine how many young people were in each cluster. Only about 8% were Activists. The Helpers

Table 1.2 **Youth Inventory of Involvement**

The following is a list of school, community, and political activities that people can get involved in. For each of these activities, please use the following scale to indicate whether in the last year:

0—You never did this	3—You did this a fair bit
1—You did this once or twice	4—You did this a lot
2—You did this a few times	

1. Visited or helped out people who were sick
2. Took care of other families' children (on an unpaid basis)
3. Participated in a church-connected group
4. Participated in or helped a charity organization
5. Participated in an ethnic club or organization
6. Participated in a political party, club or organization
7. Participated in a social or cultural group or organization (e.g., a choir)
8. Participated in a school academic club or team
9. Participated in a sports team or club
10. Led or helped out with a children's group or club
11. Helped with a fund-raising project
12. Helped organize neighborhood or community events (e.g., carnivals, hot dog days, potluck dinners)
13. Helped prepare and make verbal and written presentations to organizations, agencies, conferences, or politicians
14. Did things to help improve your neighborhood (e.g., helped clean neighborhood)
15. Gave help (e.g., money, food, clothing, rides) to friends or classmates who needed it
16. Served as a member of an organizing committee or board for a school club or organization
17. Wrote a letter to a school or community newspaper or publication
18. Signed a petition
19. Attended a demonstration

20 Collected signatures for a petition drive

21. Contacted a public official by phone or mail to tell him or her how you felt about a particular issue

(continued)

Table 1.2 **(Continued)**

22. Joined in a protest march, meeting, or demonstration
23. Got information about community activities from a local community information center
24. Volunteered at a school event or function
25. Helped people who were new to your country
26. Gave money to a cause
27. Worked on a political campaign
28. Ran for a position in student government
29. Participated in a discussion about a social or political issue
30. Volunteered with a community service organization

formed the largest proportion of the students, at 35% of the total. Responders constituted 25% of the total. Uninvolved students made up the second largest cluster of students, at 32% of the total.

In addition to having students complete the YII (and other measures), we also asked several of the students from each cluster to take part in a face-to-face interview, in which we questioned them about their community and political involvements. Their responses during this interview corresponded highly with their scores on the YII and to their cluster assignments. The following is an exchange between the interviewer and an Activist student:

INTERVIEWER: *Some people like to be really involved in the life of their school or their community. Do you consider yourself to be the kind of person who gets involved in your school or your community?*

STUDENT: *I would say yes, big time...I'm on student council here, I volunteer at the library, Sunday school teacher, I could probably go on and on about all this stuff, but hey, the tape's not long enough...I would say I'm pretty active [in] community, school, church...just about everything.*

Contrast this with the response given by one of the Uninvolved students:

INTERVIEWER: *Some people like to be really involved in the life of their school or their community. Do you consider yourself to be the kind of person who gets involved in your school or your community in this way?*

STUDENT: *Not really no.*

INTERVIEWER: *Have you been involved in any activities or anything, or special events or anything?*
STUDENT: *No, not that I can remember... I don't think I ever did anything.*

Why Is Citizenship Important?

Citizenship and civic engagement are important for many reasons. In the study I just described, we found several substantial differences between young people who were civically engaged and those who were not. The Activists and Helpers had higher levels of self-esteem, a greater sense of optimism, more social support, a greater sense of social responsibility, and more advanced identity development than the Uninvolved individuals. These results are consistent with many, many other studies (to be described in later chapters) that show that people who are civically engaged tend to be better adjusted, socially and emotionally, than individuals who are not civically engaged. While most of these studies are correlational, making it difficult to say with certainty that civic engagement causes better social and psychological health (rather than saying that psychological well-being leads to greater engagement), there are several experimental studies that indicate that civic engagement is indeed a causal factor in this relationship.

Civic engagement is linked not only to the health of individual citizens; it is strongly linked to the health of communities, as well. The noted writer and social activist Jane Jacobs, in her book *Dark Age Ahead* (Jacobs, 2004), claimed that community is one of five pillars of a healthy society, and that the most important resource of a community is "speaking relationships, among neighbors and acquaintances in addition to friends" (p. 35). These relationships and networks of acquaintances are acquired through civic engagement. They make available many critical skills that individuals and families cannot provide for themselves, skills that help community members thrive and survive. Jacobs claimed that people's lack of connection with other members of their community has placed the pillar of community in grave danger and threatens to push us into another dark age of cultural collapse.

Robert Putnam, political scientist and professor of public policy at Harvard University, makes similar claims in his seminal book, *Bowling Alone: The Collapse and Revival of American Community* (Putnam, 2000). Putnam takes a broad view of civic engagement. He sees evidence of civic engagement in people joining bowling leagues, attending church or synagogue, participating in civic organizations such as parent-teacher associations, being active members of a union, making donations, doing volunteer work, or even getting together informally with friends and neighbors. He contends that all of these activities produce social capital—"connections among individuals—social networks and the norms of reciprocity and trustworthiness that arise from them" (p. 19). This social capital, like physical or human capital, affects individual and group productivity. More important, though, it also has a profound impact on the health and welfare of entire communities. By looking across American states at things such as turnout in presidential elections, the number of civic and social organizations per 1,000 people, and individuals' responses to questions on national surveys asking how often they did volunteer work in the previous year, Putnam was able to construct an index of social capital and assign a score to every state. When he looked at the relationship between states' scores on his social capital index and several different indices of health and well-being, he found a very high correlation. States with high levels of social capital (and high levels of civic participation) had less violent crime, healthier babies, fewer school drop-outs, lower teen pregnancy rates, better school achievement, and better physical health than states with lower levels of social capital.

Perhaps the most striking set of findings that Putnam reviews in his book is that, by almost any index one would use, the level of civic engagement has been falling dramatically over the last 30 years. Over this period there has been a steady decline in membership in parent-teacher associations, church attendance, union membership, participation in professional associations, league bowling, and even in the amount of "schmoozing" (informal social interaction) that occurs among friends and neighbors. Accompanying this decline in civic engagement has been a corresponding reduction in "social trust"—the extent to which individuals feel that most people in their community are honest and can be trusted. Putnam's research, along with a growing body of work that examines well-being at a community, state, and even national level, provides strong evidence that civic engagement influences the health of communities, as well as individuals.

What Does Psychology Have to Tell Us about Citizenship?

The purpose of this book is to look at what research in psychology and related social science disciplines tells us about how civic engagement develops, the major factors that influence its development, and the impact that civic involvement can have on individuals, communities, and society. Theory and research in several areas of psychology have a great deal to contribute to our understanding of citizenship and civic engagement. In social psychology, research on topics such as attitudes and values, interpersonal relationships, social influence, and social identity help us understand how individuals relate to others in their community and come to see themselves as citizens. In developmental psychology, a prominent area of theory and research is moral development, including the ways in which young people begin to develop a sense of social responsibility (e.g., Youniss & Yates,

1997). In community psychology, a core principle guiding theory and research is that when citizens participate as partners in the development of social programs, not only will they benefit more from these programs but also better programs will result (Pancer & Cameron, 1994; Zimmerman & Rappaport, 1988). Political psychology has been concerned with topics such as nationalism and patriotism (e.g., Kosterman & Feshbach, 1989), voting behavior (e.g., Krampen, 2000), and political activism (e.g., Miller & Krosnick, 2004), all key elements of citizenship. These areas of theory and research, from four subdisciplines, represent only a portion of the work in psychology that is directly relevant to an understanding of the ways in which individuals think of themselves as citizens and participate in civic institutions and organizations. Work in several other areas of psychology, and in closely related social science disciplines such as political science and sociology, can also enhance our understanding of civic engagement. In what follows, I provide examples of work in a number of subdisciplines of psychology that relate to citizenship and civic engagement.

Developmental Psychology

Developmental psychology is the branch of psychology that studies how individuals change and mature, cognitively, emotionally, and socially, throughout their lives. Developmental psychologists are also concerned with the various contexts (such as families, schools, and neighborhoods) in which these changes occur and how these contexts affect the way people develop. One core area of research and theory in developmental psychology is moral development. How do individuals develop a sense of what is right and wrong? How do people learn to accommodate their own needs to the needs of others and to have empathy and sympathy for others? Theories in developmental psychology suggest that children adopt societal standards of what is considered right behavior through a process of "internalization" in which they come to take a societal norm or standard and adopt it as their own. Helping others is a civic behavior that is learned in this manner. Children learn to help by observing other people (in the first instance, their parents) helping others and then by imitating the helping behavior that they have seen (and sometimes being rewarded for their imitative behavior).

Several studies have demonstrated this process. In one classic study, Joan Grusec and Sandra Skubiski (1970) had third- and fifth-grade children come individually to a mobile laboratory parked in their schoolyard, ostensibly to try out a new bowling game that had been developed for children and adults. Each child played the game along with an adult of the same sex. If the child or adult playing the game achieved a certain score, they were given marbles that they could trade in for prizes at the end of the game. The more marbles they got, the better the prize they would receive. But across the room from the bowling game was a table on which sat a big blue bowl containing several marbles. A picture beside the bowl showed a young girl wearing rags. The child and adult playing the game were told that, if they wanted, they could donate some of the marbles they won so that some of the toys that were used as prizes could be given to poor children like the girl in the picture. The adult then played the game first, won 10 marbles (an outcome pre-arranged by the experimenters), and dropped half of them into the blue bowl for the poor children. The child then played the game, and it was arranged that he or she would win 14 marbles. The researchers found that children who had been exposed to the adult model donating to charity gave an average of 4 marbles to the poor, while children in a control condition who played the game on their own without witnessing an adult model donating, gave an average of fewer than 1 marble to the poor. A later study, conducted by Marnie Rice and Joan Grusec (1975), showed that children who had observed a charitable adult were more likely to behave charitably themselves even four months after they had observed the adult making a donation.

This kind of learning leads to the internalization of an important standard of behavior known as the "norm of social responsibility," which dictates that we should help those who are in need and who are dependent on us. Given the results of studies like those conducted by Grusec and her colleagues, it is no surprise that there is a strong correspondence between the extent to which parents engage in civic behaviors such as donating or volunteering and the extent to which their children engage in these behaviors, as well. These studies in the area of moral development, and research and theory in many other areas of developmental psychology, have much to tell us about the roots of civic engagement and the influence of environmental factors such as family context on how civic involvement develops.

Community Psychology

Community psychology is a subdiscipline of psychology that focuses on the interaction between individuals and the communities in which they live. The main goal of community psychology is to enhance the well-being of communities through psychological research, theory, and practice. Unlike those working in other areas of psychology, community psychologists operate on the basis of several core values. They consider it important to see social problems from an ecological perspective in which harsh social environments (in addition to individual factors) are potential causes of these problems; work to prevent problems rather than deal with them only after they have arisen; look at the strengths of individuals and communities, rather than focus only on their deficiencies, and work to build these strengths; recognize and respect diversity in the populations with whom they work; foster social change to enhance the health of communities; work toward social justice and a more equitable allocation of resources to oppressed and marginalized groups in society; and work in partnership with those who are suffering from social, emotional, and physical problems, as well as other community stakeholders, to develop solutions to these problems (Nelson & Prilleltensky, 2010).

The participation of community residents in neighborhood organizations is a key element of civic engagement that has been the focus of a great deal of research in community psychology. Community psychologist Abraham Wandersman and his colleagues have done some of the earliest and most significant work in this area. In one study (Prestby, Wandersman, Florin, Rich & Chavis, 1990), questionnaires that asked individuals about the benefits and costs of participation in neighborhood associations were administered to over 400 individuals, each of whom belonged to one of 29 different block associations in New York City. Two kinds of benefits were assessed in the questionnaire. Respondents were asked to indicate the extent to which participation in the block association produced personal benefits (e.g., by allowing them to save money, learn new skills, or gain information) and/or social-communal benefits (e.g., by allowing them to make friends, gain recognition, receive support, help others, improve the block, or fulfill a responsibility or obligation). Respondents were also asked to indicate the costs of participating in their neighborhood association. Two kinds of costs were assessed: personal costs (e.g., need for child care, time required to participate, need to attend night meetings) and social-organizational costs (e.g., need to give up activities with friends or family, not feeling welcome, disagreeing with organizational goals, not seeing any organizational accomplishments). The results indicated that both perceived benefits and perceived costs related to level of participation, although benefits were more important determinants of level of participation than were costs. Individuals who participated more reported receiving significantly greater benefits from their participation. Learning new skills and gaining information were the benefits that best discriminated among the various levels of participation. This study demonstrates how community psychology, with its focus on people's links with their community, can inform us about civic engagement and how communities can foster civic participation.

Social Psychology

Social psychology is the subdiscipline of psychology that deals with the way in which our thoughts, feelings, and behaviors are affected by other people and social situations (Allport, 1985). Social psychologists study topics such as attitudes and values, social influence, interpersonal relationships, and how individuals' membership in the various groups to which they belong affects their behavior toward members of their own groups and outsiders. One aspect of interpersonal relationships that is closely related to civic engagement, and that has been much studied by social psychologists, is altruism or pro-social behavior. Research on altruism began in the mid-1960s, sparked by an incident that horrified many because it seemingly showed how apathetic and disengaged people could be. A young woman named Kitty Genovese, on the night of March 13, 1964, had returned home from work in the early morning, and was walking from her car to her apartment building in the Queens area of New York when she was brutally (and fatally) attacked by a knife-wielding assailant. The attack lasted for over half an hour, and the *New York Times* reported that 38 people in Genovese's apartment building had heard her screams during the attack, but had done nothing. The *Times* article blamed the lack of response on citizen apathy, but social psychologists John Darley and Bibb Latané thought that there were other factors that might have prevented people from intervening. They conducted a series of studies (see Latané & Darley, 1970) that suggested that the people who witnessed the attack *were* concerned but didn't know what to do, and they failed to act because they took their cue from others who they knew must also have heard the screams but had not acted because they were also waiting to see what others would do. The research showed that social influence plays an important part in determining whether individuals will intervene when they see someone in need of help.

Darley and Latané's work spawned a large body of research into the factors that influence altruistic behavior. Some of the more recent research in this area has looked at a more common and ubiquitous form of helping than bystander intervention—the kind of helping that people engage in when they perform volunteer work. In one such study, social psychologists Allen Omoto and Mark Snyder (1995) developed a survey to tap the kinds of motivation that prompted people to work as volunteers with individuals who had AIDS. The survey, which was completed by 116 AIDS volunteers, asked them to indicate how important each of 30 factors was in motivating them to begin volunteering with an AIDS organization. Five major kinds of motivation were represented by the items in the survey: personal values ("because of my humanitarian obligation to help others"); understanding ("to understand AIDS and what it does to people"); personal development ("to challenge myself and test my skills"); community concern ("to help members of the gay community"); and esteem enhancement ("to feel better about myself"). The researchers also used a follow-up survey and agency records to get an estimate of how long the respondents volunteered with the AIDS organization. The results of the study indicated that the kinds of motivation that were most important in determining how long individuals volunteered with the AIDS organization were those relating to understanding and personal development. Those who volunteered in order to learn about AIDS and to enhance their own skills and understanding volunteered for longer periods than those who were motivated by other things. This study illustrates how research in social psychology can help inform us about key factors that influence civic behaviors such as volunteering.

Political Psychology

Political psychology is a relatively new subdiscipline of both psychology and political science that uses psychological theory, research, and constructs to examine political behavior and processes. Political psychologists have examined a wide range of phenomena, including international conflict, election campaigns, nationalism, political extremism, and terrorism. Civic engagement, and particularly political engagement, is also a topic to which political psychologists have devoted considerable energy.

Many studies of psychological factors involved in political engagement have used data collected in large national surveys conducted in the United States and other countries. For example, Elizabeth Smith used data from the American National Education Longitudinal Study (NELS) to look at the relationship between "investments in the social capital of young people" and political participation in young adulthood (Smith, 1999). The NELS surveyed a national sample of eighth grade children in 1988, and conducted follow-up surveys with a subsample of these children in 1990, 1992, 1994, and 2000. The original grade 8 survey administered in 1988 contained questions asking respondents how much their parents discussed their school activities and other topics with them, as well as questions asking the students about their involvement in extracurricular activities such as athletics or arts organizations. The follow-up survey in 1990 contained these same questions and, in addition, included questions concerning students' religious participation, such as how often they attended religious services. Smith looked at the extent to which these measures of "early investment in social capital" (i.e., parental involvement, extracurricular participation, and religious participation) predicted respondents' political participation years later, when they were surveyed in their early 20s. The results indicated that all three factors predicted later political engagement. Children whose parents had been highly involved with them, who had participated in extracurricular activities, and who had been involved in religious activities were more likely to vote or volunteer for a political organization as young adults than were those who had not participated in such activities.

An Integrative Theory of Civic Engagement

While many of psychology's subdisciplines have theories relating to behaviors such as volunteering or social activism, no one theory addresses all of the forms that civic engagement can take, from volunteering to being a member of a neighborhood organization to participating in protests or boycotts. In what follows, I outline a general conceptual or theoretical framework that attempts to integrate these forms of engagement. The framework grew out of an initial study that I and my colleague Mike Pratt conducted, in which we attempted to discover the roots of one form of civic engagement—volunteering (Pancer & Pratt, 1999). Our notion in designing the study was that the best way to find out why some people become involved in volunteering while others do not is to talk to individuals who are at the beginning of their "careers" as volunteers and ask them how they got started. Consequently, we sent letters to several community agencies and organizations that used young volunteers, asking them to nominate young people between the ages of 16 and 20 considered to be "committed volunteers" with their organization. We then contacted these individuals and interviewed several of them about their volunteer experiences. Among other questions, we asked them what they did as volunteers, how they became volunteers, what they liked and didn't like about volunteering, and how their volunteer work had affected them. We quickly discovered that what motivated young people initially to do community service was not the same as what kept them going as volunteers once they had started. For example, some of our young respondents began volunteering so that they could improve their job prospects or explore career possibilities. But what kept them going was the nature of the experience they had as volunteers and the support they felt in doing their volunteer work. We incorporated this distinction between the factors that initiated civic engagement and those that sustained them into our theoretical model.

Our theoretical framework grew and expanded as we conducted more studies of community service and other forms of civic engagement, such as social activism. The model was also informed, of course, by the research and theoretical work of others. The basic elements of the theory are presented in Figure 1.1. The theory posits that the process of civic engagement can be seen as occurring on two levels: an individual level and a systems level. On an individual level, people first become civically engaged as a result of various initiating factors. The most prominent of these are social influence, the individual's values, and instrumental motives. For example, a young person may become involved in volunteering through the influence of a parent or teacher:

> *The hospital was my first [volunteer experience]... it was my teacher. It was grade six, I think, and... we'd talk and stuff and there was a group of my friends and she [the teacher] said you know, this would be great for you guys to do this, so... I went and applied and got in and started volunteering there.*

Values can also play a role in initiating civic involvement. Social responsibility values can lead to civic behaviors such as volunteering, while social justice values might be expected to lead to involvement in social activism. Individuals may also engage in civic activities for instrumental purposes, in that they expected to receive personal benefits from their activities. We found that a number of our young volunteers began doing community service in order to improve their résumé or explore a possible career, for example:

> *I think at an early age I realized that I think I would like to go into a medicine-related field, and I figured the best way to see what was actually*

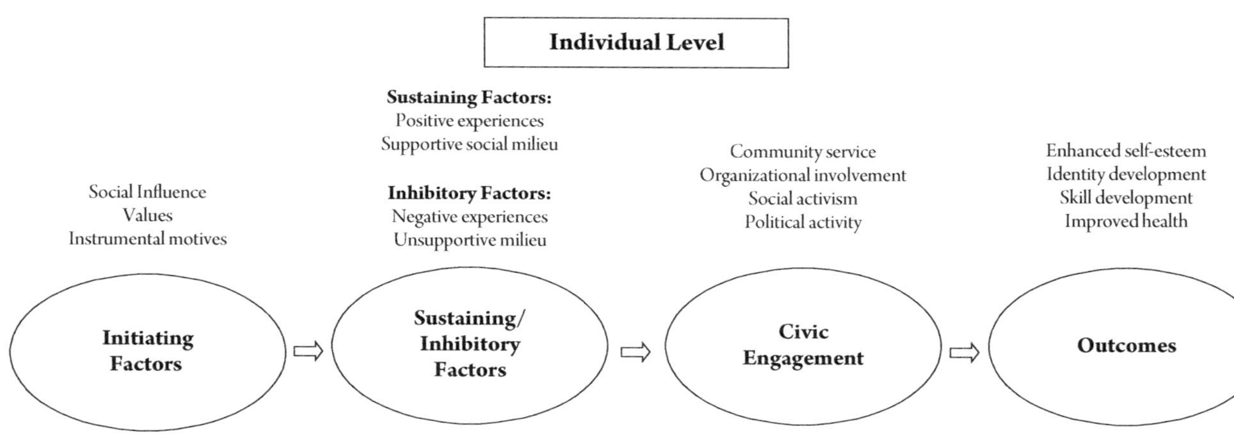

Figure 1.1 An Integrative Theory of Civic Engagement.

> *going on in the hospital was to become a volunteer. So, I called up and I asked for volunteer opportunities and they told me that there were, so I decided to go for them.*

While initiating factors are sufficient to get people involved initially, other factors are important in determining whether that civic involvement will be sustained. Our research indicates that civic engagement will continue to the extent that sustaining factors are present and that these sustaining factors outweigh any inhibitory factors that may also be present. The key factors that sustain civic engagement are positive experiences and a supportive social milieu. For example, if a young person feels that she is making a difference in the lives of others through her volunteer work (a positive experience) and is appreciated by the organization with which she works (which provides a supportive social milieu), she is likely to continue volunteering. Indeed, the feeling of having "made a difference" in people's lives is one of the most common, and most powerful, experiences that young people have reported to us about their volunteer work. As one young volunteer working with disabled children told us:

> *It was one of the most positive [experiences] of my life. It was amazing to see the difference you could make in someone's life . . . just being there . . . just giving them a hug or just making them smile is just big, and the people there are so devoted to each other. It's just amazing to see that.*

If, however, individuals have predominantly negative experiences and do not feel supported in their civic activities, they are not likely to continue. In addition, the costs of engagement may also inhibit sustained involvement. One prominent cost of engagement is the amount of time and effort it entails.

It is through sustained involvement that individuals who are civically engaged will experience outcomes related to their engagement. The kind and extent of these outcomes will depend on the nature of the involvements. For example, recent research indicates that young people who are broadly involved in a wide variety of activities will experience more positive outcomes than those who are involved more intensely in relatively few activities (Busseri et al., 2006, 2011; Rose-Krasnor et al., 2006). As I describe in detail later in the book, the majority of research on the impacts of civic engagement suggests that the outcomes associated with civic engagement are mostly positive. People (particularly young people) who are civically engaged demonstrate higher levels of well-being, more advanced identity development, fewer social and emotional problems, and a greater sense of social responsibility, among many outcomes.

Civic engagement can also be viewed on a systems level (represented in the lower half of Figure 1.1). Research indicates that social systems—the families, communities, and societies in which people live, work, learn, play, and pray—have a profound influence on civic engagement. The process through which initiating and sustaining or inhibitory factors lead to civic engagement and outcomes at the systems level is parallel to that which occurs at the individual level. Factors that initiate civic engagement at a systems level may include the presence of community organizations and leaders within those organizations who can recruit members and mentor those who participate. The more of these "opportunity structures" there are within a social system such as a school or a neighborhood, the greater the numbers of individuals in those systems who will begin to be involved (Watts & Flanagan, 2007). Other systems-level initiating factors would include the presence of programs that encourage civic engagement, such as service-learning programs in the schools, or employee volunteer programs in businesses and corporations.

Parallel to factors that sustain or inhibit civic engagement at the individual level are those that sustain or inhibit engagement at the systems level. At the systems level, engagement will be sustained if communities and community organizations have values, structures, and supports that promote engagement. For example, schools that include significant numbers of parents on their governing boards or councils serve as structures that will sustain civic involvement. Neighborhoods that have a sense of community, in which individuals feel a sense of belonging and connection with their neighbors, will also serve to sustain civic involvement. Conversely, neighborhoods with little sense of community, in which residents are mistrustful or even fearful of one another, will inhibit sustained civic involvement. According to a recent book by health scientists Richard Wilkinson and Kate Pickett (2009), income disparities are a key systemic factor relating to civic engagement. Countries with higher levels of income inequality show lower levels of social trust and less civic participation.

The work that community organizations, interest and advocacy groups, and social movements perform demonstrates civic engagement at the systems level. There is a growing body of research evidence that civic engagement at a systems level is related to positive outcomes for whole communities and even for entire states and nations. Robert Putnam's work, described earlier in this chapter, indicates that American states with greater civic participation and more community organizations are "healthier" states, in that they have lower rates of violent crime, better educational achievement, and fewer health problems compared to states with less civic participation and fewer opportunities for civic engagement (Putnam, 2000).

Organization of the Book

This first chapter of the book introduces the concepts of citizenship and civic engagement, shows how different areas of psychological research relate to civic participation, and provides a theoretical framework concerning the individual and systemic factors that influence civic involvement. Chapters 2 to 5 look at how civic participation develops throughout the lifespan and the role that families, peers, schools, neighborhoods, workplaces, religious organizations, and society play in its development. In chapters 6, 7, and 8, I discuss the impacts of civic engagement on young people, adults, and the communities in which they live. Chapter 9 discusses the "why's and wherefore's" of civic engagement—how civic participation achieves the many positive outcomes with which it is associated, and the kinds of civic involvements that lead to the greatest benefits. In the final chapter of the book, I talk about how what we have learned through research can help us develop programs and policies that will build and enhance civic engagement and redress some of the gaps in civic participation that we see between rich and poor, marginalized and non-marginalized individuals, and other social divides.

One cannot approach a topic such as citizenship and civic engagement without bringing a certain set of values or perspectives to bear on the subject. The reader will notice several of these values and perspectives in reading through this book. First, I consider civic engagement to be a broad set of behaviors that link individuals to others in their community and serve to enhance community life, rather than a narrow set of behaviors having to do with only the more legalistic aspects of citizenship (such as voting). Second, I see people's notions of citizenship and their civic involvements as developing and changing throughout their lives; consequently, I will be looking at the influences on and outcomes of civic engagement throughout the lifespan in this book. Third, I believe that using a wide range of research methodologies is necessary and important to gain a full understanding of civic engagement. In my own research I use quantitative methods such as surveys and experiments, but I also make extensive use of qualitative methods, such as individual interviews, focus groups, and action research, in which I and my research partners have talked to people about issues such as their community service work, their experiences with corporate social responsibility programs, and their involvement in protests and civil disobedience. I will be quoting frequently from these interviews and discussions throughout the book. Fourth, I consider it critical to look at civic engagement at the social systems level, as well as from an individual perspective, by examining the various social contexts in which engagement occurs. For example, civic engagement will be very different for those who live in impoverished environments, or for those who are oppressed and lack political power, than for those who come from more privileged social backgrounds. Finally, given what we know about the many positive impacts of civic engagement, I believe that it is incumbent upon those who do research in this field to consider the ways in which their research can be translated into policy and practice that will enhance and increase civic participation and to work hand-in-hand with practitioners, policymakers, and citizens, young and old, to make this happen.

2

The Influence of Parents, Families, and Peers on Civic Engagement

As the theory of civic engagement presented in the last chapter implies, our level of civic involvement is strongly influenced by the different systems and environments in which we live our daily lives. Our families, the schools we attend, the neighborhoods in which we live, the places where we work, the religious institutions where we worship, the cultures to which we belong, and the political structures that govern us—all have a profound impact on how we connect with others in our communities. It is not surprising that our families and peers are the most powerful of these influences, since family and friends are our first community, and they envelop us for our entire lives.

Impacts of Parents and Families on Civic Engagement

Recent studies confirm the importance of parents and families in the development of civic participation. Duke, Skay, Pettingell, and Borowsky (2009), for example, used data from the Longitudinal Study of Adolescent Health (Add Health) to look at adolescents' family and community connections and how they related to their civic engagements as young adults. The adolescents who were tracked by Add Health were first contacted when they were about 15 years old; they took part in a 90 minute interview in which they were asked, among other things, about their connections with their families, peers, schools, and neighborhoods. Connection with parents and family was assessed by asking the young respondents to indicate how close they felt to their parents, how much love, warmth, and caring they thought their parents provided, and the extent to which their family understood them and gave them attention. The youth were also asked how many different activities they had engaged in with their parents over the previous four weeks. Parallel measures tapped interviewees' connections with their peers, schools, and neighborhoods. Six years later, when they were young adults of 21 years of age, they participated in another interview, which included several measures of civic engagement. Among other questions, they were asked if they had voted in the last presidential election, done unpaid volunteer or community service work, been involved in political clubs or organizations, attended a political march or rally, or participated in a social action group. Analyses of the data collected at ages 15 and 21 showed that those who had shared more activities with their parents and felt a stronger connection with their families when they were 15 years of age were more likely to have voted, volunteered, participated in political groups, and engaged in social activism more than 6 years later, when they were young adults of 21 years of age.

One of the most telling signs of the influence that parents have on their children's civic development is the fact that civic engagement appears to run in families (Duncan & Stewart, 1995; Janoski & Wilson, 1995; Jennings, 2002; Mustillo, Wilson & Lynch, 2004). Studies of volunteering, for example, have shown that children of parents who volunteer are twice as likely to volunteer themselves, compared to children of parents who do not volunteer (Mustillo, Wilson & Lynch, 2004). Indeed, sociologists who have studied volunteering have talked about a "legacy of volunteering" that adults who do community service provide for their children. Other forms of civic engagement also seem to run in families. Kelly (2006), in a survey of American young people between 15 and 25 years of age, found that individuals who reported that their parents voted in most or every election were more likely to value voting and to intend to vote themselves than were young people who reported that their parents voted rarely or not at all. Duncan and Stewart (1995) found that students who participated in protests against the (first) Gulf War initiated by US President George H. Bush in 1991 were more likely than non-protesting individuals to have had parents who had been active in protests against the Vietnamese war a generation earlier.

We have found a similar correspondence in the civic engagement of parents and children in our own research. In our study of community and political involvements of adolescents (the Futures Project; Pancer, Pratt, Hunsberger & Alisat, 2007), we administered our Youth Inventory of Involvement (YII) to young people in their next to last year of high school, and calculated a total score for each youth as an indicator of the youth's overall level of civic engagement. We also used their scores on subscales of the inventory to categorize the young people into four groups: Activists, Helpers, Responders, and Uninvolved. The Activists and Helpers were the most civically engaged of the four groups, the Responders less engaged, and the Uninvolved, as their name implies, were the least civically engaged. In addition to having young people respond to the YII, we created an adult version of the inventory (the Adult Inventory of Involvement, or AII) to assess the overall civic engagement of the youths' parents, and we sent the adult inventory to the parents of a subsample of our youth respondents. Our analyses of the involvement inventories indicated a high degree of correspondence between the parents' and children's scores. The correlation between both mothers' and fathers' level of involvement with their children's level of involvement was substantial ($r = 0.40$ and 0.44 for mothers and fathers, respectively). Also, the pattern of mothers' involvement corresponded to the pattern of involvement found for the four clusters of youth (there were too few fathers in our sample to conduct this analysis with fathers' data). The mothers of the more engaged Activists and Helpers reported significantly greater involvement than did the mothers of the less engaged Responders and Uninvolved youth.

It should come as no surprise that there is also a correspondence in civic involvement between spouses and partners in a family. Research indicates, for example, that if one spouse volunteers, the other is likely to volunteer as well (Freeman, 1997; Thompson, 1993). Interestingly, this correspondence is somewhat asymmetrical in terms of the number of hours of volunteer work contributed by the man and woman in a marital relationship. As a husband's volunteering hours increase, so do his wife's. In contrast, as a wife's volunteering hours increase, her husband's volunteer hours tend to decrease. Wilson (2000) suggests that a wife's volunteer contributions are seen to complement her husband's, while a husband's contributions are seen as a substitute for his wife's. If the wife contributes more hours, then the husband doesn't have to contribute as much because his wife has already made a sufficient contribution for the family.

How Do Parents and Families Influence Civic Engagement?

Social Influence

Through what processes and mechanisms do parents and families influence civic engagement? The theoretical model outlined in the last chapter suggests several ways in which families may contribute to the initiation and sustainment of civic behaviors. According to the model, one of the ways in which civic involvement is initiated is through a process of social influence. Parents exert considerable influence on their children, especially when their children are young. One of the most direct ways in which parents wield this influence is through the suggestions and exhortations that they make to their children. Recent surveys of volunteering in the United States and Canada, for example, indicate that half of those who volunteer initially became involved in volunteer activity because someone asked them to (U.S. Department of Labor, 2013; Vezina & Crompton 2012). The person doing the asking and suggesting is often a parent or family member. This was evident in what the young participants in our own study of the roots of volunteering said about how they first became involved as volunteers:

> *I guess one of the things that kind of influenced me is my mom. I wasn't really into sports, so I was looking for something to do in school, so my mom ... we*

were just talking about school groups and that, like the Sunnyside group [that made visits to help out at a local seniors residence]...and she was encouraging me to try and get involved in that group, since I wasn't really into sports. So...we have quite a few seniors in my family, so, you know, I usually get along well with them and interacting with them, so I thought maybe I'd try to volunteer at the seniors residence.

Social Learning

Parents also serve as important role models for their children. Many studies show that children adopt behaviors and standards of behavior through a process of social learning, by observing the behavior of others (Bandura, 1977, 1986). When children see their parents and other family members acting charitably, helping others, or engaging in social activism, they are more likely to attempt these kinds of behaviors themselves (Mussen & Eisenberg-Berg, 1977). When such behaviors lead to positive outcomes and are supported and reinforced by their parents and others, they are even more likely to be performed in the future and can lead to the internalization of norms of social responsibility that become part of the individual's moral or civic identity (Youniss & Yates, 1997). We found many instances of parents serving as models of civic responsibility in our research on adolescent volunteers. One of our interviewees, for example, talked about how important her father was in setting an example for her own community service work:

My dad, you know, he's only been a member Rotary for a few years, but he made me realize I guess that there are people out there that are less fortunate than we are and that, you know, we should be lucky for what we have and thankful for what we have.

This kind of learning can last a lifetime. Studies of Christians who risked their lives to hide and rescue Jews during the Second World War indicate that many of these individuals had close relationships with at least one parent who had also been involved in humanitarian causes, modeling the kinds of behavior that the rescuers exhibited themselves as adults (London, 1970; Oliner & Oliner, 1988).

Family members may also serve as negative role models, in that they demonstrate values and behaviors that inspire aversion rather than admiration. In these instances, the individual may consciously try to behave differently from those family members. We found this to be the case in a number of individuals whom we interviewed in a study of the roots of social activism (Pancer & Eckerle-Curwood, 2009). For example, one young woman who had been very involved in activities on behalf of Canadian First Nations or aboriginal groups told us how the values espoused by some members of her family made her want to work to change those kinds of values and beliefs:

> *I have cousins that are kind of organized racists... And seeing racism and how it's derived so much from ignorance, and a sense of superiority—the way I see it, it's an illegitimate sense of superiority—just seeing that, maybe, gave me a sense of urgency that something needed to be changed.*

Parent-Child Interaction and Discussion

It would seem to make sense that the more opportunities parents have to interact with their children, the more influence they will have on their children's civic behavior. Research certainly supports this supposition (Duke et al., 2009; Hart, Atkins & Ford, 1999). Hart, Atkins, and Ford (1999) used data from the American National Longitudinal Study of Youth (NLSY) to look at the relationship between several different measures of parent-child relations (collected when the children were about 13 years of age) and the children's volunteer work two years later, when they were about 15 years old. Among the measures collected when the youth were 13 was one that the parents completed, assessing the kind of cognitive, emotional, and social support that they provided in the home, and a measure administered to the youth asking them to report on the quality of their relationship with their parents (e.g., how much autonomy their parents allowed them, how close they felt to their parents). The 13-year-olds were also asked how often they had done things together with their parents (e.g., worked on schoolwork, played a game or sport) over the previous week. Analysis of this information indicated that it was the frequency of the youths' interactions with their parents that was the best predictor of their volunteer activities two years later. Indeed, the amount of time the parents and their adolescent children spent doing things together was a better predictor of volunteering than any of the other measures of parental support and parent-child relations that were collected.

One of the things that happen when parents and children participate in activities together is that they talk with one another. These kinds of informal discussions that occur at the dinner table, when playing games together, and during other activities, play an important role in influencing children's civic behaviors. We found this in our own Futures Project research (Pancer, Pratt, Hunsberger, & Alisat, 2007). For this study, we assessed parent-child interaction by asking our respondents, in their second-last year of high school, to indicate how often they discussed each of six topics (school work, family issues, personal friendships, religion, moral values, and politics) with their parents. We also asked them to rate how much they enjoyed discussing each of these topics with their parents, and how much influence they felt their parents had on their thinking about each of these topics. We computed a "parent interaction" index by summing all of the ratings that youth made about their discussions with their parents. We then looked at how our parent interaction index related to the young people's civic involvements, assessed with our Youth Inventory of Involvement (YII). We found a strong and significant correspondence between our parent interaction index and young people's scores on the YII. Those youth who were more civically engaged (those whom we labeled "Activists" and "Helpers") reported much more frequent discussions with their parents than did the youth who were less engaged (those whom we labeled "Responders" and "Uninvolved").

Other studies have looked specifically at the kind of discussions that parents have with their children, and how the content of these discussions influence their children's civic engagement (Andolina, Jenkins, Zukin & Keeter, 2003; Kelly, 2006; McIntosh, Hart & Youniss, 2007; Zukin, Keeter, Andolina, Jenkins & Delli Carpini, 2006). Andolina and her colleagues (2003), for example, surveyed American young people between 15 and 25 years of age, asking them about their involvement in a wide range of civic activities and how often their family discussed politics in their home. They found that young people who heard frequent discussions about politics in their home were much more likely to be engaged in several kinds of civic activities. Among those who were eligible to vote, 38% of those whose families discussed politics frequently said that they always voted, compared to only 20% of those whose families didn't discuss politics. Compared to young people whose families rarely discussed politics, those whose families frequently discussed politics were more likely to follow politics themselves (44% vs. 18%), sign petitions (30% vs. 11%), boycott a product (54% vs. 25%), and serve regularly as a volunteer (35% vs. 13%).

The political discussions that parents have with their children may be particularly influential when parents are well-informed about political matters. McIntosh, Hart, and Youniss (2007) utilized data from the US Department of Education's National Household Education Survey, administered in 1996, to look at "civic outcomes" (interest in national news, political knowledge, involvement in community service) in young people and how these outcomes related to the frequency of political discussions with their parents. Consistent with other studies, McIntosh and colleagues found that young people who had frequent political conversations with their parents reported greater interest in national news, more knowledge about politics, and higher levels of community service than did youth who had these kinds of conversations infrequently. In addition to surveys being sent to young people to ask them about their political interests and activities, surveys were also administered to their parents, asking the parents about their own interest in and knowledge about politics. Analyses including these variables showed that parents' discussions with their children had the greatest impact on their children's civic behaviors when the parents were knowledgeable about politics.

In what way do discussions with parents influence children's civic engagement? One school of thought, deriving from theories of political socialization, holds that these discussions allow parents to transmit their knowledge and values about politics and civic affairs to their children. Through discussion with their parents, children learn about the major political figures and institutions in their country and around the world, the key social and political issues of the day, and the community in which they live. They also pick up on their parents' values. One of the values that children can learn from what their parents discuss is that their connection to their communities, their country, and the world around them is important and warrants their attention.

Another school of thought views children and youth as being more active in the processing of information about their social and political worlds. According to this cognitive developmental perspective, rather than merely being passive recipients of civic and political information, young people are actively working to construct their own understanding and meaning from the information they get from their parents and from other sources, such as their peers, teachers, and religious leaders (Flanagan & Faison, 2001; McIntosh, Hart, & Youniss, 2007; McLeod, 2000). Indeed, there is good evidence that when political discussions occur in families, it is not just the parents who influence the children. Children often influence their parents, as well. This is evident from studies of the Kids Voting USA program in operation in several American states (McDevitt & Chaffee, 2000; McDevitt & Kiousis, 2007; Saphir & Chaffee, 2002). This school-based program was designed to encourage high school students to take an interest in political affairs. Studies of the program's impact found that the program not only affected the students who took part in it, but affected their parents, as well. Students who participated in the program began to initiate political discussions with their parents, and these discussions, in turn, enhanced their parents' interest in and knowledge about politics. McDevitt and Kiousis (2007) describe this phenomenon, in which young people initiate discussions and influence their parents, as a "trickle up" process of family communication.

Transmission of Values

According to the integrative theory of civic engagement presented in the last chapter, another key influence on people's initiation of civic activities is their values. It is no surprise that parents and families play an important role in the development of individuals' values. Evidence for the influence that parents have on their children's values comes from the many studies that show a significant, though variable, degree of congruence between the values that parents hold and those that their children hold (Bengtson, 1975, Jennings & Niemi, 1968; Jennings, Stoker & Bowers, 2009; Knafo & Schwartz, 2008; Rohan & Zanna, 1996). Interestingly, it appears that the correspondence between parents' and children's values increases with age (Rohan & Zanna, 1996). Rohan and Zanna found a very substantial correlation of ($r = 0.54$) between parents and their adult children in core values assessed using Shalom Schwartz's Value Inventory (Schwartz, 1992, 1994). There is also evidence that there may be more parent-child concordance on some values than others. Troll, Neugarten, and Kraines (1969) found a higher degree of correspondence between parents and children with regard to dedication to causes than with regard to materialist values.

Theories about the transmission of values from parents to children generally hold that for children to adopt the values of their parents, two things are required (Grusec & Goodnow, 1994; Knafo & Schwartz, 2008; Westholm, 1999). First, the child must accurately perceive what the parents' values are. Second, the child must accept those values as his or her own. The more parents interact with their children, and the more they discuss topics such as politics and the importance of being involved in community, the more likely it is that children will form accurate perceptions of their parents' values, meeting the first requirement for parent-to-child value transmission. The more persuasive parents are in convincing their children that their (the parents') values are important, the more the children are likely to accept these values, meeting the second requirement. As the research on the Kids Voting USA program suggests, the transmission of values may also proceed in the other direction; the more accurately parents perceive their children's values, and accept those values, the more likely that values will be transmitted from children to parents. One would expect more reciprocal influences between parents and children as the children became older and more skilled at expressing their values and beliefs (Wintre et al., 1995).

Theory and research on human values suggest that there are key values that relate to civic engagement. In Shalom Schwartz's "Theory of Human Values," it is the value of universalism (one's concern for the welfare of all people and nature) that relates most directly to civic involvement (Schwartz, 2010). In our own research, we identified value orientations relating to social justice and citizenship as the most important influences on people's civic involvements (Pancer, 2004; Pratt, Hunsberger, Pancer & Alisat, 2003). Ervin Staub (1991) talks about a "prosocial value orientation," comprising a positive evaluation of human beings, a concern about other people's well-being, and a feeling of personal responsibility for others' welfare, as the key value that underlies people's connections with others in their community and the world. Staub asserts that parents are especially important in establishing this prosocial value orientation in their children, by providing a "caring context" for their families. We found evidence of the importance of this kind of caring context that parents and families can provide in our own work. In our Futures Project (Pancer et al., 2007), we had 17-year-old high school students complete the Youth Inventory of Involvement, along with measures designed to assess the kind of parenting that their parents provided and their general feelings about their family. We used a scale developed by Lamborn and colleagues (Lamborn, Mounts, Steinberg, & Dornbusch, 1991) to assess parenting style. This measure yields a score for parental warmth and involvement and a score that reflects the amount of structure or "demandingness" provided by the parents. Together, these two qualities define an "authoritative" style of parenting that has been shown in many studies to contribute to healthier adjustment in children (Baumrind, 1991). We found a strong relationship between research participants' perceptions of their parents' style of parenting and the youths' civic involvements. Children of authoritative parents, whom the youth perceived to be warm, involved, and demanding, showed significantly higher levels of civic engagement. Similarly, youth who had positive feelings about their families were also more civically engaged. Other analyses we have conducted on data from youth who participated in our Futures Project suggest that it is at least partly through the transmission of values that children of authoritative parents come to be more civically engaged. These analyses showed that there was greater parent-child congruence in values among families with more authoritative parents than in families with less authoritative parents (Pratt et al., 2003).

Community and Cultural Norms

In addition to transmitting values to their children, parents and families serve as vehicles through which community and cultural norms and standards are passed along to children (Yagmurlu & Sanson, 2009). Parents and members of one's immediate and extended family are the first and most prominent representatives of community that a person encounters. Authoritative parents who listen to and reason with their children, and who encourage them to participate in family decision-making and discussion, model the democratic process, and the children in such families begin to see participation and discussion with others as the norm, not just for their family, but for the wider society as well. When parents and other family members are actively engaged in civic activities such as volunteering and participating in political or community organizations, they are also conveying norms with regard to civic involvement to their children. We found many examples of this kind of familial norm transmission in the young people we interviewed in our study of the roots of volunteering. For example, one young woman who was heavily involved in several volunteer activities talked about how her family members had influenced her:

> *My family... has definitely had a big influence on me... especially my father's family. He comes from a Mennonite background and he had fifteen brothers and sisters... I have an aunt and uncle in Mexico who are missionaries, I have an aunt and uncle who are going back and forth to the Ukraine with a mission there... and a cousin who was doing prison ministry... he had a group that went and sang and worked with people in prisons... that family is just an amazing family and very giving... it's a way of life, it's, you know, it's just understood that you do these kinds of things.*

Parents and Families as Links to Community

Parents also affect their children's connection with community through the links they provide with other members of the community and with community organizations and institutions. We found many examples of this in a study of a mandatory community service program for high school students introduced in the province of Ontario, Canada, in 1999. Beginning in that year, all high school students were required to complete 40 hours of community service during their high school years in order to obtain their high school diploma. Unfortunately, the provincial policy did not provide any infrastructure or guidance to students that would help them find an appropriate service opportunity, and many students had difficulty finding service placements. We conducted a detailed study of the mandatory service program, and, as part of the study, we interviewed over 100 students about their experiences with the program (Pancer, Brown, Henderson, & Elllis-Hale, 2007; Henderson, Brown, Pancer, & Ellis-Hale, 2007). One of the questions we asked them was how they found a community organization with which to perform their service. In conducting our interviews, it became very clear that it was often the students' parents who provided this connection. For example, a student who did her community service at a local hospital described how she had come into contact with the hospital:

> *My mother was a nurse so she suggested it and then I got into contact with a friend of my mother's, who also worked as a nurse, and she set it up.*

Parent and Family Support

According to the model of civic engagement presented in the last chapter, there are two stages in the development of long-term civic involvement. Individuals first participate in civic activities through a process of social influence, in order to express their values, or to gain personal benefits. As we have seen, parents and families can influence all of these "initiating" factors that start people on the road to civic participation. In order for this civic participation to be sustained, however, the model indicates that the individual needs to experience positive outcomes within a supportive social milieu. Parents and families can and do provide this kind of supportive social milieu. This was demonstrated in a study by Fletcher, Elder, and Mekos (2000). The participants in this study were adolescents, whose parents were part of the Iowa Youth and Families Project, a longitudinal investigation of American families living in rural communities in the north central part of the state of Iowa. The adolescents completed measures assessing their community involvement in activities such as sports teams or community groups such as the Future Farmers of America when they were in grade 9 and again when they were in grade 10. Their parents completed a parallel measure of their own involvement in the community when their children were in grade 9. The parents also completed a scale designed to assess how much support they provided for their child's interests and activities. This scale included questions such as, "How often do you let your child know that you appreciate her, her ideas, or the things she does?" Consistent with other studies, the results of this study showed that the more parents were involved in community activities, the more their children were. The results also showed that the more support parents provided their children, the more involved their children were. Interestingly, parental support appeared to have a greater impact on the school and community activities of children whose parents were not highly involved compared to the children of parents who were highly involved.

Impacts of Peers on Civic Engagement

As individuals move into adolescence, their friends and peers begin to exert considerable influence on their values, attitudes, and behaviors, and the influence of their parents and families begins to wane (Catalano & Hawkins, 1996; Erikson, 1974). The influence of friends and social networks on a wide variety of civic activities can be potent. McLellan and Youniss (2003), in a study of volunteering among students in two Washington, DC high schools, found that students whose close friends volunteered were three times more likely to volunteer themselves than were students whose friends did not volunteer. We found similarly strong influences of friends when we interviewed young volunteers for our study of the roots of volunteering (Pancer & Pratt, 1999). Many of the young people we interviewed, who had been nominated as exemplary volunteers by local health and social service organizations, had close friends who also volunteered:

> *I have one friend who volunteers at the Sunbeam Centre for children who are mentally challenged and physically as well. And then there's the Red Cross. I have friends who volunteer through the Red Cross and some at the hospital. And I have one who does work with the Multicultural Women's Association.*

Peers and social networks affect other areas of civic activity, as well. Political scientist Christopher Kenny, in a study of political activities prior to the 1984 American presidential election campaign, found that individuals were more likely to put up an election sign, work on a political campaign, or vote if they had a friend who performed these same activities (Kenny, 1992). Michael Gross, in a study of 174 individuals from France and Holland who had aided Jews in hiding or escaping from the Nazis during World War II, found that the more friends that individuals had who participated in the rescue of Jews, the more involved those individuals were themselves in the rescue attempts (Gross, 1994).

How Do Peers Influence Civic Engagement?

Social Influence

Friends and peers influence civic engagement through many of the same processes that parents and families do. Like family members, friends often exert this influence quite directly, by making requests and suggestions. As mentioned earlier in this chapter, nearly half of all people in the United States and Canada doing volunteer work started volunteering because someone, often a friend, asked them to (U.S. Department of Labor, 2013; Vezina & Crompton 2012). In fact, the majority of individuals who become involved in a wide range of civic activities and organizations, including social movements, peace groups, political protest, political campaigning and lobbying, neighborhood and school associations, and religious organizations, do so through the influence of individuals from their networks of friends and acquaintances (Klandermans & Oegema, 1987; Schussman & Soule, 2005; Verba, Schlozman, & Brady, 1995). In many of these activities, this is by far the most common route to participation. Sociologists Alan Schussman and Sarah Soule note, for example, that "individuals rarely participate in protest and other political activities unless they are explicitly asked to do so" (2005, p. 1086). In his study of rescuers of Jews in France and Holland during World War II, Gross found that among the 175 individuals he interviewed who had been involved in the rescue attempts, 75% said that they had been enlisted by others to participate (Gross, 1994). Political parties, of course, are quite aware of the importance of social influence in getting people involved in the political process, particularly on election day, and exert considerable effort to "get out the vote" by having volunteers call supporters to make sure they have voted and bring them to the polling station if they have not.

Peer Interaction and Discussion

Discussion with peers is an important way in which people, young and old, begin to construct a notion of how they are connected to their community and society. There is considerable research evidence that the more these discussions occur, the more civic engagement also occurs. Zaff, Malanchuk, and Eccles (2008) consider one's peers (along with parents, supportive adults outside the family, and religious influences) to constitute a "civic context" that needs to be present in order for a person to develop a strong civic identity. To demonstrate this, they conducted surveys of American young people in the state of Maryland when the youth were in the 8th and 11th grade. They assessed the youths' civic participation in both grades by asking them about their involvement in volunteer work and other civic activities. They also asked their research participants how often they discussed with their friends subjects such as problems in school or how things were going in their families. The results indicated that young people who frequently discussed these kinds of things with their friends were more civically engaged than were young people who had these kinds of conversations less frequently.

We found similar effects in our study of young people's involvements in our Futures Project research (Pancer et al., 2007). In addition to completing our Youth Inventory of Involvement to assess their overall level of civic engagement in a wide variety of activities (e.g., volunteering, political work, participation in youth organizations), the young people who took part in this study also completed a "peer interaction" measure, which asked them to indicate how often they discussed each of several different topics (school work, family issues, personal friendships, religion, moral values, and politics) with their friends. We found that youth who were more civically engaged reported much more frequent exchanges with their peers about a wide variety of topics than did the youth who were less engaged.

What people talk about in their conversations with friends and acquaintances may also be an important factor in determining people's civic involvements. Political scientist Scott McClurg (2003) suggests that, with regard to political participation, discussions with peers will only influence participation if those discussions "carry political substance" (p. 449). He argues that these kinds of conversations provide individuals with information and stimuli that they would not have been exposed to had those conversations not taken place, and this information changes the way individuals think about their participation. Conversations devoid of political substance do not provide this kind of information, and therefore, are not likely to influence an individual's political activities. To confirm these notions, McClurg used data from a survey conducted during the 1984 American presidential election. Respondents to the survey were asked two questions about their discussions with friends. One question asked respondents how often they had spoken to three individuals in their social network. The other question asked the respondents how frequently they had discussed politics with these individuals. The survey also asked respondents about their involvement in the electoral process—whether they had worked for one of the candidates, attended a meeting or rally, displayed a political "bumper" sign on their car, or contributed money to a campaign. McClurg found that the more people had discussions with peers about political matters, the more involved they were in political activities. The frequency with which they had had social discussions, devoid of political content, bore no relationship to the frequency of their political activities. These findings are similar to studies of the influence of family discussions, which suggest that family conversations about civically or politically related themes will have a greater impact on civic behavior than conversations that do not address these topics (Andolina, Jenkins, Zukin, & Keeter, 2003; Kelly, 2006; McIntosh, Hart, & Youniss, 2007; Zukin, Keeter, Andolina, Jenkins, & Delli Carpini, 2006).

The nature and tone of the political discussions that one has with friends and acquaintances can also influence civic participation. What happens, for example, when individuals encounter disagreement with their views when they discuss politics with those in their social networks? A number of studies suggest that encountering disagreement in political discussions can dampen people's civic participation. Mutz (2002) and others (McClurg, 2006; Pattie & Johnston, 2009) have found, for example, that the more individuals encounter disagreement in their discussions about politics, the less likely they are to vote. Pattie and Johnston claim, however, that the impact of disagreements on civic participation is small, and is confined to what they refer to as "low cost" individual behaviors such as voting. In their examination of British voters participating in the 2005 British Election Study, they found that, while political discussions with individuals who disagreed with them was associated with a small decrease in voting, the frequency of political discussion with others (who agreed or disagreed with them) was associated with higher rates of other kinds of civic participation, such as political and community volunteering.

Transmission of Values and Norms

Peers exert considerable influence on individuals' values and play a significant role in the transmission of social and cultural norms. Cialdini and his colleagues (Cialdini, Reno, & Kallgren, 1990; Reno, Cialdini, & Kallgren, 1993) distinguish between two kinds of norms that can affect individuals' behavior: descriptive norms, which have to do with what most people do in a particular situation, and injunctive norms, which have to do with beliefs about what others consider to be moral or acceptable behavior in a given situation. Research suggests that it is a person's perception of what peers consider to be acceptable behavior that has the greatest influence on behavior, regardless of the accuracy of those perceptions. These injunctive norms affect many different behaviors, including civic participation. Smith and McSweeney (2007) demonstrated this in research involving a sample of adult Australians. They found that individuals with strong intentions to donate money to charity within the subsequent month perceived that their friends also valued donating to charity, while those not intending to donate perceived that their friends did not value this activity as much. Our own research (Pratt, Hunsberger, Pancer, & Alisat, 2003) showed a high degree of correspondence between young adults' perceptions of their friends' moral values, and their own values and behavior. In this research, we had young adults, about 19 years of age, rate the extent to which 12 values were important to them in their lives, as well as rating the extent to which they thought these values were important for their friends. We categorized the values into two types: "moral" values, such as being a good citizen and showing kindness and caring for others, and "non-moral" values, such as being independent or having ambition. We computed a "moral value emphasis" index by subtracting ratings of the non-moral values from those of the moral values; this index reflected the extent to which individuals considered moral values to be more important than non-moral values. Our analyses indicated a strong correspondence between the values our respondents perceived their peers to have and their own values. The more young people perceived their peers to emphasize moral values, the more they considered these values to be important themselves. Moral value emphasis, in turn, was significantly correlated with respondents' levels of civic engagement, as assessed by our Youth Inventory of Involvement.

Peer Support

The integrative model of civic engagement presented in the last chapter indicates that, in order for civic participation to be sustained, individuals must experience positive outcomes (and relatively few negative outcomes) in an atmosphere of social support. Peers, especially during adolescence, when peer acceptance is particularly valued, can provide this supportive milieu. This was demonstrated in a study of Australian youth conducted by Lisa da Silva and colleagues (2004). Their study employed data collected from 16- to 17-year-old youth, as part of the Australian Temperament Project, a longitudinal study that tracked a cohort of Australian children from birth to young adulthood. "Civic responsibility" was assessed in the survey that the young people completed by asking them how often over the past 6 months they had participated in volunteer work and political activity. The survey also contained questions about the amount of encouragement and support they had received from their peers for their involvement in these activities, as well as the degree to which their peers also participated in volunteering and politics. The researchers' analyses indicated that peer encouragement, and to a somewhat lesser extent, the involvement of their peers in these activities, were the most powerful predictors of civic engagement of any of the predictors that they tested (other predictors included measures of family support and environment, as well as school and community attachment).

Summary

Family and friends are our first community, and they exert a powerful influence on our connections to the broader community. The impact of parents and families on civic engagement is evident from the fact that parents who are involved in their communities through volunteering, social activism, and political activities tend to have children who are more likely to be involved in these kinds of activities, as well. Parents influence their children's civic activities in a number of ways: they influence them directly through their suggestions and exhortations, they serve as models of civic engagement, they transmit values and norms of behavior through discussion with their children, they help link children to community organizations, and they provide support for their children's involvements. Peers and friends have a similarly powerful impact on people's civic engagements. Individuals whose friends are civically engaged are much more likely to be civically engaged themselves. Peers and friends exert their influence in a manner similar to the ways in which parents do. They provide direct social influence, they serve as models of behavior, they transmit values and norms, and they provide support for one's civic activities.

3

The Influence of Schools and Neighborhoods on Civic Engagement

As we age and develop, we become part of many different kinds of communities. The most significant of these communities are those which almost all of us will encounter; we will attend school, live in a neighborhood, and have a job or career in a workplace. Most of us will also belong to a church, synagogue, mosque, or other religious organization. The kind of school, neighborhood, workplace, and religious organization in which we learn, live, work, and worship will have a profound effect on our connections with community. In this chapter, I discuss the ways in which schools and neighborhoods can influence civic engagement.

Schools

The school is the first real community that a person encounters. Indeed, it is the school setting in which most of us learn what a community is and how to navigate our way through the complexities of community life. Schools vary significantly in the kind of learning and social environment they provide for children and in the extent to which they teach and foster the kinds of skills that individuals need to adapt to community life. According to the integrative theory of civic engagement presented in chapter 1, two key elements or factors must be in place to produce long-term, committed civic engagement. Initiating factors, the first element, are those which prompt the first acts of participation. These acts of participation will only continue in the long term, however, if sustaining factors (the second element) are also present. Schools can provide both elements. For example, over the last several years, schools have increasingly required their students to participate in some form of community service as part of course requirements or in order to obtain a diploma or degree. A study commissioned by the Corporation for National and Community Service (Spring, Grimm & Dietz, 2008) found that, in the United States, more than two out of every three schools either organized or supported their students' involvement in community service activities. In many of the schools (and nearly half of all high schools), this service was part of a "service-learning" program, in which the community service was integrated with the school curriculum. The presence of such programs in schools serves as a strong "initiating" factor for the development of civic engagement, in that these kinds of requirements often serve to initiate young people's first meaningful engagement with their community. Schools can also provide "sustaining" elements that promote long-term civic involvement. McLellan and Youniss (2003), for example, argue that when schools help students reflect on their service activities, students are more likely to learn from their experiences and see themselves doing community service in the future. The support that schools provide in helping students understand the significance of what they are doing serves as a "sustaining" factor that can lead to long-term civic engagement.

Mandatory Service Programs

There are many different kinds of school-based programs that can influence young people's civic participation. One way of categorizing these programs has to do with whether students are mandated to participate in the programs or are only encouraged to be involved. In many schools, students are mandated or required to perform community service to complete course or even diploma or degree requirements. The recent survey of American schools by the Corporation for National and Community Service indicated that 43% of American high schools have a requirement that all or some of their students participate in community service activities (Spring, Grimm, & Dietz, 2008). A survey on volunteering in Canada in 2000 indicated that nearly one in three high school students in the country participated in a mandatory service program in the year the survey was administered (Hall, McKeown, & Roberts, 2001). Mandatory service programs have been implemented at the class, school, school district, and even the state or provincial level. My own university, for example, requires students in a number of degree programs, both undergraduate and graduate, to perform community service as part of their degree requirements. An example of a provincewide program is the policy enacted by the province of Ontario, Canada, in 1999, requiring every high school student in the province to complete a total of 40 hours of community service as one of the requirements for obtaining a high school diploma.

These kinds of requirements have generated considerable debate among researchers, policymakers, and others about the impact such programs have on students' interest in and long-term commitment to volunteering and civic participation. On one side of the debate are those who argue that mandating community service creates a negative attitude toward service, which reduces the likelihood of individuals' civic involvement in the future. As evidence for their claim, these individuals cite research in social psychology showing that mandating or forcing people to perform a particular task tends to reduce their "intrinsic motivation" for performing the task, that is, their interest in performing the task for its own sake (see, for example, Deci & Ryan, 1987). There is some empirical support for this assertion with regard to community service. Stukas, Snyder, and Clary (1999), for example, examined the impact of a mandatory service requirement implemented at the University of St. Thomas in St. Paul, Minnesota in 1993. Between 1993 and 1995, business students enrolled in a course requiring community service completed surveys during the first and last class of the course. In the survey administered in the first class, students indicated how much prior volunteer experience they had and the extent to which they were participating in the service course only because they had to. In the survey administered in the last class, after students had completed their service requirement, they indicated how likely they were to volunteer in the future. The results indicated that the more students felt that they were taking the course only because they were required to, the less they intended to volunteer in the future. Moreover, the feeling that they were performing service only because they were required to appeared to undermine future intentions to volunteer, particularly among those who had volunteered in the past. Students appear to be quite conscious of the fact that the service they provide under a mandated program is not the same as service that is freely given. As one student participating in a qualitative study of mandatory service programs in Australian schools said:

> *Sometimes people come to assembly and say, we need to raise money. You know, it'd be great if you could volunteer. And then it's your decision to think, hey I'd like to help that cause. So then you go up and you organize it. But with this* [mandatory] *programme it sort of you have to do this, you know. It's like—it's not volunteering... immediately you're thinking, oh my goodness, you know, something else I've got to do. So it's got the negative perspective on it from the beginning.* (Warburton & Smith, 2003, p. 779)

On the other side of the debate are those who claim that mandatory service programs, especially those with certain characteristics (for example, those which are integrated into the school curriculum), do not reduce people's motivation to volunteer, but enhance it. Metz and Youniss (2003, 2005) demonstrated the positive impact that a well-designed mandatory service program can have in a study they conducted in a high school near Boston. In the fall of 1997, the school implemented a mandatory community service program in which students were required to complete 40 hours of community service during their high school years. The adoption of this program allowed the researchers to compare students who started attending the school before the service requirement began with those who started school after the requirement was in place. They further compared students who already had experience performing service with those who had not. The results of the study showed that, for students who had previous service experience, the mandatory program made little difference; these students, whether in the mandatory service program or not, showed a high level of interest in civic affairs and expressed the intention to become civically engaged in the future. It was among the students who had little community service experience that the greatest differences were evident. Among these students, those who participated in the mandatory service program showed a marked increase in their interest in politics and their intentions to become civically involved by voting, volunteering, and/or joining civic organizations after they completed their mandatory service, while those not participating in the program showed a decline in civic interest and intention over the same period.

Our own research has examined the impact of mandatory service programs on a much larger scale (Henderson, Brown, Pancer, & Ellis-Hale, 2007). The policy implemented by the province of Ontario, Canada, in 1999, mandating all high school students to complete 40 hours of community service as part of the requirements for their high school diploma, provided a unique opportunity to study how such programs influence civic engagement. Ontario, the largest province in Canada, with a population of over 11 million, has about 700,000 students attending more than 850 publicly funded secondary schools. When the province enacted its mandatory service requirement, it also reduced the number of years required for a high school diploma from five to four. This meant that, for one year, there would be a "double cohort" of students graduating from high school—one part of the double cohort having completed high school in five years, and one part having completed high school in four years. The students from the two parts of the double cohort were from the same neighborhoods, attended the same schools, and were similar in almost all respects. The main differences were their ages (those in the older cohort were about a year older when they graduated) and the fact that the older cohort had not been required to perform community service, while the younger cohort had.

Eighteen months after students in the double cohort completed high school, we administered a detailed survey to nearly 1,300 of these individuals; half had been required to perform community service, and half had not. Among other things, we asked them about their community service experiences during and after high school, their attitudes towards community service, and their intentions to perform service in the future. Our results indicated that the mandatory service requirement served as a strong "initiating" factor for many students. Almost all (95%) of those mandated to perform service indicated that they had indeed done so while in high school, while a substantially smaller proportion (76.7%) of those not mandated indicated that they had performed community service, a difference of nearly 20%. We found very few differences between the mandated and non-mandated group on any of the measures we collected. Mandated and non-mandated students did similar kinds of community service during high school, and they did not differ from one another in the kind or amount of service they did after high school, their attitudes toward performing service, or their intentions to do service in the future. These results lend support to the claim that mandating service does not reduce people's intrinsic interest in service or their intention to perform service in the future.

As a supplement to our survey, we also conducted face-to-face interviews with a subsample of students who had been involved in the mandatory program. We asked them to describe how they had chosen the service they had performed to complete their requirement, how they felt about their service experience, and how they felt about the mandatory program itself. The great majority reported having a positive experience performing their service. For example, one student who completed the requirement by working in a nursing home said:

> *It was just really rewarding to see with just a small amount of time for me, to make such a big difference for other people.*

When asked how they felt about the mandatory nature of the requirement, there were a few students who expressed a dislike for having to perform community service, rather than doing it freely of their own accord:

> *I think that if volunteering is required then it's not really the same. I think that volunteering is for people that want to be there to help someone, you know what I mean? So if you have to volunteer for 80 hours, then some people may be in a position where they don't really want to be there, so they are not really benefiting anyone.*

However, it was only a very few students who expressed these kinds of feelings about the program. Indeed, several students thought that the 40 hours mandated by the program were not sufficient and suggested that the requirement be increased:

> *It's not difficult at all to get 40 hours in the 4 years, that's like, what, 10 hours a year, so I personally would double or even triple it. You know, it's a really good thing.*

One of the most frequent complaints about the program was the lack of infrastructure supporting it. For example, many students described having difficulty finding an appropriate placement, because their school didn't help them in this process:

> *I think the teachers could make it easier to find volunteer work, because they just sort of said to us, go volunteer somewhere. They didn't really give us any opportunity or say OK, here are some things you can do. I think teachers or*

principals need to sit down and be like OK, if you are interested in this, do this, maybe associate it with some kind of a career goal. I think that would be really useful.

Service-Learning

One of the most popular kinds of community service programs operating in schools is the "service-learning" program. A recent report on service-learning in American schools indicates that nearly one in four schools had service-learning activities for their students and that over 4 million students participated in service-learning programs during the 2007–2008 academic year (Spring, Grimm, & Dietz, 2008). The key feature of this type of program, as its name implies, is the integration of community service with structured learning activities. Rather than merely requiring students to perform community service, the service-learning program, in addition, gives students the opportunity to reflect on and learn from their service experiences through activities such as classroom discussion, presentations, and journaling. The kind of service that students perform is typically organized so that it relates to the subject matter in a course or curriculum, and it is expected to enhance learning. For example, as part of a high school unit on poverty in a social studies course, students might work in a soup kitchen or tutor children from poor neighborhoods, so that they can learn about the impacts of poverty first-hand. According to widely accepted definitions of service-learning, the service that students engage in as part of a service-learning program should involve more than participating in a one-time event such as a fundraiser or park clean-up; it should occur over a sustained period and address real community needs (Scales & Roehlkepartain, 2004).

Are service-learning programs effective in promoting civic engagement? Many studies indicate that service-learning programs do indeed enhance civic participation. Westheimer and Kahne (2004), for example, assessed the impact of a service-learning program run by two teachers of an American civics course in a rural East Coast community. As part of their course requirements, students worked in small teams on a variety of public service projects in local government offices. One team of students, for example, investigated the feasibility of a recycling program for their community. They solicited the opinions of residents by means of a phone interview, and they collected data on the costs of the program and its potential environmental impact. In the process of working on their project, students interacted with government agencies, wrote a report, and presented their findings to their county's board of supervisors. Interviews with students involved in the program indicated that the service experience had a profound effect on their sense of civic responsibility. As one student said:

Everyone needs to do their part if they want something to be done... In politics, the people always say their opinions and get mad about this and that but then

> *they never do anything about what they feel... This [experience] makes me feel like you have to do your part.* (p. 250)

In addition to the interviews, the researchers administered surveys to students participating in the program and to a control group of students, taught by the same teachers, who did not undergo the service-learning program. The results showed that students participating in the service-learning program made significantly greater gains than students in the control group on several measures relating to civic participation, such as their sense that they could make a difference in their communities and had a personal responsibility to help others.

Other studies, however, have found little or no impact of service-learning on civic participation. Billig, Root, and Jesse (2005), for example, compared over 1,000 high school students participating in classes that had a service-learning component with students who were similar in age and school achievement but were enrolled in classes that did not have a service-learning component. Students in both types of classes completed a survey at the beginning and the end of the school year. The surveys assessed students' civic knowledge (e.g., their knowledge about the three branches of American government), their sense of attachment to their community (e.g., the extent to which they felt they had contributed to their community), their sense of civic responsibility (e.g., the extent to which they had acted to help the needy), and their civic engagement (e.g., the extent to which they had discussed politics, raised funds for a cause, sent a letter to a public official). The results of the study revealed very few differences between service-learning students and non-service-learning students on any of these indicators.

Why are there such conflicting results in studies of the effects of service-learning? A large part of the problem may be that there seems to be a wide variation in the way service-learning programs are implemented. Many are not really service-learning programs at all, in that they do not meet the key requirements considered to define a true service-learning program. As discussed earlier, these requirements are that the program is part of a course or curriculum, has clearly stated learning objectives, addresses real community needs, occurs over an extended period, and involves structured reflection on the experience (Skinner & Chapman, 1999; Scales & Roehlkepartain, 2004; Spring, Grimm, & Dietz, 2008). Janet Eyler, a prominent researcher in the service-learning field, suggests that many programs describing themselves as involving service-learning have only "brief 'add on' service activities largely unconnected to classroom discourse," and that "there is reason to believe that reflection gets rather short shrift in the typical service-learning experiences" (Eyler, 2002, p. 518).

When programs do meet these requirements, research evidence suggests that service-learning can indeed be effective in enhancing civic engagement. Alan Melchior (1999) administered pre- and postprogram surveys to students in 17 high-quality service-learning programs in middle and high schools across the United States, as well as to a comparison group of students not involved in service-learning. The programs were deemed high quality in that they had been in operation for more than a year, required above-average contributions in terms of service hours, had students regularly reflecting on their service experiences (in both oral and written form), and were linked to a formal curriculum. The survey results indicated that after completion of the program, those involved in service-learning were more likely to have been involved in voluntary service activities, and performed more hours of voluntary service, than did those in the comparison group. A longer-term follow-up, one year after the end of the program, however, indicated that many impacts of the program had dissipated.

A study by Conway, Amel, and Gerwien (2009) used meta-analysis, a statistical technique that combines the results of several studies of the same type of program, to make an overall determination of the effects of service-learning on citizenship and other outcomes. They included over 100 studies of service-learning in their analysis; these studies were undertaken in schools ranging from the elementary through middle and high school to higher education levels. The results indicated that service-learning programs do have a small but statistically significant impact on citizenship outcomes, which included activities such as volunteering and social activism. The outcomes were larger for those programs that included structured reflection on student experiences as part of the service-learning process. A number of studies have found that reflection on one's service experiences, particularly through discussion with others, is a critical component of effective service-learning programs (e.g., Astin, Vogelsan, Ikeda & Yee, 2000; Andolina et al., 2003).

Civic Education

The early 1900s saw great waves of new immigrants coming from Europe to the United States. They came knowing little about their new country. They had scant knowledge of its history, the way its government worked, or their rights and responsibilities as citizens. Education was seen as a powerful antidote to this lack of knowledge. It was assumed that if people were taught about the political structures of their new country and their role as citizens, they would participate more fully in national life. Research does indeed show that those who know more about their country's politics are more likely to participate (Delli Carpini & Keeter, 1996; Galston, 2001; Torney-Purta, & Amadeo, 2003). Delli Carpini and Keeter (1996), in their analysis of more than 50 years of survey data concerning people's knowledge of political institutions, leaders, processes, and policies, found that political knowledge was a highly significant predictor of voting. Torney-Purta and Amadeo (2003), analyzing data from a 28-country study of civic education sponsored by the International Association for the Evaluation of Educational Achievement (IEA), found that the strongest predictors of American 14-year-olds' intentions to vote were their level of civic knowledge and the extent to which they learned about elections and voting in their classes at school.

Civic education has been a part of the school curriculum in many countries for over 100 years. In the United States, the earliest courses in civics or government involved rote learning about the three main branches of American government (the judicial, the legislative, and the executive branch [i.e., the president]), the rights and responsibilities of citizens (such as the responsibility to vote), and the history of the United States, focusing on key figures such as Lincoln or Jefferson. One of the main goals of such courses was to instill a sense of patriotism and national identity in young citizens. Civic education in other countries appears to utilize this same approach and cover the same kinds of content. The IEA study of civic education in 28 democracies found that in most of the countries participating in the study, "teacher-centered" methods and the use of recitation were the most prevalent modes of instruction in the civics classroom (Losito & Mintrop, 2001), while the use of more student-centered activities such as student projects was much less prevalent. A comparative report on civic education in Europe stated that "all too often, civic education in European schools remains isolated from the outside world, aside from a one-day visit to city hall or to a parliament building" (Hooghe & Claes, 2009, p. 233).

What impact do such courses have on civic knowledge and engagement? A well-known study by Langton and Jennings in 1968 found that participation in civics or government courses in American schools had no significant impact on political involvement (though there was some indication that there were effects for children from ethnic minority backgrounds). A later study by Jennings and Niemi (1974) found a similar lack of impact for civic education as it was practiced at the time. More recent studies, however, have found that civic education courses do have a significant impact on civic knowledge and practice (Conover & Searing, 2000; Niemi & Junn, 1998). Niemi and Junn (1998), for example, in a major study of civic education based on data collected for the American National Assessment of Educational Progress (NAEP) in 1988, found that the more courses in civics that students took, and the more recently they had taken these courses, the more political knowledge they had. They determined that civics course work raised overall political knowledge by 4%, and that when course work was combined with regular classroom discussion of current events and other social issues, it raised political knowledge by as much as 11%.

Niemi and Junn's study suggests that a key factor in determining whether civic education is effective or not is the nature of the courses that students take. The kind of rote learning that was typical of American courses in civics from the very beginnings of such courses in the early 1900s up until the 1970s and beyond (and is still prevalent in many American and European courses) appears to have little impact on civic knowledge and engagement. In contrast, classes that involve active discussion of issues that students care about, that engage them in activities that allow them to develop civic participation skills and expose them to the political process, can have profound effects on students' civic knowledge and participation. This has been demonstrated in evaluations of innovative educational programs such as the CityWorks curriculum adopted in several Los Angeles high schools (Kahne, Chi, & Middaugh, 2006), the Student Voices curriculum followed in Philadelphia high schools (Pasek, Feldman, Romer, & Jamieson, 2008), and the KidsVoting USA classes operating in several American states (McDevitt & Kiousis, 2007).

The CityWorks curriculum, for example, had students engaging in active discussions about issues that mattered to them, such as teen pregnancy and drug use. Rather than learning about how government works from a textbook, students participated in simulations in which they took on roles such as those of lobbyists or local politicians involved in debates about public policy. They met with community leaders such as elected officials, media representatives, and community activists. In addition, they took action to address a local issue of their choice. Kahne, Chi, and Middaugh (2006) compared students who participated in classes in government that used the CityWorks curriculum with students who took a government course taught in the traditional manner (involving more textbook study and less active learning). They found that students in the CityWorks classes showed significantly greater gains on civic outcomes such as their future commitment to participate in their communities and work for social justice than did students in government classes taught in the traditional manner. As one CityWorks student said:

> *If I was never in this class, if something was wrong in my neighborhood, I wouldn't have known what to do. But now, since I'm in this classroom, if I think something's wrong in my neighborhood or something, I know where to go. Go to the City Council, call the Chamber of Commerce.* (p. 397)

School and Classroom Climate

Just as family climate and the nature of parent-child interactions influence civic engagement of young people, so, too, do the climate of the school and the nature of teacher-student interactions. This was certainly the opinion of American educational reformer, John Dewey, writing in the early 1900s. He saw the school as the "nurse of democracy," a place where students should be engaged in "active inquiry and careful deliberation in the significant and vital problems" that confront their communities, so that they would develop into active members of society when they became adults (Dewey, 1910, p. 55).

Recent research lends support to Dewey's notions (Campbell, 2008; Duke et al., 2009; Torney-Purta, Lehmann, Oswald, & Shulz, 2001). Political scientist David Campbell (2008), using data from the IEA Civic Education study, looked at the extent to which students experienced an "open" classroom climate in school, and how this related to their civic knowledge and expectations about future political participation. The IEA study defined an open classroom as one in which students felt free to express their opinions and to make up their own minds about issues. Students participating in the study indicated their perceptions of how open the climate of their school classrooms was by responding "strongly disagree," "disagree," "agree," or "strongly agree" to each of six statements, such as, "Students are encouraged to make up their own minds about issues," and, "Teachers respect our opinions and encourage us to express them during class." Campbell found that the more open the classroom climate was, the more political knowledge the students had, the greater their intention to vote when they became adults, and the more they said they would seek out information about candidates before voting. Another finding, both interesting and important, was that an open classroom climate had a much greater impact on students with lower socioeconomic status. This finding suggests that classrooms that encourage all students to express their opinions openly may be effective in reducing the differences in political engagement often seen between those who are low and high in socioeconomic status.

The classroom and the school serve as an important model of the larger society. If young people experience their school as democratic, in that teachers respect their students, expect students to treat each other with respect, and treat everyone fairly and equally, students will come to expect to see these democratic principles (of respect, fairness, and equality) in operation in other communities of which they become a part and in society-at-large. Students in such a school environment are more likely to see themselves as citizens of their school and to participate in school activities. Students' experiences as citizens of a school, in turn, influence their sense of citizenship in society and their commitment to civic life in general. This link between students' perceptions of their school and their societal commitments was demonstrated in a study by Flanagan, Cumsille, Gill, and Gallay (2007). They administered a survey to American high school students (ranging from 11 to 18 years of age) that assessed students' perception of the "democratic ethos" of their teachers. The measure of "democratic ethos" required students to indicate their agreement or disagreement with statements relating to their teachers' respect (e.g., "teachers expect students to listen to each others' opinions"), fairness (e.g., "teachers give all students a fair chance"), and tolerance (e.g., "teachers won't let students make fun of other students") in their dealings with young people. Students also completed a measure of "civic commitment" by indicating how important it was for them, in their future life, to do things such as work to stop prejudice and help those who are less fortunate. The results indicated a strong relationship between the democratic practices of teachers and students' future civic commitments.

A positive school climate can also produce an emotional connection and a sense of belonging between the student and the school and can enhance participation through this emotional connection, as well. Health researcher, Naomi Duke, and her colleagues (2009), using data from the National Longitudinal Study of Adolescent Health (Add Health), found that young people who experienced a sense of connection with their school at age 15, in that they felt close to the teachers and students at the school and perceived that the teachers cared about them and treated them fairly, were significantly more likely to be civically engaged when they were assessed six years later, as young adults. Among other actions, they were more likely to have volunteered, donated blood, worked with a political organization, and participated in a social action or community group.

School Norms

Adolescence is a time when individuals are particularly sensitive to the norms or traditions of the communities to which they belong. Schools, for most people, are the preeminent community to which they belong during this period of their lives. If one's peers at school believe that civic participation is important, this will have a powerful influence on one's own beliefs. Individuals who subscribe to normative beliefs will be accepted by their peers at school, while those who do not face the possibility of censure or rejection. Over time, these norms become internalized, and the individual subscribes to the belief without the need for peer acceptance or the threat of rejection. This line of reasoning suggests that if a student attends a school with a strong norm of civic participation, in which the majority of the student body believes that civic engagement is important, then that student will endorse and then internalize that belief.

Support for these ideas come from David Campbell's analysis of data from the Youth-Parent Socialization Study (YPSS), which he presents in his book, *Why We Vote: How Schools and Communities Shape Our Civic Life* (Campbell, 2006). The YPSS involved the administration of a survey to all students in the graduating classes of 77 American high schools in 1965, asking them, "What three things about a person are most important in showing that he is a good citizen?" Included in the list of possible choices was the response, "He votes in elections." High schools varied considerably in terms of the percentage of students who selected this response (from 46 to 85%), indicating wide variation in the extent to which there was a norm within each school regarding voting and civic participation. In a subsequent survey, administered more than 15 years later, these individuals were asked if they had voted in the presidential election of 1980. The results indicated that students who had attended a high school with a strong civic participation norm were significantly more likely to have voted in the presidential election held 15 years after they graduated from high school. Individuals from high schools with these norms were also more likely to be involved in volunteer work at the time of the follow-up survey.

Extracurricular Activities

The community of the school includes much more than classrooms and curricula. It also includes a wide variety of school clubs, teams, arts and cultural groups, and governing bodies in which students participate outside of the regular curriculum. Participation in these kinds of extracurricular activities can be seen as a form of civic participation in the school community, and there is strong evidence that participation in these activities can lead to civic engagement outside of the school, and in later life, as well (Glanville, 1999; Hart, Donnelly, Youniss, & Atkins, 2007; Smith, 1999; Youniss, McLellan, & Yates, 1997; Zaff, Moore, Papillo, & Williams, 2003). Jonathan Zaff and his colleagues (2003), for example, using data from a longitudinal study of American high school students (the National Education Longitudinal Study), found that students who had consistently participated in extracurricular activities in grades 8, 10, and 12 were nearly twice as likely to vote or volunteer two years after they had completed high school, compared to students who had not been involved in extracurricular activities. Dan Hart and colleagues (2007), also using data from the National Education Longitudinal Study, found that students who had participated in extracurricular activities when they were in grade 12 of high school were more likely to have voted in local and national elections and volunteered in their community, eight years after they had graduated from high school, at 26 years of age.

While a significant proportion of adolescents (70%, according to Feldman & Matjasko, 2005) do participate in structured extracurricular activities, there is considerable variation in the number of activities in which students participate, and a substantial proportion of students do not participate at all. Why is it that some students participate in extracurricular activities and others do not? Unfortunately, there is very little research into the factors that may initiate and sustain students' involvement in these kinds of activities (Feldman & Matjasko, 2005). The few studies that do address this issue suggest that schools themselves play an important role in determining how many of their students will engage in these kinds of activities. For example, it has been known for some time that the level of participation in extracurricular activities is much higher in small schools than it is in large schools (Barker & Gump, 1964; McNeal, 1999).

Research indicates that school climate may also play an important role in determining the proportion of students who participate in extracurricular activities. Sociologist Ralph McNeal examined the relationship between school climate and participation in extracurricular activities using data from the "Highschool and Beyond" study, gathered from tenth grade students from 281 high schools across the United States (McNeal, 1999). He found that students in schools with a problematic climate, characterized by conflict among students, students feeling unsafe while at school, and high levels of problems such as theft and drug use, were less likely to participate in extracurricular activities than were students in schools with less problematic climates.

Research suggests that one of the most important determinants of how many students in a school will participate in extracurricular activities is the number of such activities that are on offer in a particular school. Stearns and Glennie, in a recent study of high schools in the state of North Carolina, collected yearbooks from over 200 of the 300 high schools in the state, and used these yearbooks to determine how many extracurricular activities were offered at each school (Stearns & Glennie, 2010). From the North Carolina Education Research Data Center, they obtained the extracurricular activity participation rate for grade 9 students in each of the schools. They found that the more activities there were in a school, the greater the proportion of grade 9 students that participated in extracurricular activities, and this was true of almost every type of activity, from sports to the arts to community service.

Neighborhoods

For many of us, the community that is most important to us is the one in which we live—our neighborhood. If someone were to ask us how involved or engaged we were in our neighborhood, we would probably think of our relationships with our neighbors, our (and our children's) participation in local organizations or associations, or perhaps the kinds of things we do to help make our community a better place to live (for example, by participating in a neighborhood clean-up). Just as the kinds of schools our children attend affect participation in their school communities, so too do the kinds of neighborhoods in which we live affect our involvement in our local community and in the wider community, as well. Neighborhoods in which people know and trust one another, feel safe and secure, and have a variety of community groups and organizations to which they can belong are more likely to have residents who participate actively in community life.

This link between the nature of one's community and civic engagement was demonstrated in the recent study by Naomi Duke and her colleagues, using data from the National Study of Adolescent Health (Add Health), a longitudinal study of the causes and contexts of health-related behaviors of American adolescents (Duke et al., 2009). In this study, 15 year-old youth were asked a number of questions about the neighborhoods in which they lived. Among other things, they were asked if they knew most people in their neighborhood, if people in their neighborhood looked out for one another, and if they felt safe in their neighborhood. Several years later, when they were young adults of 21 and 22 years of age, they were asked about their current civic involvements—whether they had voted in the last presidential election, volunteered for a community organization, or contributed their time to a political organization, among other activities. The results showed that individuals who had lived in a safe and supportive community when they were 15 years of age were more likely to be civically engaged as young adults.

Like schools, neighborhoods can provide the two key elements outlined in our integrative model (see chapter 1) that encourage long-term, committed civic engagement. They can initiate civic involvement through the network of connections that individuals have with their neighbors or the activities and organizations available to them in their neighborhood, and they can sustain these involvements by providing a supportive environment and positive experiences to those who participate.

Relationships with Neighbors

Community psychologists Donald Unger and Abraham Wandersman use the term "neighboring" to refer to the extent to which neighbors interact with one another and feel a sense of attachment to their neighbors and to the neighborhood (Unger & Wandersman, 1985). Neighboring can involve chatting with the person who lives down the street, borrowing tools or baking supplies from the person next door, asking someone on your block to keep an eye on your house while you are away, or just feeling that there are people in your neighborhood who would support you if you needed them. Early research on this topic indicated that the more neighboring that occurred, the more likely individuals were to get involved in neighborhood organizations and work to improve their neighborhoods. Wandersman and Giamartino (1980), for example, looked at neighboring in two adjacent blocks in Nashville, Tennessee, to see if it related to residents' willingness to get involved in a neighborhood organization. This research was part of the Neighborhood Participation Project, a longitudinal study of resident participation in block organizations. The researchers measured neighboring by asking residents to respond to questions such as how many people on their block they would consider to be close friends and how often they socialized with people on their block. They also asked residents, "Do you feel a sense of community with other people on this block?" Shortly after completing these measures, all of the homes on each of the two blocks were approached by a community organizer, who talked about common concerns faced by block residents and tried to find someone who would be willing to host a block meeting in their home to discuss ways in which residents might work together to deal with these concerns.

The response of residents on the two adjacent blocks could not have been more different. In one of the blocks, not one person was willing to host a block meeting. When the organizer finally gave up on finding someone to host the meeting and scheduled it in a local housing services office, no one showed up. In the other block, by contrast, a meeting was scheduled at a resident's home and was attended by almost half the residents on the block. Why was there such a difference between the two blocks? The study results suggest that the amount of neighboring that went on in the two blocks played an important role. Residents of the block that held the successful meeting had shown much higher levels of neighboring and had a significantly greater sense of community than residents of the other block, according to their responses to the questions asked prior to the organization attempts.

Neighbors can help initiate civic participation in many ways. They can inform each other about opportunities for civic engagement and encourage one another to get involved. They can also establish norms relating to civic involvement; if one sees one's neighbors participating actively in civic life, this can create a norm of participation and enhance one's sense of responsibility to become involved oneself. Neighbors can also support one another in their initial involvements; it is much easier to attend a meeting of a block association if one knows and feels comfortable with others who will also be attending the meeting. It is no surprise, then, that residents of a block with high levels of neighboring and a greater sense of community would attend a meeting about neighborhood concerns.

More recent research indicates that neighboring is related to other forms of civic participation, in addition to becoming involved in neighborhood organizations. Bolland and McCallum (2002) assessed neighboring in six low-income, public housing neighborhoods in Hunstville, Alabama, using a scale that asked respondents whether, during the past year, any of their neighbors had asked them to do things such as lend them food or take care of their children while they ran an errand. They found that individuals who had engaged in more neighboring activities were more likely to have talked with their neighbors about issues such as violence and teen pregnancy, worked with others in their neighborhood to try to solve a neighborhood problem, and contacted an elected official to talk about a need or problem. Xu, Perkins, and Chow (2010) used data from the 2005 Chinese General Social Survey, an annual survey of a representative sample of rural and urban residents of China, to examine the relationship between neighboring and political participation. The survey included questions asking respondents, "How well do you know your neighbors?" and "How much do neighbors help each other or expect to be helped?," which provided an index of neighboring and sense of community. They found that individuals who engaged in more neighboring and had a stronger sense of community were significantly more likely to have voted in the last election for members of their Urban Neighborhood Committee or their Rural Villager Committee. A study by Lewis and Noguchi (2008), using data from the American Social Capital Benchmark Survey, found that males (but not females) who felt that their neighbors gave them a sense of community were more likely to have participated in a march, boycott or demonstration over the previous 12 months, compared to those whose neighbors did not give them a sense of community.

Neighborhood Activities and Organizations

Neighborhoods can affect civic involvement in other ways, as well. The mere presence of opportunities for neighbors to get together, whether just to socialize with one another or to work together in an organization or on a project, may serve to enhance the amount of neighboring that goes on and increase civic participation. A recent study by Dan Hart suggests that the availability of local social institutions that promote connections among neighbors can have an impact on civic engagement (Hart, 2011). Using data from the American National Longitudinal Study of Adolescent Health (Add Health), Hart looked at civic participation in young adults (18 to 26 years of age) and how it related to the distance from their home to the closest YMCA. The "Y" is one of the most prominent and ubiquitous neighborhood institutions in America, and Hart considered the presence of a YMCA to be an index of the availability of social institutions within a neighborhood. Results of the study indicated that the closer one lived to a YMCA, the more likely one was to have participated in a range of civic activities, such as volunteering or attending a public meeting, over the previous year.

What is it about neighborhood organizations that foster civic engagement? The key to producing long-term civic participation is to first get people involved but then to ensure their continued involvement by supporting their activities and providing them with positive experiences. Neighborhood organizations can provide both support and positive experiences; indeed, the extent to which they do this is an important determinant of residents' continued involvement and even the viability of the organizations themselves. This was demonstrated in a study by Prestby, Wandersman, Florin, Rich, & Chavis (1990). They administered questionnaires that asked individuals about the benefits and costs of participation in neighborhood associations to over 400 individuals, each of whom belonged to one of 29 different block associations in New York City. Respondents were asked to indicate the extent to which participation in the block association produced a variety of benefits or positive outcomes (e.g., learning new skills, gaining information, making friends, gaining recognition, improving the block), as well as the costs of participating in their neighborhood association (e.g., child care, time, giving up activities with friends or family, not feeling welcome, no organizational accomplishments). The results indicated that both perceived benefits and perceived costs related to level of participation, although benefits were more important determinants of level of participation than were costs. Individuals who experienced more positive outcomes participated more. In another phase of the study, the investigators compared 8 block organizations that were no longer functioning with 20 that had continued to function one year after the study's initial phase. They found that the more viable associations that had continued to function had leaders who had used a range of strategies to ensure positive outcomes for association members.

Another constellation of factors that seems to be related to residents' participation in neighborhood organizations is the climate of support in those organizations. Giamartino and Wandersman (1983) asked members of 17 block organizations in Nashville, Tennessee to complete Moos & Humphrey's (1973) Group Environment Scale. This scale assesses the perceived climate of a group or organization along ten dimensions, including cohesiveness within the group, supportiveness of the group's leader, the extent to which practical tasks are emphasized, and the degree to which the group's activities are organized and structured. Research participants were also asked to indicate how involved they had been in their organizations and whether their involvement had been increasing, decreasing, or unchanging. The results indicated that organizations that were perceived to provide a friendly, caring environment but at the same time had a clear and formalized structure and focused on practical, down-to-earth tasks, had higher levels of involvement than neighborhood organizations that did not have these characteristics.

Our own investigation of the Better Beginnings, Better Futures Project provides additional evidence of the importance that positive experiences and a climate of support have in enhancing participation in neighborhood organizations (see Cameron, Peirson, & Pancer, 1994; Nelson, Pancer, Hayward, & Peters, 2005; Pancer & Cameron, 1994; Peters et al., 2010). Better Beginnings, Better Futures is a neighborhood-based initiative designed to reduce social, emotional, and academic problems in children and youth in socioeconomically disadvantaged communities in the province of Ontario, Canada. Provincial funding was used to create neighborhood organizations in eight communities in the province, and these organizations worked with local schools and social service agencies to provide a wide variety of programs for children and families living in the community. One of the unique features of the Better Beginnings project was the participation of neighborhood residents, not just as participants in programs but also in creating, developing, implementing, administering, and evaluating the programs offered in their communities. Indeed, one of the requirements for receiving funding was that at least 51% of the members of the steering group coordinating activities at each Better Beginnings site had to be neighborhood residents. Residents, consequently, played an active role in activities such as hiring project staff, managing budgets, making presentations on behalf of the project, and strategic planning. A key factor in soliciting and sustaining the participation of residents in these activities was the welcoming climate of the projects and the opportunities they provided for residents to have positive experiences. This was amply demonstrated in residents' responses to questions in the many interviews we conducted to document the development of the initiative:

> *At the meetings, the community is heard and listened to, but also there is a response to what we've said from staff and fellow board members that are representing agencies... Community members are made to feel welcome and agency people are not agencies, but just like us.*

Youth Organizations

Neighborhood organizations are particularly influential with regard to the civic engagement of young people, especially organizations such as 4-H, Boy Scouts and Girl Scouts, and the "Y" that focus on youth. Many of these organizations have civic participation as one of their core objectives. For example, the mission of the Woodcraft Folk, a child and youth organization based in the United Kingdom, is "to educate and empower young people to be able to participate actively in society, improving their lives and others' through active citizenship." All of the many thousands of young people who join 4-H clubs recite a pledge that prominently features service to their community and their nation: "I pledge my head to clearer thinking, my heart to greater loyalty, my hands to larger service, my health to better living, for my club, my community, my country and my world." Several studies show that young people who are involved in these kinds of organizations are significantly more likely to become civically engaged (e.g., Lerner et al., 2009; McFarland and Thomas, 2006; Rosenthal, Feiring, & Lewis, 1998).

Richard Lerner and his colleagues, for example, examined the impact of youth organizational participation on civic engagement as part of their large-scale 4-H Study of Positive Youth Development, launched in 2002 (Lerner et al., 2005). In the first wave of this study, over 1,700 fifth graders and 1,100 of their parents from 13 American states completed questionnaires that asked about the young people's involvement in youth organizations and their "contribution" to community. They looked at involvement in four youth organizations, in particular 4-H, Boy Scouts or Girl Scouts, YMCA or YWCA, and Boys and Girls Clubs. These are among the most popular youth organizations in the United States and, in addition, they all have a focus on positive youth development, in that they build young people's life skills, involve positive and sustained relationships between youth and adults, and give youth an opportunity to use their skills "as both participants and leaders in valued community activities" (Lerner et al., 2009, p. 12).

The researchers assessed community contribution in two ways. First, they asked the young respondents questions such as, "If you imagine yourself doing well in all areas of your life, what would you be like? What sorts of things would you do?" Answers were given a score of 0 for contribution if they contained no mention of others or of community or society (e.g., "gets an A on every test"), a 1 if they indicated that the youth cared about those around him or her (e.g., being "kind to others"), or a 2 if they indicated that the youth wanted to contribute significantly to society (e.g., by "talking to the governor about school issues"). Respondents also completed a scale designed to assess their sense of social responsibility (the Social Responsibility Scale, Greenberger & Bond, 1984) in which they indicated their agreement or disagreement with statements such as, "It is important to me to contribute to my community and my society." The results indicated that the more time young people had spent participating in one of the youth organizations, the more important they considered contributing to their community to be.

Participation in a youth organization can have long-lasting effects on young people's civic participation. Analysis of subsequent waves of data collected in the 4-H study indicated that youth who had participated in 4-H activities in grade 5 scored 25% higher on the community contribution measure four years later, when they were in grade 9, compared to youth who had not participated in 4-H (Lerner et al.,

2009). Other research indicates even longer-term effects. McFarland and Thomas (2006), in their analyses of data from the American National Longitudinal Study of Adolescent Health (Add Health), found that young people who were involved in local youth centers such as the YMCA when they were high school students were significantly more likely to vote, volunteer with a community organization, and/or get involved in a political campaign seven years later, when they were young adults of 18 to 26 years of age. Ladewig and Thomas (1987) administered a survey to adults in their 40s and 50s, asking them whether they had belonged to youth organizations such as 4-H, YM-YWCA, or Boys and Girls club. They found that adults who had belonged to these organizations in their youth were twice as likely to be civically active in organizations such as political groups, chambers of commerce, and community committees, compared to individuals who had not been involved in youth organizations as adolescents. They even seem to have passed their civic activism on to their children; even the children of youth group alumni were more active in youth organizations than were the children of non-alumni.

Summary

Schools and neighborhoods are the first real communities that an individual encounters, and the nature of these communities has a profound impact on civic engagement. Schools play an active role in promoting civic participation through the curricula and programs that they provide, such as mandatory service programs, service learning programs, and courses in civic education. Research tells us that these kinds of programs can be effective in producing long-term civic participation if they adhere to certain principles, such as having students reflect upon and discuss their experiences. The research also shows that the climate of schools and classrooms can also have an impact on young people's civic engagement. Schools that encourage respect among students, allow students to express their views openly, feel safe, and offer a wide range of extracurricular activities will have students that go on to be active citizens when they become adults.

Neighborhoods, too, influence civic engagement. Neighborhoods characterized by high levels of "neighboring," in which individuals know and trust one another, tend to have more civically involved residents. The presence of neighborhood organizations, particularly those that provide a welcoming, supportive environment, also encourages civic participation. Youth organizations, in particular, can have a long-lasting impact on individuals' civic involvements. Youth who get involved in organizations such as the "Y," 4H clubs, or Scouts show greater involvement in civic activities well into adulthood.

4

The Influence of Places of Work and Worship on Civic Engagement

In the last chapter, I discussed the ways in which schools and neighborhoods can affect our participation in civic life. We all participate in other communities that also have a profound influence on our lives. Most of us will spend a large proportion of our adult life in a workplace. A large majority of us will grow up in a religious tradition and have at least some involvement in a church, synagogue, mosque, temple, or other religious institution. Our relationship with these communities of work and worship cannot help but affect how we participate in the other communities of which we are a part.

Religion and Civic Engagement

While there are large variations in religious observance around the world, a significant proportion of individuals in almost every country participate in some kind of religious activity on a regular basis. In a survey of Americans conducted by the Gallup polling organization, 62% of the respondents said they were members of a "church or synagogue," and 44% reported that they attended religious services every week or almost every week. Fifty-six percent of respondents indicated that religion was "very important" in their lives, and only 17% stated that it was "not very important." Taking all of their results into consideration, the Gallup report claimed that more than 8 in 10 Americans identify with a religion, say that religion is import in their lives, and attend church at least occasionally (Newport, 2007).

Religion is a significant force in the lives of people living in other nations, as well. Gallup's International Millennium Survey, which polled people in 60 countries around the world in October of 1999, found that 87% of the respondents thought of themselves as being part of some religion. Nearly a third of those surveyed reported that they attended religious services regularly. In some parts of the world, religious observance is remarkably high; 99% of the respondents from

West Africa saw themselves as being part of a religion, and 82% reported attending religious services at least weekly (Carballo, 2000).

People's religious beliefs and practices have been linked to every form of civic participation. Several studies have shown an association between religion and volunteering (e.g., Lam, 2002; Wilson & Musick, 1997; Smetana & Metzger, 2005; Smith & Faris, 2002). Sociologists Christian Smith and Robert Faris, for example, examined data from the "Monitoring the Future" (MTF) survey administered to a nationally representative sample of American high school students to look at the association between religion and community service. They found that students who attended religious services weekly were more than twice as likely to participate regularly in community affairs or volunteer work compared to students who never attended religious services (Smith & Faris, 2002). Wilson and Musick (1997) found similar results in a survey of American adults; those who attended religious services frequently were more likely to have done volunteer work during the previous year than those who had attended less frequently. Other indices of religiosity, besides frequency of attendance at religious services, also correlate with volunteering. Pui-Yan Lam (2002), using data from a 1996 survey on "God and Society in North America," found that individuals who were members of a religious or church-related[1] organization were much more likely to have done volunteer work than were those who were not members. She also found that individuals who prayed frequently and read religious materials were more likely to volunteer than were those who did not. Smetana and Metzger (2005), in a study of middle-class African American youth, found that young people who considered themselves to be more spiritual, endorsing statements such as "I maintain an inner awareness of God's presence in my life," were more likely to have engaged in volunteering and community service, among other civic activities. Youniss, McLellan, and Yates (1999) report results from the Monitoring the Future survey of American high school students indicating that young people who believe that religion is important in their lives are almost three times more likely to have performed community service compared to youth who don't believe that religion is important to them.

Religion has also been associated with political participation. Jonathan Zaff and his colleagues (Zaff et al., 2003), using data from the American National Educational Longitudinal Study (NELS), found that youth who attended religious services when they were in grade 10 were 24% more likely than youth who did not attend religious services to have voted four years later, when they were young adults. Verba, Schlozman, and Brady, in their landmark study of adult political participation in the United States, found that the more individuals attended religious services, the more likely they were to have voted in local and

[1] In this chapter, I will be using "church" as the generic term referring to a place of worship of any faith (e.g., church, mosque, synagogue, temple, etc.).

national elections (Verba et al., 1995). Other research indicates that individuals who attend religious services regularly are more likely to engage in a wide range of political activities, such as attending a public meeting, writing a letter to an elected official, or signing a petition (Jones-Correa & Leal, 2001).

Other forms of civic participation, such as social activism and community organizing, have also been strongly linked with religion. One of the most powerful figures in the history of the civil rights movement in the United States was Martin Luther King, the Baptist minister who, in 1957, helped found an organization of African-American ministers and religious leaders known as the Southern Christian Leadership Conference (SCLC). King and the SCLC advocated non-violent protest to redress civic ills and organized some of the largest and most effective protests that America had ever seen, such as the march of over 200,000 people on Washington, DC in August of 1963 in support of changes in civil rights legislation. The SCLC spearheaded the march, which culminated in Dr. King's famous "I have a dream" speech, envisioning a future in which people would be known for "the content of their character" and not "the color of their skin." Religion has continued to be strongly associated with social activism and community organizing to the present day. One example of the link between religion and social action is the Faith-Based Community Organizing (FBCO) groups (Wood & Warren, 2002). These are local groups of Christian and non-Christian congregations in the United States that have banded together and hired professional community organizers to help them wield the political force necessary to address important social problems facing their communities. Wood and Warren (2002) estimate that there are about 3,500 religious congregations that are members of FBCOs. These organizations have tackled a wide range of issues, including public school reform, affordable housing, a reduction in gang violence, and services for seniors. For example, one Texas-based FBCO group, working since the early 1980s to influence policy at the state level, led a drive that resulted in the state allocating an additional 2.8 billion dollars to poor schools in the state as part of an educational reform package.

What is it about people's religious beliefs and practices that motivates individuals to be more civically engaged? The theoretical model presented in chapter 1 suggests that individuals will begin to be involved in civic life when "initiating" factors are present, such as their values, the influence of others, or social norms relating to civic participation. They will continue to be involved if "sustaining" factors are also present. These sustaining factors include the experience of positive outcomes as a result of civic involvement and feeling a sense of community within the social milieu in which they perform their civic activities. Religion and religious organizations provide elements that both initiate and sustain civic involvement. They help initiate civic participation through the values of social responsibility that they espouse, the influence of clergy and co-religionists, and the wealth of opportunities they provide for involvement, among other things. They also serve to sustain civic engagement by providing a sense of community among those who participate in civic activities both within and outside the church.

Social Influence and Social Networks

People don't just pray when they attend a mosque, church, or synagogue. They talk with one another about a wide range of subjects, form friendships, ask for and give each other advice, and enlist the help of fellow congregants with both church and non-church activities and organizations. The most common way in which people become engaged in civic organizations, political activities, or social activism is by being asked by a friend or acquaintance to participate. Because churches are places where people form friendships and make acquaintances, they become an important setting for the "recruitment" of individuals for civic activities. This was forcefully demonstrated in the study of civic participation in the United States by Verba, Schlozman, and Brady (1995). Among the questions asked in their survey of a random sample of over 15,000 Americans was whether they had been asked personally by a co-religionist to do political campaign work, contact a public official, get involved in a protest, or participate in a community organization. Nearly one in four individuals indicated that they had been asked to do one or more of these things. The percentage was much higher for those individuals who belonged to a church that sanctioned political activity, in that the clergy (at least sometimes) discussed political issues. Of those who belonged to these kinds of churches, 50% indicated that they had been asked to take part in some kind of political action, compared to only 11% who belonged to churches where the clergy never discussed local or national political issues from the pulpit.

The network of friends and acquaintances that are established through one's religious affiliations exert influence on individuals in a more indirect manner, as well. Simply engaging in a discussion about civic affairs or politics with fellow congregants can provide information and reinforce the notion that awareness of and involvement in civil society is important. Scheufele, Nisbet, and Brossard (2003), using data from the 2000 American National Election Study, found that individuals who attended church frequently were more likely to engage in political discussions with fellow church members, and that these discussions were related to more viewing of national television news, greater political knowledge, and enhanced political participation. McKenzie (2004), in a study of African American churchgoers, found that individuals who indicated that they had "talked to people about political matters" at their church or place of worship were more likely to vote and to engage in a number of other political activities such as attending political fundraisers, driving people to the polls on election day, and helping with voter registration.

Church-based social networks are also important in the establishment of social norms that compel civic action without the need for direct persuasion.

When one sees individuals in one's church network working together in a soup kitchen, helping immigrants adjust to their new community, or providing clothing for the poor, this establishes a norm of social responsibility that acts as a strong incentive for one's own involvement. The normative influence of religious social networks on civic participation, in the form of volunteering, was examined by Becker and Dhingra (2001), using data from a survey of residents in four communities in the state of New York. In their survey, they asked residents several questions about their religious beliefs, affiliations, and practices, such as how frequently they attended church and how important their religious beliefs were to them. They also asked a number of questions about their social networks, such as how many of their good friends (none, hardly any, some, many, nearly all) they had met through their church congregation. They found that among individuals who attended a church, those who had large numbers of church members in their network of close friends were significantly more likely to volunteer than those who had fewer church members in their friendship network. They claim that the "church effect" in volunteering (the fact that churchgoers volunteer in larger numbers than non-churchgoers) happens mainly because of these church-based friendship networks and the norms established in these networks.

Values and Beliefs

Every major religion has a set of beliefs that lie at the core of how that religion defines itself. These beliefs have to do with the need for people to reach out beyond themselves and their families and to form a relationship with God. They also have to do with reaching out to others and to the wider community through acts of charity and compassion. Individuals who identify with a religious tradition, then, are subscribing to a set of beliefs that emphasize a concern for others and active involvement in improving their communities and the world around them. A central tenet of Judaism, for example, is a belief in *tikkun olam,* which means "repairing the world." Jews are expected to act to repair the world through the performance of *mitzvot,* or "good deeds." These deeds involve not only helping those who are in need but also working for social justice by advocating for the economic and political rights of oppressed groups.

Given the centrality of the belief in service to others in major religions, one would expect that religious individuals would be more likely to subscribe to this core belief, and seek out opportunities to help others. This indeed appears to be the case. Robert Serow and Julia Dreyden conducted a survey of nearly 2,000 students attending university in the southeastern United States (Serow & Dreyden, 1990), asking them to select from a set of eight choices "the single value they expected to be most important over their adult lives" (p. 559). The three values that respondents most frequently selected were professional satisfaction, family, and spiritual fulfillment/religion. They also asked respondents how often they had participated in unpaid community service or volunteer work off-campus. They found that of those who indicated that religion was the most important value, 52% performed community service at least monthly; of those who named another value as most important, only 32% engaged in service that often. The researchers also found that students attending a college with a strong religious emphasis were significantly more likely to be involved in community service than were students who attended institutions with less religious emphasis.

Of course, religion does much more than provide individuals with a belief system that emphasizes helping others or seeking social justice. According to Youniss, McClellan, and Yates (1999), belonging to a religious tradition helps individuals feel that they are a part of something with a set of traditions and a history that transcends the self. In this context, their acts in the cause of service or social justice are imbued with a deeper meaning and serve to connect individuals not only with their fellow human beings but with their cultural traditions and history. Youniss and Yates saw evidence of this in their study of high school students who had worked at a soup kitchen near their school in Washington, DC (Youniss & Yates, 1997). Students' involvement with the soup kitchen was one of the requirements of their high school religion course on social justice. In addition to serving in the kitchen, the students discussed their experiences at the soup kitchen in small group sessions and wrote essays reflecting on what their service meant to them. These discussions and essays indicated that the students frequently (and spontaneously) saw their service as part of a religious tradition that emphasized people's common humanity. For example, one student's essay stated

> *I'm being grateful for what I have and to know that someone cares for me. These people are like you and me, but the only difference is that they have to sleep on hard cold cement and we sleep with our eyes closed on soft beds... We should take a moral stand to what's happening in our community and try as decent human beings to fix up our gift from God.* (Youniss & Yates, 1997, p. 96)

Religions and denominations within religious traditions, of course, differ with one another on certain core values and beliefs, and these differences most certainly have an impact on the nature and level of their civic engagement. Several studies indicate that individuals belonging to churches that espouse more conservative or fundamentalist religious beliefs will be less likely to participate in secular community organizations or in social activism (e.g., Schwadel, 2005; Sherkat & Blocker, 1993). Sherkat and Blocker, for example, using data collected by the University of Michigan's Survey Research Center in the 1960s and 1970s, found that individuals who expressed more literal beliefs in the Bible (i.e., they endorsed the statement "The Bible is God's word and all it says is true") were less likely to have participated in environmental activism or protest activities such as antiwar or civil rights demonstrations than were individuals with less literal beliefs. Schwadel (2005), using data from a survey administered in the midwestern United States, found that individuals with more literal views of the Bible were less likely to participate in non-church community organizations. At the same time, however, individuals belonging to fundamentalist or evangelical churches spend significantly more time volunteering within their church than do members of more mainstream congregations (Campbell, 2004). Evangelical churches have also been very successful in mobilizing their congregants for political action. For example, the "Christian Right," a network of fundamentalist individuals, churches, and organizations operating in the United States, has wielded considerable political power since the 1970's.

Role Models

Many individuals throughout history have served as significant role models of civic engagement and concern for their communities. Mahatma Gandhi, Martin Luther King, Mother Theresa, Nelson Mandela—all of these individuals have been a source of inspiration through their selfless work for the poor, indigent and powerless, and for the cause of social justice. Psychologists have described these individuals as "moral exemplars" who have committed their lives to helping others and advocating for human rights (Colby & Damon, 1992; Carlo, Hardy, & Albert, 2006). For every Ghandi and Martin Luther King, whose names are recognized throughout the world, there are thousands of other individuals, some well-known and others much less well-known, who have shown the same kind of commitment to human welfare. Developmental psychologists Ann Colby and Bill Damon (Colby & Damon, 1992) describe 23 of these individuals in their book, *Some Do Care: Contemporary Lives of Moral Commitment.* One of the striking things that Colby and Damon noted was that 80% of the individuals they studied saw their religion as the basis for their values and their commitment to helping others.

Colby and Damon's work inspired many subsequent studies of individuals who have shown exemplary moral behavior, and several of these studies have shown a strong link between moral exemplarity and religious faith. Matsuba and Walker (2004), for example, studied young adults, 18 to 30 years of age, who had been nominated by the executive directors of a variety of social organizations (e.g., Big Brothers, youth service agencies, crisis centers) as having shown "extraordinary moral commitment." These individuals were compared on several variables with a group of individuals who were matched in age, gender, level of education, and ethnicity but who had not demonstrated the same kind of moral commitment. The variable that most distinguished the moral exemplars from the comparison individuals was their high level of faith development.

This research indicates that religious beliefs frequently serve as the foundation of civic action in individuals who have shown exemplary commitment to human welfare. These individuals are often inspired by role models within their faith. We found this in our own study of young people who had been nominated as "committed volunteers" by local service agencies (Pancer & Pratt, 1999). For example, one young woman in our study, when asked what got her started as a volunteer, said

> *I think that behind everything has been my faith...I want to do things because Christ did so much for me and because that's what he's told us to do and to use our gifts...with other people and so...working in the community and helping other people has come really out of my Christian background and my faith.*

In turn, those who are inspired to contribute to society by religious role models become models of civic participation and community-mindedness themselves, thus inspiring others to emulate them.

Opportunities for Engagement

Historically, it was churches, not governments, that established the first organized social services for the poor, the sick, the elderly, orphaned children, and others in society who were in need. Even after governments took over many of these services, providing unemployment insurance, old-age pensions, and disability allowances, churches maintained an active role in helping those in need. A survey of a nationally representative sample of American religious congregations indicated that 92% of congregations are involved in social service projects, ranging from the provision of food, clothing, and housing to dealing with domestic violence and substance abuse (Saxon-Harrold, Wiener, McCormack, & Weber, 2000). In my own community, it is the local churches that have organized most of the soup kitchens that feed those who are hungry and cannot afford to buy food, provide shelter in "out-of-the-cold" programs for homeless people with nowhere warm to sleep on frigid winter nights, and play a prominent role in advocating for improved benefits for the poor.

In order to staff these programs, clergy and church members who organize the programs seek out fellow congregants as volunteers. It also means that, within churches, there are many opportunities for members to become involved in community service and other civic activities. Individuals who belong to churches, then, are more likely to be asked to participate in community services provided by the church and have more opportunities to provide service. It is not surprising that when teenaged volunteers are asked how they got involved in community service, one of the most frequent ways they mention is through a church group (Hogdkinson & Weitzman, 1997). Research also indicates that students who attend church-affiliated schools are significantly more likely to perform community service than are students who attend public schools, probably because of the greater opportunities for service at the church schools (Youniss, McLellan, & Yates, 1999).

Churches offer opportunities for other forms of civic involvement as well. Beyerlein and Chaves (2003) studied the political activities of religious organizations in the United States with data from the National Congregations Study. This study involved interviews with a key informant, typically a minister, priest, rabbi, or other religious leader, from a representative sample of nearly 1,500 religious congregations across the country. Those interviewed were asked whether members of their congregations had been informed during worship services within the previous 12 months about opportunities to engage in political activities such as demonstrating or lobbying, and whether the congregation had a meeting, group, class or event focusing on discussing political issues or engaging in political activities such as getting people registered to vote, lobbying elected officials, or participating in a demonstration. While there were differences in these kinds of activities among different religious traditions, the results indicated that a substantial proportion of congregations from all major religious traditions provided opportunities for political involvement. Forty-one percent of the congregations had provided at least one kind of opportunity for political involvement to their members; 26% had informed congregants about political activity opportunities during a worship service; 17% had distributed voter guides to congregants; and nearly 10% of congregations organized groups to participate in a march or demonstration.

In many ways, churches provide the ideal setting for political mobilization. They serve as significant sources of political information. Their congregants constitute networks of friends and acquaintances in which information and influence can be quickly and efficiently communicated. They have leaders, both among their clergy and among lay members, who have the ability to influence and organize congregants for political activity. They also provide space for meetings, administrative capacity, and even financial support that can be utilized for political action. Political scientist and commentator Anna Greenberg describes churches as "political institutions," which serve as "sources of political information, opportunities, resources and incentives to engage the political process" (Greenberg, 2000, p. 378).

The Development of Civic Skills

People are involved in varying ways and degrees with the religious organizations to which they belong. Some will merely attend religious services (sporadically or regularly). Some will also take part in other church-related activities; they may sing in a choir, teach religious school, do outreach or missionary work, or sit on a church committee or board. Verba, Schlozman, and Brady (1995) suggest that these latter activities build important skills that enable individuals to participate in civic affairs in the broader community. In their survey study of American civic activities, Verba and colleagues asked respondents affiliated with a church whether, in the previous six months, they had done things within their church such as writing a letter, attending a meeting where they took part in making a decision, or giving a presentation or a speech. They found that a substantial percentage of church members had done one or more of these things. For example, nearly a third had attended a church meeting where decisions were made. These activities, the researchers suggest, help develop individuals' organizational and communication skills, which allow them to participate effectively in community activities both within and outside their church. Analyses of their survey data indicated that it was the skills that church members learned through their church activities, rather than just their attendance at church, that resulted in greater civic engagement for church members compared to those unaffiliated with a church.

Recent research supports these ideas. Driskell, Lyon, and Embry (2008), using data from a nationally representative survey on religion and politics in America, looked at different kinds of church involvement and how these activities related to involvement in a wide range of civic organizations outside of the church (e.g., arts organizations, service clubs, ethnic associations, neighborhood groups, political parties). They examined three aspects of religious involvement: frequency of attendance at religious services, religious "participation," and religious "involvement." Religious participation was measured by simply summing the number of different church activities (e.g., choir practice, outreach programs, committee work) in which the respondent had participated over the previous month. To assess religious involvement, respondents were asked *how* involved they were in each activity, by indicating if they belonged, volunteered, contributed, or led the activity they were involved in. The results indicated that, while attendance at religious services and religious participation were only modestly related to civic organizational activity, religious involvement was highly related to civic activities. Individuals who contributed to or led church activities were much more likely to participate in civic activities outside the church.

The Workplace and Civic Engagement

A number of things that happen in churches and other religious organizations also happen within workplaces. We have conversations with our colleagues and fellow workers about a wide range of subjects, both work related and non–work related, and form networks of friendship and support. Our supervisors and coworkers, intentionally and unintentionally, influence our thinking and behavior relating to our jobs and to the outside world. We have the opportunity to learn skills such as organizing meetings or making presentations that we can utilize within the workplace and in other settings. And while the kinds of values endorsed within a workplace are often more heterogeneous than those that are found within groups of individuals who have common religious beliefs, there are often shared beliefs and values in many kinds of work settings. All of these things that happen in workplaces have the potential to influence civic participation.

Social Influence and Social Networks

The most common way in which individuals get involved in civic activities such as volunteering or political activism is by being asked. Like churches, workplaces are settings in which people form friendships and make acquaintances. These friends and acquaintances are important sources of recruitment for civic participation. Earlier in this chapter, I discussed some of the results of the study conducted by political scientists Sidney Verba, Kay Schlozman, and Henry Brady (1995), in which they looked at the influence of Americans' organizational affiliations, such as church membership, on civic participation. Their study showed that nearly one in four individuals had been asked by a coreligionist to participate in some form of political activity. Verba and his colleagues found that these kinds of requests were also made in work settings, though to a lesser degree. Of the respondents to their survey, 13% indicated that they had been asked by a fellow worker to engage in political activities such as voting, contacting a public official, or signing a petition. Interestingly, 30% of those requests came from individuals' supervisors, and, of those requests, 70% were successful in getting the individual to participate.

Workplace friends and acquaintances influence one's civic participation in a less direct manner, as well, through the process of discussion and social interaction. Discussions at the water cooler (or on the assembly line) aren't always about things like sports, recipes, and home repairs; they often are concerned with community and political affairs, as well. In fact, a number of studies show that individuals are more likely to discuss politics with their coworkers than with friends, neighbors, or other individuals, with the possible exception of their spouses (Beck, 1991; Wyatt, Katz, & Kim, 2000). But the people one encounters at work are different from those one encounters in one's church or community organization in one key respect—they tend to be more diverse in both background and belief. One's church is typically populated by like-minded individuals who share one's political, as well as spiritual, beliefs. By contrast, at work, one encounters individuals who may differ considerably in terms of not only political beliefs, but other characteristics, such as race and ethnicity, as well. This means that, at work, one can expect to discuss politics and social issues with individuals whose opinions and political affiliations are very different from one's own.

Sociologist Dietram Scheufele and his colleagues (Scheufele, Nisbet, Brossard, & Nisbet, 2004) consider this kind of discussion among individuals with different opinions and political affiliations to be the "soul of democracy" (p. 332). They suggest that discussions with non-like-minded individuals have two important effects. First, the exposure to differing points of view forces one to consider others' perspectives and possibly reevaluate and reformulate one's own views. Second, these kinds of discussions motivate individuals to become better informed about the issues involved, through reading newspapers, watching the news on TV, and consulting other sources of information. This increase in knowledge, in turn, produces greater political involvement. Scheufele and colleagues found evidence supporting their views in a national survey they conducted in 2002. They asked survey respondents who they talked to at work about political issues and candidates; how often they read about national or international affairs or watched the news about these affairs on TV; and whether they had been involved in activities such as voting in the last election, working for a political campaign, or contacting a public official. They found that the more individuals had talked with people of diverse backgrounds and political views at work, the more they read the newspapers or watched TV news. And the more they became politically informed, the more likely they were to become engaged in political activities such as working on a political campaign.

The Development of Civic Skills

Work settings provide individuals with opportunities to learn a wide variety of skills. At work, individuals are often required to make presentations, take part in decision-making meetings, and work with a team to achieve a goal or make a product. The skills acquired in performing these tasks are very similar to the kinds of skills that are required when one engages in civic or political activities. This suggests that individuals who learn these skills in the workplace will feel comfortable and efficacious in civic or political settings that require similar skills; in other words, there will be spillover from the work to the civic setting (Greenberg, Grunberg, & Daniel, 1996). Experience with such tasks, which require actively working with others, may also enhance people's appreciation for the importance of participation in general.

This kind of theorizing forms the basis of the "civic voluntarism model" outlined by Verba, Schlozman, and Brady in their book *Voice and Equality: Civic Voluntarism in American Politics* (Verba et al., 1995). They assert that individuals who acquire "civic" skills in churches, workplaces, and other settings will be more likely to participate in political affairs than will individuals who have not acquired these skills. Results of their survey of civic activities in the United States indicate that individuals who had done things at work such as attending a decision-making meeting, writing a letter, or making a presentation were significantly more likely to have participated in civic activities such as voting, contacting a public official, taking part in a demonstration, or serving on a local board or council. Verba and colleagues suggest that among the various kinds of institutions with which individuals are affiliated, workplaces offer the greatest number of opportunities to learn civic skills. For example, 69% of those affiliated with a workplace indicated that they had attended a decision-making meeting at work within the previous six months, compared to only 32% of church-affiliated individuals who had attended such a meeting at their church over the same period.

While several studies indicate that participation in the workplace is linked to greater civic engagement, the relationship found is typically small, and some studies have found no relationship at all between workplace involvement and civic participation (Ayala, 2000; Adman, 2008). Ayala (2000), for example, using data from the 1990 American Citizen Participation Study, looked at the extent to which individuals participated in decision making in three settings: their workplace, their church, or a community organization. Respondents to this survey indicated whether they had been involved in activities such as planning a meeting, making a presentation, or attending a decision-making meeting in each of these settings. They also indicated the extent to which they had been involved in political activities such as voting, working on a political campaign, or serving on a local community board. Ayala's analyses indicated a strong link between political involvement and participation in church and community organizations but a much weaker link between work-setting participation and political involvement. The reason for this, Ayala suggests, is that the workplace is a less "voluntary" setting than one's church or community organization. Even though individuals may practice and learn the same kinds of civic skills by participating in planning and decision making in each type of organization, participation in these activities in the workplace is a requirement of the job rather than freely chosen. Consequently, participation in the work setting will be less effective in motivating individuals to practice these skills in other arenas, such as political and community life.

Opportunities for Civic Engagement: Corporate Volunteer Programs

Over the last 20 years or so, it has become common to think of not only individuals but also corporations and businesses as "citizens." "Corporate citizenship" or "corporate social responsibility" has to do with how corporations relate to the communities (usually local but also global) of which they are a part. The good corporate citizen contributes to the well-being of its community, not just by providing employment but also by working in partnership with community agencies and organizations to enhance the lives of all community members. One of the ways in which companies do this is through corporate volunteer programs. These programs can take many forms. Some companies give their employees days off from work to volunteer with community agencies and organizations. Others have taken part in disaster relief. Some have focused on particular issues such as health care or education and have their employees take part in events such as fundraisers that support these causes.

Corporate or employee volunteer programs are becoming an increasingly prominent feature of corporate life across North America. Fifty-eight per cent of the 248 companies surveyed in 2000 by the Points of Light Foundation in the United States had formal volunteer programs (Points of Light Foundation, 2000). Over half of the companies surveyed incorporated a commitment to community service in their mission statements. Canadian businesses and corporations have also demonstrated significant support for volunteering. The 2001 National Survey of Giving, Volunteering, and Participating in Canada (Hall, McKeown, & Roberts, 2001) reported that 27% of employed volunteers indicated that their employer had given them approval to modify their hours of work so that they could volunteer.

These kinds of programs provide all the elements necessary to produce committed, life-long volunteers among employees. The programs initiate volunteering through a process of social influence, in that supervisors and fellow employees encourage individuals to take part in the program. Also, when large numbers of employees participate, this creates strong social norms that also encourage individuals to take part. On a systemic level, employee volunteer programs create more opportunities for civic engagement. The programs also serve to sustain volunteering by acknowledging, supporting, and, sometimes, rewarding employee volunteer efforts.

My own research, with colleagues Mark Baetz and Evelina Rog, provides evidence that corporate volunteer programs can indeed motivate increased civic engagement through volunteering among employees (Bart, Baetz, & Pancer, 2009; Pancer, Baetz, & Rog, 2002; Rog, Pancer, & Baetz, 2004). To assess the impact of corporate volunteer programs, we conducted interviews with over 100 employees of the Ford Motor Company of Canada. Ford is one of the largest companies in Canada to embark on a significant corporate volunteer program. The program originated from a 1998 team-building exercise, known as the Business Leadership Initiative (BLI). The initiative involved three days of meetings and activities designed to share the corporate vision with all its salaried employees. One aspect of Ford's vision was its desire to demonstrate "corporate citizenship." On the first day of the meetings, teams of employees traveled on a fleet of buses to volunteer at nonprofit organizations to experience what corporate citizenship was all about through a hands-on experience of giving back to the community. The event was so successful that many employees asked how they could get more involved in the community. Sensing an opportunity for team-building, as well as for enhancing its image as a responsible corporate citizen, Ford began its formal corporate volunteer program in 2000.

The program allows salaried employees to spend up to 16 hours per year, on company time, volunteering in the community. For a community organization to qualify for support by Ford volunteers, it has to be a registered nonprofit, charitable group. Qualifying projects have to involve teams of at least five employees to facilitate team-building and leadership skills. Other requirements are that all work has to be completed during regular business hours and that projects must encompass four-hour, one-day, or two-day off-site tasks and projects. Volunteer opportunities, including all of the details that potential volunteers need—the organization, the type of work, where to show up—are listed in detail on a website on the company's intranet, and employees register for the projects that interest them. Occasionally, employees find opportunities on their own and make their own arrangements for volunteering.

Ford's program had a marked impact on those employees who participated. The employees we interviewed indicated that it made them feel good about the company they worked for, helped them build stronger relationships with their fellow employees, and gave them a greater respect for those in need and the people they had helped with their volunteer efforts. It also enhanced their connections with the community, and, in many, it created an interest in community service that they felt would last a lifetime. As one employee said:

> *I'm glad they did come out with the [corporate volunteer] program, because they've got me involved and interested... You know, if I left Ford tomorrow, I would probably still go to Run for the Cure and Juvenile Diabetes and that type of thing.*

Another employee whom we interviewed talked about how his experience affected his feelings about his employer, as well as impressing upon him the need to help others in the community:

> *Now I go out and do what I can, but I also encourage family and others too. [It] makes me feel good to be part of an organization that is contributing back to the community and to do something valuable in a non-work setting with my work colleagues.*

Opportunities for Civic Engagement: Labor Unions

Labor unions serve as another work-related context in which individuals are provided the opportunity to become civically engaged. Although union membership in the United States has been declining, there are still a large number of workers who belong to unions—approximately 14.5 million (11.3% of all workers), according to statistics provided by the US Department of Labor (2014). Many other countries have higher rates of membership; for example, 27.5% of Canadian workers and 70% of Finnish workers, belong to a union (Organization for Economic Cooperation and Development, 2014).

Unions were established primarily to represent their members in seeking fair wages and healthy working conditions. But they also serve as places where individuals can learn civic skills and exert social influence on one another. Similar to religious organizations and workplaces, unions give their members opportunities to participate in meetings where decisions are made, work with other members on a committee, or take on leadership roles. These kinds of activities provide individuals with skills that can be transferred to other areas of civic life and make them more likely to participate in community organizations. Verba and colleagues, in their study of civic participation in American adults, found that 56% of union members reported that their participation in a union had given them a chance to develop civic skills (Verba et al., 1995). Unions can also serve as places where members influence on one another, for example, by recruiting fellow members to participate in activities both within the union and outside the union in the community. The study by Verba and colleagues found that 66% of union members had been asked by a fellow union member to participate in activities such as working on a political campaign.

Recent research indicates that membership in a union does indeed relate to a variety of civic activities. Kerrisey and Schofer (2013), using information from three large-scale national surveys of American adults, found that union members were significantly more likely than non-union members to have voted in a presidential election, worked on an election campaign, participated in a protest, or become involved in a community organization. Interestingly, the relationship between union membership and civic engagement was stronger for those with low levels of education than for those with higher levels of education. For example, among individuals with no formal education, union members were five times as likely as non-union members to have participated in a protest. Among those with a college degree or post-college education, there was no difference between union members and non-union members in their likelihood of participating in a protest.

Summary

Recent surveys indicate that a large majority of the world's population is affiliated with a religious tradition of some sort. A significant proportion of religiously affiliated individuals attend services regularly and participate in many other activities and organizations centered around their mosque, church, or synagogue. Membership in a religious group or organization influences civic participation in a number of ways. Religious leaders and fellow congregants become part of one's social network, and this network often serves as a source of recruitment for civic and political activities. Almost all religious traditions espouse a belief in service to others, and they convey these values to their adherents. Religious leaders serve as role models, moral exemplars who inspire others through their commitment to bettering society. Being involved in religious groups also provides individuals with the opportunity to be involved in a wide range of community projects and to learn skills that can be used in other civic organizations and activities.

Workplaces can influence civic participation in many of the same ways that religious organizations do. They, too, serve as a place where individuals can be recruited by friends and coworkers to participate in community and political organizations. Individuals learn many skills in the workplace, such as decision making and teamwork, that are also useful in civic settings. Workplaces encourage civic participation through corporate or employee volunteer programs. Unions, too, serve as work-related settings that can increase civic involvement.

5

Societal Influences on Civic Engagement

In the first few months of 2011, thousands of people took to the streets of Tunis, Cairo, Tripoli, Damascus, and other cities in the Middle East and North Africa in an attempt to remove the autocratic leaders that, for decades, prevented them from asserting their rights as citizens. When Haiti, the poorest nation in the Western Hemisphere, was struck by a magnitude 7.0 earthquake in 2010, killing an estimated 200,000 people and making a significant proportion of the Haitian population homeless, people working on their own and with scores of nongovernmental organizations travelled to the country to help. And in September of 2001, soon after two airplanes piloted by terrorists struck the twin towers of the World Trade Center in New York, there was a huge spike in volunteering, with nearly twice as many Americans performing community service after 9/11 compared to the numbers who had volunteered before the event. These actions leave no doubt that events and circumstances at the national and international level can have a profound effect on people's civic involvement, whether through protest, participation in community and political organizations, or helping those who have been stricken by disaster or conflict. In this chapter, I discuss some of the ways in which social and political systems and events influence individuals' participation in their countries and in their communities.

National Differences in Civic Participation

One indication of the impact that social and political systems can have on civic participation is the number of citizens who turn out to vote in different countries. In many Western democracies, voter turnout has been steadily declining for decades and has been strikingly low in recent elections. In the US presidential election of 2008, only 57.5% of eligible voters cast a ballot. In the most recent federal election in Canada, in 2011, voter turnout was a dismal 61.4%. The United Kingdom's last general election saw 65.1% of the electorate turn out to vote. But contrast these elections to Denmark's general election in September of 2011, where 87.7% of voters came to the polls on election day, or to Sweden's 84.6% of eligible individuals who voted in 2010.

Substantial differences among countries are also evident when one looks at other forms of civic participation, such as volunteering. Between 1999 and 2002, the European Values Survey and World Values Survey collected information on volunteering in 47 countries (Hodgkinson, 2003). The survey results indicated large differences among countries in every region of the world. In North America, 66% of Americans and 47% of Canadians reported that they had done volunteer work. In Western Europe, volunteer rates ranged from a high of 54% in Sweden to a low of 12% in Portugal. In Eastern Europe, levels of volunteering were generally lower, with volunteer rates below 20% for the majority of countries. Flanagan and colleagues, in their seven-nation study of adolescents' civic commitments, found similarly large differences in volunteering rates among adolescents across countries, although their study showed relatively high rates of volunteering among adolescents in the Eastern European countries of Hungary, the Czech Republic, and Bulgaria (Flanagan et al., 1999).

Inequality and Civic Participation

Why is it that individuals participate more in political and community life in some countries than in others? Why has civic participation declined in countries such as the United States and the United Kingdom? Finding an answer to these questions requires an understanding of political and social systems, as well as human behavior. One of the systemic factors that have been discussed as possible causes of declining civic participation is the steady increase in economic disparities seen in a number of countries, particularly in the United States. From 1930 to the mid 1970s, income inequality in the United States was relatively stable. The wealthiest 10% of Americans got a bit less than 35% of all income. That changed around 1979, when the gap between those with the highest and lowest incomes began to increase dramatically. By 2007, the wealthiest 10% of Americans were earning close to 50% of all income. The growth in income inequality can also be seen by examining how much company CEOs earn relative to the average worker employed by those companies. In 1978, the average CEO earned about 35 times as much as the average worker. By 2005, that ratio had soared to 262 to 1. In that year, the average worker earned a little over $41,000, while the average CEO earned over $10,000,000 (Mishel, Bernstein, & Allegretto, 2007). Nobel-winning economist Paul Krugman calls this widening of the income gap "the great divergence" (Krugman, 2007, p. 124).

Income inequality has been linked to a wide variety of health and social problems. In their seminal book, *The Spirit Level: Why More Equal Societies Almost Always Do Better,* Richard Wilkinson and Kate Pickett (2009) look at the relationship between income inequality and social problems across countries in the developed world and across states within the United States. One way of assessing income disparity is to look at the earnings of the top 10% of earners relative to the bottom 10%. This is one of the indices contained in the Human Development Report of the United Nations Development Programme in 2009. According to this report, the top 10% of earners in the United States received almost 16 times as much income as the bottom 10% of earners. The United Kingdom had a similarly high ratio of 13.8. In contrast, the ratio for Canada was 9.4, and for Norway and Sweden, the ratio was just above 6. When Wilkinson and Pickett examined countries in the developed world, they found that the greater the income disparity in a country, the more health and social problems experienced in that country. Countries with greater income inequality had higher rates of infant mortality, obesity, school dropout, homicide, teenage births, school bullying, drug abuse, and mental illness, compared to countries with less inequality. In contrast, more equal countries had citizens who lived longer, attained higher levels of education, and were more literate.

Wilkinson and Pickett (2009) also found that income inequality in a country or state was linked to "social trust." Social trust is typically measured by asking individuals how much they think other people can be trusted. Using information from the European and World Values survey, Wilkinson and Pickett looked at how social trust related to economic inequality. What they found was that individuals in more economically equal countries trusted one another more than did individuals in economically unequal countries. For example, in Norway, Sweden, and Finland, which are among the most economically equal of developed countries, more than 60% of respondents agreed that most people could be trusted, while in Portugal, one of the most economically unequal countries, fewer than 20% agreed that most people could be trusted. Wilkinson and Pickett found a similar relationship between income inequality and social trust among states in the United States. States with greater income equality, such as Utah or New Hampshire, were three times as trusting as states with high levels of inequality, such as Alabama or Mississippi. About 60% of Utah and New Hampshire citizens thought that "most people can be trusted" compared to around 20% of citizens living in Alabama or Mississippi.

Why is there a link between economic equality and social trust? Political scientist Eric Uslaner (Uslaner, 2002; Uslaner & Brown, 2005) suggests that individuals in more equal societies feel a sense of "shared fate" with their fellow citizens and greater optimism about the future. It is these feelings that lead to greater trust in one's neighbors and compatriots. Social trust, in turn, leads to greater civic participation; if one is to get involved with one's neighbors and fellow community members, one has to feel that these individuals are trustworthy. This suggests, then, that economic inequality, through its impact on social trust, affects levels of civic engagement.

Harvard political scientist Robert Putnam also saw a strong link between economic equality and civic participation. He saw the decline in economic equality that started in the late 1970s as going hand-in-hand with the decline in civic participation that began around the same time:

> *The timing of the two trends is striking: Sometime around 1965–70 America reversed course and started becoming both less just economically and less well connected socially and politically. This pair of trends illustrates that fraternity and equality are complementary, not warring values.* (Putnam, 2000, p. 359)

Putnam also saw a link between economic inequality and differences in civic participation among states in America. His examination of economic equality within states showed that the more income equality there was in a state, the more citizens of that state participated in civic life by attending public meetings, volunteering, joining local organizations, and other forms of civic behavior. Others have found similar links between economic equality and different forms of civic participation. Ichiro Kawachi and his colleagues found that Americans (of all income levels) were more likely to vote and to belong to civic groups and associations such as church groups, labor unions, professional societies, and political organizations if they came from states with greater economic equality than if they lived in more economically unequal states (Blakely et al., 2001; Kawachi et al., 1997).

What is it about income inequality that makes people less likely to participate in political and community life? One possible explanation has to do with people's sense that their actions can actually influence what happens in their community and their nation, such as who gets elected to public office, or what kinds of policies are enacted by politicians and other decision makers. In the political realm, this feeling that one's actions can have some influence on political decision making is referred to as "political efficacy." Political efficacy (or rather, the lack of political efficacy) has been measured in every American presidential election year since 1952 by having people indicate their agreement or disagreement with statements such as, "People like me don't have any say about what the government does," or "I don't think public officials care much what people like me think" (American National Election Studies, n.d.). Throughout the 1950s and 1960s, 65 to 75% of those responding *disagreed* with these statements; most people felt that they *did* have a say in what their government did. This percentage has decreased steadily. During the presidential election of 2008, only 38% disagreed with the statements; a large majority of individuals felt that they *didn't* have a say in what their government did.

It has been well-established in many studies that the more people feel that they have a say in what their governments do, the more they participate actively in political and community affairs (e.g., Morrell, 2003; Pattie & Johnston, 1998, Karp & Banducci, 2008). It is not surprising, therefore, that the decline in political efficacy has been paralleled by a decline in voting and other forms of political participation. If what you do doesn't matter, why do anything? Sadly, research indicates that, for many people, what they do in the political realm really doesn't matter to their political leaders and representatives. This is especially true for those who are poor, but it is also true for those in the middle income brackets. In his 2008 book, *Unequal Democracy,* Larry Bartels describes his analysis of voting patterns in the United States Senate from the late 1980s to the early 1990s. On issues such as civil rights, the minimum wage, and government spending, Bartels found that the senators were much more responsive to wealthy voters than to those who were less well off. Indeed, he determined that those in the upper third of income levels wielded 50% more influence than those in the middle third in terms of their effect on voting patterns. Those in the bottom third wielded no influence at all.

Political Structures and Participation

Participation in civil society, and particularly in the political process, is most certainly influenced by the structures and processes by which a country is governed. This is obvious when one compares countries that have autocratic and democratic governments. Nations with autocratic leaders have less civic participation than those with democratically elected leaders, because citizens of autocratic nations are prevented from choosing their political leaders and participating freely in other political institutions and organizations, like opposition parties or advocacy groups. But important differences in political systems also occur among democratically governed countries. One of the key differences among democratic countries is the way in which people's votes are used to determine who is elected to public office. Countries like the United States, Britain, and Canada use a "first-past-the-post" (FPP) or "winner-takes-all" system, in which the candidate receiving the most votes gets elected. In elections where there are more than two candidates for office, this can mean that a candidate with fewer than 50% of the votes can be elected. This happened in the 2000 American presidential election, in which Democratic candidate Al Gore narrowly lost to Republican George W. Bush. A small proportion (2.7%) of voters in that election voted for Ralph Nader of the Green Party. Exit polls indicated that a large majority of those who voted for Nader would have voted for Gore if Nader had not been in the race, and this may have swung the election in Gore's favor. Instead, George Bush was elected president, even though he received fewer than 50% of the votes and even though a majority of individuals would have preferred Gore as their president.

The FPP system creates even greater distortions when there are more than two viable, popular parties fielding candidates in an election. For example, in the 2005 general election in the United Kingdom, the Labor Party only received 36.1% of the votes, but it got a majority of 56.5% of the seats in the House of Commons and formed the government. In contrast, the Conservative Party, which received 33.2% of the votes, had 31.5% of the seats in the House of Commons, and the Liberal Democrats, who received 22.6% of the votes, got only 9.9% of the seats. It becomes clear that under this system, individuals whose sympathies lie with less popular parties may feel that their votes don't count as much. Even though nearly a quarter of electors voted for the Liberal Democrats, they received fewer than 10% of the seats. Political commentators often talk about votes for unelected candidates being "wasted" in this system.

The major alternative to the first-past-the-post system is proportional representation. In this system, the number of seats that a party wins is proportionate to the number of votes it receives. If a proportional representation process had been used in the 2005 British election, the Labor party would have had 36.1% of the seats in the House of Commons, the same as the proportion of votes it received in the general election, rather than having a majority of 56.6% of the seats, and the Liberal Democrats would have had 22.6% of the seats, considerably more than the 9.9% they actually elected. Under this system, there are no "wasted" votes, as every vote contributes to the election of candidates from the party for which one votes. Proportional representation is the most common format for elections in Europe and in almost every country in South America.

So what do voting systems have to do with civic participation? A great deal, as it turns out. Studies of voter turnout across countries consistently show that a greater proportion of the electorate votes under proportional representation systems than under nonproportional systems such as "first-past-the-post" (Blais & Carty, 1990; Jackman, 1987). Some analyses indicate that the difference in voter turnout may be as large as 9% in favor of proportional systems (Jackman, 1987). Why does this happen? Recent research suggests that the prospect of "wasting" one's vote by not having one's vote translated into seats may decrease one's sense of political efficacy, which in turn reduces one's motivation to vote. Karp and Banducci (2008) found evidence supporting this explanation. They examined political efficacy and voter turnout in 27 democracies with varying voting systems and found that individuals in countries with proportional systems had a greater sense of political efficacy than did individuals in nonproportional systems, and were also more likely to have voted.

The Electoral Process: Negative Campaigning

Another way in which the electoral process can influence civic participation in democratic countries is through the way in which political campaigns are fought. It seems that in many countries, political campaigns are becoming increasingly personal and increasingly malicious (Pancer, Brown, & Barr, 1999; Pancer & Landau, 2009). The use of "attack ads," advertisements designed to tear down the personal character of political opponents, has become commonplace, particularly in countries with FPP electoral systems, such as the United States. Darrell West, vice president and director of Governance Studies at the Brookings Institution in Washington, DC, began a recent article of his with the line "Negative attacks are as American as apple pie" (West, 2009). Many times, these attack ads have seemed to be very effective. For example, several attack ads were aimed at the Democratic candidate for president, John Kerry, in the 2004 presidential election. These ads were paid for by a group calling itself the "Swift Boat Veterans for Truth," named after the "Swift Boat" class of naval vessel that Kerry had commanded during the Viet Nam war. The ads painted veteran Kerry as unpatriotic for discussing the war crimes he had witnessed while in combat and for giving back the medals he had received. They also attempted to paint Kerry as unpatriotic by questioning the legitimacy of his combat record. One of the legacies of this campaign was the new term "swiftboating," which refers to the use of vicious and often fallacious claims about a political opponent in an attempt to smear the opponent's reputation.

Research on attack ads and other kinds of negative campaigning suggest that these kinds of ads may indeed be effective in producing a negative impression of a candidate in the minds of voters. The research indicates that they may produce negative attitudes toward the perpetrator of the attacks, as well as the victim (Roese & Sande, 1993). But the greatest victim of negative campaigning may be democracy itself. Political psychologists Lau, Sigelman, and Rovner (2007) examined 111 published and unpublished studies of negative advertising and its impact on candidate impressions, as well as its impact on voter turnout, trust in government, and political efficacy. They found that negative ads had a consistent and "overwhelmingly negative" impact on individuals' trust in government and on their sense of political efficacy. They conclude that "negative campaigning has the potential to do damage to the political system itself, as it tends to reduce feelings of political efficacy, trust in government, and perhaps even satisfaction with government itself" (p. 1184).

This reduced sense of efficacy and trust in government has consequences for civic participation. For example, one casualty of negative campaigning is voter turnout (Allen & Burrell, 2002; Kahn & Kenny, 1999). This was demonstrated in a study by Kahn and Kenney (1999), who interviewed individuals who had been campaign managers during the 1990 Senate elections in the United States. Based on their interviews and an analysis of the media coverage of the campaigns, they constructed a "mudslinging" rating for each of the campaigns. Higher ratings of mudslinging occurred when a candidate's campaign used deceptive messages and personal attacks in an attempt to smear the rival candidate. The results indicated that there were significantly lower levels of voter turnout in campaigns characterized by mudslinging compared to campaigns that were relatively free from mudslinging.

Social Norms and Civic Participation

In earlier chapters, I discussed the ways in which social norms or expectations established in one's family, school, neighborhood, place of worship, and workplace can influence an individual's level of civic participation. Social norms can be more broadly based, as well. Whole cities, states, countries, and even regions of the world may have social norms that influence their citizens, and these norms can differ substantially from one area to the next. These differences are likely to play an important role in producing the variations in civic participation that we find among cities, states, or provinces within a country or among different countries. David Campbell provides a graphic example of how the city one lives in can influence civic participation (Campbell, 2006). He recounts the story of Traci Hodgson, who was the only person from her precinct of 275 registered voters to cast a vote in Boston's City Council election of 1989. He suggests that the reason Traci voted was that she came from a town (Little River in Kansas) that had a strong norm of civic participation and that she had internalized this norm.

Recent research seems to support the notion that norms of participation can vary widely among states and countries. Fieldhouse, Tranmer, and Russel (2007), for example, looked at variations in civic participation among European countries, in terms of voter turnout. They were particularly concerned about voter turnout among young people, who tend to vote in much lower percentages that other eligible voters. Using results from the European Social Survey of 2002 and 2003, they examined some of the possible causes of low voter turnout in young people. They found large differences in voter turnout in national elections among the countries surveyed, ranging from a low of just over 43% in Switzerland to over 90% in Belgium. As expected, young people (18 to 24 years of age) voted in lower percentages than older individuals. But the most important determinant of young people's likelihood of voting was the overall voter turnout in their country. Young people in countries with higher overall turnout rates voted in higher percentages than young people in countries with lower overall turnout. Fieldhouse and colleagues also found that young people in countries with higher turnout were more likely to believe that voting was an important part of citizenship and that it was important to belong to voluntary organizations. These results support the idea that countrywide social norms can influence civic participation. In countries with a strong norm of civic engagement, where participation in civil society is seen as important and there is an expectation that people will engage in civic life, larger numbers of the population will demonstrate active citizenship.

Individualism-Collectivism

As we have seen, societies can differ in many ways. They differ in wealth, economic equality, governmental structures, and in the kinds of norms that govern civic behavior. Another fundamental way in which societies differ has to do with the cultural values that predominate among their citizens. One of these cultural values, commonly referred to as individualism-collectivism, concerns people's views about independence and their relationships with others. In individualist societies, people tend to value self-reliance and independence. Individual rights are paramount, and the greatest successes are seen to be those that individuals achieve on their own. In contrast, those in collectivist societies value cooperation and working with others. Their identities have more to do with their relationships and their membership in a family, work group, and community than with who they are individually or what they have done on their own. People in collectivist societies are encouraged to consider what is best for their community over what is best for them as individuals (Triandis, 1995). The United States, Canada, and many of the countries in Western Europe have generally individualist cultures, while countries in the Far East, such as China, Korea, and Japan, have generally collectivist cultures.

Not surprising, individualist and collectivist societies differ in terms of the civic participation of their citizens. Those living in countries with a more collectivist culture, for example, are more likely to engage in volunteering than are individuals living in countries with more individualist cultures. Parboteeah, Cullen, and Lim (2004) found this in their examination of volunteering across 21 countries participating in the World Values Survey, a cross-national survey of social values and practices including countries from every continent and of varying levels of development (e.g., Australia, Brazil, Germany, Japan, Mexico, Nigeria, Russian Federation, Phillipines, South Korea, Turkey, United States). Respondents to the survey were asked how active they had been with several voluntary organizations, ranging from arts and recreational organizations to labor unions and political parties. They were also asked how much they agreed with statements relating to the individualist-collectivist orientation of their country, such as "leaders encourage collective loyalty even if individual goals suffer." The results indicated a strong relationship between the individualist-collectivist culture of a country and the extent to which citizens of that country were active as volunteers. Citizens of countries with a collectivist culture were significantly more likely to volunteer than were citizens of countries with an individualistic culture.

Religiosity

Another cultural value that varies across societies has to do with the importance of religion. In their examination of volunteering across countries, Parboteeah and his colleagues also looked at how countries varied in terms of the religiosity of their citizens. They used the percentage of individuals within a country who attended religious services weekly as an indication of each country's religiosity. As I noted in the last chapter, religiosity is strongly linked to volunteering and other forms of civic participation for a number of reasons. Almost all religions have service to others as one of their core beliefs, and religious institutions and organizations provide many opportunities for individuals to engage in service through volunteering. It makes sense to assume, then, that societies that have greater numbers of religious individuals will show higher levels of volunteering, because they have more individuals who will be influenced by the values of service espoused by their religion and will have more opportunities (through their religious affiliations) to volunteer. This is what Partboteeah and his colleagues found. Among the countries they examined, more religious countries had higher levels of volunteering than did less religious countries.

Living in a religious or "devout" country influences not only those individuals who are religious, but those who are not religious, as well. Ruiter and deGraaf (2006), using data from the European and World Values surveys, looked at volunteering among both religious and nonreligious individuals in countries that varied in "devoutness" (measured by assessing the average frequency of church attendance). They found that among both religious and nonreligious individuals, those who lived in a devout country were more likely to volunteer than were individuals living in more secular countries. Indeed, they determined that people living in the most devout country examined in their study were more than four times as likely to volunteer compared to people living in the most secular country, regardless of whether they themselves were religious. They suggest that the reason for even secular individuals being influenced by the devoutness of their society is that in more religious societies, nonreligious people will have greater numbers of religious individuals in their social networks, and these religious network members will, through a process of social influence, recruit them for volunteer work. They also suggest that the high level of civic involvement among religious individuals in devout societies will create norms of participation and social pressure to volunteer.

Materialism

Many individuals around the world live in societies that are highly materialistic. Individuals residing in such societies feel pressure to acquire material goods, in the form of money and possessions, and to compete with others for wealth, power, and status. They are bombarded with thousands of advertisements every day, exhorting them to purchase the newest electronic gadget, appliance, or automobile so that they can lead happier lives. Unfortunately, that just doesn't happen.

Research by social psychologist Tim Kasser and others shows that those for whom materialistic goals such as the acquisition of wealth or status are the major driving forces in their lives actually lead lives that are impoverished in many ways (Kasser, 2002). They suffer from higher levels of depression and anxiety, and they have more health problems. They have poorer relationships with their friends and romantic partners. They even have more nightmares. Most important, as far as active citizenship is concerned, the pursuit of materialistic goals appears to leave little time and inclination for other pursuits, such as connecting with one's community or contributing to its well-being (Kasser, 2002, 2011; Rahn & Transue, 1998). Wendy Rahn and John Transue (1998), using data from the Monitoring the Future survey given annually to American high-school students, found that students who indicated that "having lots of money" was very important to them were less likely to feel that people could be trusted than were students for whom having lots of money was less important.

Studies that have looked at materialism across countries have found that some nations are much more materialistic than others. American society, for example, is highly materialistic. Americans are more likely than individuals from other countries to agree with statements such as "When friends have things I cannot afford, it bothers me" (Ger & Belk, 1996). Individuals in other countries, such as Sweden, France, or India, are much less materialistic. Rather than valuing things such as the acquisition of wealth, power, and possessions, citizens of those countries are more likely to value having strong relationships and a close-knit community. In a recent study, Kasser (2011) looked at the relationship between materialistic values relating to self-interest and power and the extent to which a country had policies and practices that demonstrated a concern for children and future generations. He found that countries whose predominant values were power and self-interest had fewer of these practices, and consequently they had children with lower levels of well-being. What this suggests is that materialistic societies are less likely to have policies and regulations that promote individuals connecting with their communities and being concerned with future generations.

Kasser and his colleagues Steve Cohn, Allen Kanner, and Richard Ryan (2007) suggest that the materialism of a society is closely linked to the economic system in which people live and work. They claim that the system of capitalism that governs the economy of the United States and many other countries in the world (a form that they call "American Corporate Capitalism") actively fosters a set of values in the citizens of those countries, values that center around self-interest, competition, the acquisition of material goods, and the pursuit of financial success. These values, they say, "crowd out" other kinds of values that focus more on things such as contributing to and connecting with one's community. Award-winning scholar and film-maker Saul Landau suggests that the American economic system has turned the country from a nation of "citizens" into a nation of "consumers" (Landau, 2004). Research supports these claims. McHoskey (1999), for example, found that individuals who agreed with the statement "The most important goal in life is financial success" were less likely to be involved in civic behaviors such as volunteering.

World Events

Sometimes a single world event can have a profound effect on our collective consciousness. Such events are so significant that they are seared into our memories. We can almost see them unfolding, even decades later, and we recall in detail what we were doing when they occurred. For those of us who were around during the 1960s, the assassinations of John F. Kennedy, Robert Kennedy, and Martin Luther King Jr. continue to live in our memories. For North Americans living in the 21st century, it is the events of September 11, 2001, that will live on in our consciousness. On that day, now known simply as 9/11, two airplanes, hijacked by terrorists crashed into the World Trade Center buildings in New York City, bringing them tumbling down in a cloud of dust and debris. A third plane crashed into the Pentagon, and a fourth, targeted at Washington, DC, crashed instead into a field near Shanksville, Pennsylvania, after its passengers tried to overcome the hijackers. In total, including hundreds of first responders, over 3,000 people were killed. The world has not been the same since. Two wars, one in Afghanistan and one in Iraq, can be directly linked to 9/11. The United States enacted major changes in both foreign and domestic policy, which included the establishment of the Office of Homeland Security, the world's largest counter-terror organization. Air travel has changed profoundly, with markedly heightened security measures. A wave of anti-Islamic prejudice, sometimes known as "Islamophobia," was also ushered in by 9/11 in North America and Europe.

But the attacks had other effects, as well. Soon after the events of 9/11, social psychologist Louis Penner contacted VolunteerMatch, an organization devoted to increasing volunteering in the United States. VolunteerMatch operates a website that lists hundreds of volunteer opportunities across the United States. Individuals consulting the website can find out about a wide range of organizations seeking volunteers in their community and can sign up for volunteer work with one of the organizations listed. When Penner contacted VolunteerMatch, he discovered that they kept a daily record of the number of people who had offered to volunteer and decided to analyze these records to see what had happened to volunteer rates after 9/11 (Penner et al., 2005). He found that volunteering surged to more than double what it had been before 9/11, and this increase persisted for weeks. Moreover, volunteering didn't increase just for crisis-related helping. It increased for all kinds of service activity, from working with refugees and immigrants to educating voters.

Similar increases in volunteering and helping have been seen in other recent disasters. In the year following the tsunami that devastated large swaths of Southeast Asia in 2004, more than $13 billion from around the world was pledged for disaster relief (Inter Press Service News Agency, 2005). After hurricane Katrina struck New Orleans and other parts of the Gulf Coast of the United States in August 2005, more than a million people gave up their weekends and vacations to help the citizens rebuild homes and communities destroyed by the floods. Thousands of these individuals drove long distances from other states to provide their help (Corporation for National and Community Service, 2008). Such events, in which innocent individuals suffer through no fault of their own, evoke high levels of sympathy, which in turn provide strong motivation to help (Marjanovic, Greenglass, Struthers, & Faye, 2009).

Other kinds of events can also lead to increases in civic participation of many kinds. It is interesting to note that while young people were shunning the polls on election day in democratic countries such as the United States, Canada, and the United Kingdom, young people in Tripoli, Cairo, and Damascus were out on the streets in large numbers, fighting for the right to participate more meaningfully in the governing of their countries. This movement for the establishment of more democratic government was part of what is now called the "Arab Spring." It began with protests and street demonstrations in Tunisia in December of 2010, which led very quickly to the ouster of Tunisia's autocratic president of 24 years, Zine El Abidine Ben Ali. The events in Tunisia started a wave of massive demonstrations for greater democracy across the Arab World. How did this happen? Unfortunately, little, if any, psychological research has been published concerning the attitudes and emotions of those participating in the protests. But psychological theories and principles can be readily applied to explain these events. One of the most plausible psychological constructs that can be used to explain the Arab Spring is the notion of political efficacy, the feeling that citizens have that their actions can make a difference in the political decisions that affect them. When the citizens of Tunisia were so quickly successful in forcing their autocratic leader out of power, this increased the feeling among citizens of other Arab countries that their involvement in protests and demonstrations could similarly result in the overthrow of their own despotic regimes. In other words, the enhanced feeling of political efficacy created by witnessing the effects in Tunisia led to civic engagement in the form of participation in demonstrations in other Arab countries.

Summary

Social and political systems, as well as world events, can have a profound effect on civic engagement. Evidence for this comes from the fact that individuals in different countries show wide variations in their likelihood of voting or of volunteering.

A number of factors may account for these kinds of differences in civic participation. One of them has to do with levels of economic inequality. Countries with high levels of economic inequality tend to have citizens who participate less in civic life than do countries with greater economic equality. The political structures and processes by which countries are governed also appear to influence civic participation. There is greater civic involvement in countries where politicians are elected through proportional representation processes than through "first-past-the-post" systems, in which only the candidate receiving the most votes gets elected. Research also indicates that in political systems characterized by vicious partisanship and mudslinging at political opponents, citizens will spurn government and participate less in political life. National character and countrywide norms can also influence civic participation. Countries with norms that promote civic involvement, more collectivist values, higher levels of religiosity, and less materialism have higher levels of civic engagement. World events can also have a strong impact on civic participation, as indicated by the dramatic increase in volunteering that occurred after 9/11, the Asian tsunami of 2004, and the Haitian earthquake of 2010. Another example of world events that can influence civic activity is the Arab Spring, in which the overthrow of a dictatorial government in Tunisia through popular uprising inspired individuals throughout the Arab world to rise against their autocratic leaders and governments.

6

Impacts of Civic Engagement on Youth

Many people engage in their first civic activities when they are young; they may join a team or a club at school, participate in a youth group at church or synagogue, volunteer at a food bank, become a member of a youth organization such as girl guides or 4-H, or protest against harmful environmental practices as part of an environmental action group. These activities provide young people with their first links to their communities and their first experiences as active citizens. There has now been a considerable body of research that has examined the impacts of this kind of early civic participation on individuals. What this research shows is that these impacts are almost always positive, they are frequently profound, and they can last a lifetime.

Engagement and Problem Behaviors

Several studies have looked at the relationship between young people's civic participation and a wide range of "problem behaviors" such as alcohol and drug use, delinquency, and school dropout. A large majority of these studies show that the more involved young people are in their schools, neighborhoods, religious groups, and other organizations, the less likely they are to engage in problem behaviors.

Alcohol Use

Alcohol abuse is one of the most common of these problem behaviors, in both young and older individuals. According to the American National Institute on Alcohol Abuse and Alcoholism (NIAAA), one in four American adults reports having a drinking problem or reports a pattern of drinking that would put them at risk for developing a serious problem (NIAAA, 2005). These patterns of alcohol abuse frequently begin in the teenage years. The consequences of alcohol abuse are devastating. In the United States, nearly 2,000 people each year die in car crashes in which underage drinking was a causal factor. Alcohol abuse is related to a wide range of physiological and psychological problems, including heart and liver disease, as well as relationship, employment and financial difficulties.

Many studies have looked at the link between alcohol use in young people and their participation in a range of civic activities (Barber et al., 2001; Denault et al., 2009; Eccles et al., 2003; Harrison & Narayan, 2003). These studies consistently show that civically engaged youth are less likely to use and abuse alcohol. One of the researchers who has done extensive research on the impact of young people's involvements on problem behaviors is Jacquelynne Eccles, a developmental psychologist and former president of the Society for Research on Adolescence. In one of her studies, Eccles and her colleagues (Eccles, Barber, Stone, & Hunt, 2003) used data from a longitudinal survey of young people to look at a range of problem behaviors (including alcohol use) and the relationship of these problem behaviors with different kinds of youth activities. The results of this study showed that young people who had been involved in prosocial activities such as church groups or community service when they were in grade 10 were significantly less likely to have drunk alcohol, gotten drunk, or driven a car while under the influence of alcohol when they were young adults of 21 to 22 years of age. Harrison and Naryan (2003), in a study involving over 50,000 grade 9 students in Minnesota, determined that young people who had been involved in volunteering and youth organizational activities were half as likely to have drunk alcohol over the previous year or to have engaged in binge drinking over the previous two weeks. While most types of youth engagement are associated with lower levels of alcohol consumption, the one type of organized activity that seems to be associated with higher alcohol use is participation in team sports, probably because a norm or tradition of consuming alcohol has become associated with this kind of team membership (Barber et al., 2001; Denault et al., 2009).

Drug Use

Alcohol is only one of many substances that individuals can abuse. Drug use is another scourge that often begins in adolescence. The most recent survey by the American National Institute on Drug Abuse (NIDA) indicated that more than one in four grade 12 students had used illicit drugs within the previous year. The human and financial costs of drug use are substantial. The estimated costs associated with the use of illicit drugs in the United States, in terms of crime, lost work productivity, and health care, are nearly $200 billion a year (National Drug Intelligence Center, 2011).

Civic participation, in the form of extracurricular activities, appears to be associated with lower rates of drug use (Barber et al., 2001; Bohnert & Garber, 2007; Eccles et al., 2003; Elder et al., 2000; Youniss et al., 1999). The study by Eccles and her colleagues (Eccles et al., 2003), described earlier, in addition to looking at links between civic participation and alcohol use also examined the link between civic activities and drug use. This study found that young people who had participated in activities such as community service or religious organizations when they were in grade 10 were significantly less likely to have used drugs nearly 10 years later, when they were young adults of 25 to 26 years of age. Elder and colleagues (2000) determined that young people who were involved in only one or two civic activities, such as clubs or organizations within or outside of school, were 2.5 times less likely to use marijuana than were youth who were not involved in such activities. The link between civic participation and reduced drug use holds not only for so-called "soft" drugs, such as marijuana, but "hard" drugs, as well (Eccles & Barber, 1999).

Delinquency

Delinquent or "antisocial" behavior is another significant problem associated with young people. A recent study by American criminologist Robert Brame and colleagues (Brame, Turner, Paternoster, & Bushway, 2012), using data from the National Longitudinal Survey of Youth, estimated that one in three American young people under the age of 23 had been arrested or taken into custody for illegal or delinquent offences. Youth who have been arrested often face a lifetime of hardship, involving unemployment, diminished educational attainment, family violence, and further criminal activity.

Research on young people's involvements suggests that civic participation, in the form of membership in organized groups and activities both within and outside of school, can protect young people from being involved in delinquent activity (Busseri et al., 2006; Crean, 2012; Harrison & Narayan, 2003; Mahatmya & Lohman, 2011; Mahoney, 2000; Mahoney & Stattin, 2000; Uggen & Janikula, 1999). Yale University psychologist Joseph Mahoney has done considerable research on the impacts associated with young people's extracurricular involvements. In one of his studies, Mahoney (2000) examined school yearbooks to obtain a measure of the extent to which students had participated in extracurricular activities during their years in high school. He then looked at arrest records from the State Bureau of Investigation to determine which of the students who had been part of the study had been arrested for criminal activities such as homicide, burglary, assault, rape, and vandalism by the time they had reached the age of 23. The results showed that students who had participated in one or more extracurricular activities were significantly less likely to have been arrested than were students who had not participated in extracurricular activities.

My own research corroborates these findings. Over the last two years, I and my colleagues Karen Hayward and Dianne Heise Bennett (Pancer, Hayward, & Heise Bennett, 2013) conducted an evaluation of a gang-prevention program called "inREACH." One of the key goals of inREACH was to prevent gang involvement and criminal activity in poor, high-risk communities by providing young people with opportunities to participate in organized community endeavors such as an art or music studio. We interviewed several of the young people involved in the project to assess the impact it had had on them. Here is what one of them said:

> *I loved Kitchener [the city in which the program operated] because it was a great place to sell drugs... Then I got connected with them [inREACH] and I swear I don't know what the hell happened. I started going to programs. Art programs and video programs... I performed live rapping at the church... I realized there are a lot of other fun things to do... I didn't know that was there until they showed me... there is a graffiti thing on Friday and I am going to go... at City Hall and it is going to be cool... instead of spray painting on walls I am getting put in the gallery... So instead of illegal I get to make it legal... they helped me to find out a whole bunch of different things that I get to interact with without selling drugs... and it is all free and I'm just having a good time... it changed my mind about Kitchener cause I wanted to leave.*

School Problems, Failure, and Drop-Out

Recently, in the province of Ontario, Canada, where I live, there was a job action, or slowdown, by the province's teachers. As part of the job action, teachers stopped running all of the extracurricular activities normally available at their schools. There were no practices for athletic teams, no music rehearsals or concerts, no clubs—no before- or after-school activities of any kind. Teachers did continue all their teaching activities as usual, however, so that students wouldn't suffer academically. Unfortunately, however, according to what the research tells us, students who don't participate in extracurricular activities do suffer academically. Young people who do not participate in extracurricular activities have more negative attitudes toward school (Fredricks & Eccles, 2008), do less homework and studying (Harrison & Naryan, 2003; Marsh, 1992; Marsh & Kleitman, 2002), and skip classes more often (Harrison & Naryan, 2003; Marsh, 1992) compared to youth who do participate in these activities. They are also more accepting of cheating on tests and assignments (Anderson-Butcher et al., 2003), more likely to be suspended from school (Allen et al., 1997), and more likely to be bullied by other students (Jimenez et al., 2009). It comes as no surprise, then, that uninvolved students also get lower grades (Fredricks & Eccles, 2006, 2008; Schmidt, Shumow, & Kackar, 2007), are more likely to fail courses (Allen et al., 1997), and are more likely to drop out of school (Mahoney, 2000; Mahoney & Cairns, 1997).

Sexual Behavior

While births to teenage mothers have been declining steadily since the 1950s (Hamilton & Ventura, 2012), there are still substantial numbers of teenagers who have babies. In the United States in 2010, there were nearly 400,000 births to teenagers, one of the highest rates in the industrialized world. According to a recent report by the United Nations, more than 7 million girls under the age of 18 are giving birth each year in the developing world, and 2 million of these births are to girls 14 years of age or younger. Teenage childbearing poses risks for the health of both the mother and her baby. For example, teen mothers are more likely to have low birth-weight babies.

Another risk associated with teenage sex is sexually transmitted disease. A 2008 study by the Centers for Disease Control and Prevention (CDC) in the United States indicated that 1 in 4 women between the ages of 14 and 19—over 3 million teen girls—had a sexually transmitted disease (CDC, 2008). The CDC also has reported that young people between the ages of 13 and 29 accounted for nearly 26% of all new HIV infections in the United States in 2020 (CDC, 2014).

A number of studies that have examined youth who participate in activities such as school clubs, community service, and youth organizations suggest that such youth are less likely to engage in high-risk sexual behavior. A study by Allen and colleagues (Allen et al., 1997), for example, looked at the rate of teen pregnancies in high school students who participated in Teen Outreach, a program in which students volunteered with local community organizations over the course of their school year. Students in the study were randomly assigned to work as volunteers through the Teen Outreach program or to a control group that did not volunteer but completed the same measures as students in the program. At the end of the program, all students were asked if they had ever been pregnant (females) or been responsible for a pregnancy (males). The results of the study indicated there had been twice as many pregnancies (nearly 10%) among girls in the control group (and who had not done volunteer work) as there had been among girls who had volunteered through the Teen Outreach program (just over 4%).

Research has identified other ways in which civic participation among young people yields benefits in terms of risky sexual activity. A study of young teens in Oklahoma City (Aspy et al., 2010) found that teenagers from 12 to 14 years of age who were not involved in their communities were more than 2.5 times more likely to have had sexual intercourse than were teens who were involved in their communities. A study of African-American teenagers aged 14 to 18 (Crosby et al., 2002) found that teens who had participated in African-American groups or organizations were significantly less likely to have had sex with more than one partner and were more likely to have used contraception and discussed ways of preventing STDs and pregnancy with their sexual partners, compared to teens who were not active in these kinds of organizations.

Smoking

Smoking has well-known harmful effects on people's health and longevity. The great majority (88%) of adult smokers begin smoking in their teens. Consequently, many of the programs designed to prevent smoking are targeted toward young people. Unfortunately, these programs typically have only limited success (Rooney & Murray, 1996). There have now been a number of studies that suggest that young people who participate in extracurricular school and community activities are much less likely to smoke (Anderson-Butcher et al., 2003; Bohnert & Garber, 2007; Elder et al., 2000; Marsh & Kleitman, 2002; Metzger et al., 2011). Anderson-Butcher, Newsome, and Ferrari (2003), for example, found that American youth who regularly attended Boys and Girls Clubs were less likely to have smoked cigarettes compared to youth who had not attended or had infrequently attended club meetings and activities. Elder and colleagues (2000), using survey date from over 3,500 high school students in the southeastern United States, determined that young people who participated in organized activities such as clubs or organizations, either within or outside of school, were two times less likely to smoke cigarettes, compared to peers who hadn't participated in these kinds of activities.

Mental Health

A report by the United States Surgeon General indicated that more than 1 in 5 children and youth between the ages of 9 and 17 had a mental health disorder that was serious enough to warrant treatment (U.S. Department of Health and Human Services, 1999). Mental health problems can have devastating effects on young people and can last a lifetime. Young people with mental health problems are more likely to drop out of school, be incarcerated, and commit suicide than are young people without mental health disorders.

Research suggests that civic involvement can protect young people from developing mental disorders (Bartko & Eccles, 2003; Bohnert et al., 2008; Fredricks & Eccles, 2006). Fredricks and Eccles (2006), for example, examined the link between participation and mental health problems using data from a longitudinal study of American adolescents from the state of Maryland. As part of this study, youth in grade 11 were asked about their participation in extracurricular activities such as sports teams, school clubs, student government, community service, and civil rights groups. The parents of these youth were asked to complete ratings of the extent to which their children showed mental health difficulties such as anxiety, depression, aggression and behavior problems. The results of the study indicated that students who were engaged in a broad range of extracurricular activities were significantly less likely to experience both "internalizing" problems, such as anxiety and depression, and "externalizing" problems, such as fighting and bullying, compared to students who were engaged in fewer or no extracurricular activities. Participation in extracurricular groups and activities appears to be particularly effective in the reduction of depression among young people (Bartko & Eccles, 2003; Denault et al., 2009; Mahoney et al., 2002). A study of youth in the province of Quebec, Canada by Denault and colleagues (2009) found that young people who participated in youth clubs such as Scouts, service clubs, or Boys' and Girls' Clubs when they were in grade 7 were less likely to show symptoms of depression from grades 7 to 10.

Engagement and Positive Youth Development

There is strong evidence, then, that young people who are engaged in their communities through their participation in extracurricular groups and activities are less likely to experience a wide range of problems. But avoiding problems is only one aspect of healthy development. Young people who are truly thriving not only have few problems but also have developed strengths and capacities that will enable them to become emotionally healthy adults who contribute to the creation of healthy societies. Developmental psychologist Richard Lerner (Lerner et al., 2005) has identified five major capacities (which he calls the "5 Cs") that mark the healthy, positive development of young people: Confidence (a sense of positive self-worth and self-efficacy); Connection (positive bonds with peers, family, school, and community); Caring (a sense of empathy for others); Competence (social, academic, cognitive, and vocational skills); and Character (integrity and a sense of right and wrong). Research on young people's involvements in the communities both within and outside their schools provides strong, consistent evidence that civic engagement enhances the development of all of these capacities and more.

Confidence, Positive Identity, and Life Satisfaction

Many studies provide evidence that engaged young people have greater self-esteem and self-confidence, a better sense of who they are and what they want out of life, and more life satisfaction (Barber et al., 2001; Jimenez et al., 2009; Johnson et al., 1998; Rose-Krasnor et al., 2006; Zeldin, 2004). A number of my own studies (Henderson, Pancer, & Brown, 2014; Pancer & Pratt, 1999; Pancer et al., 2007) confirm the link between youth civic engagement and self-esteem. In one study, I and my colleagues Mike Pratt, Bruce Hunsberger, and Susan Alisat had students in their second to last year of high school complete several scales, one of which was the Youth Involvement Inventory, a measure designed to assess the extent to which young people were involved in a wide range of civic activities, from community service to school clubs to neighborhood organizations (Pancer et al., 2007). We also had our research participants complete scales that measured self-esteem and optimism. In completing these scales, they indicated the extent to which they agreed with statements like, "On the whole, I am satisfied with myself," and "I'm always optimistic about my future." Our results showed that youth who were more involved in civic activities had greater self-esteem and were more optimistic than were youth who were uninvolved.

In other studies, we interviewed young people who were involved in community service and social activism, asking them what impact their experiences had had on their lives. In one of our earliest studies on civic engagement in young people, Mike Pratt and I (Pancer & Pratt, 1999) asked local religious, health, education, and social service organizations that used volunteers to nominate young people whom they considered to be "committed volunteers" with their organization. We wanted to find out how these youth had first become involved in community service in an attempt to identify some of the key factors that initiate this kind of community engagement in young people. We interviewed 20 volunteers between the ages of 16 and 20, and we ended our interview by asking them what changes they had undergone as a result of their volunteer experiences. Every one of these youth indicated that their volunteer work had produced profound changes in them. One of the most common changes they mentioned was an increase in self-confidence and self-esteem:

> *I think through volunteering...I gained a lot of confidence in myself and just what I can tackle and the challenges that I can take on in my life and...I guess I just totally...feel like I can take on any challenge now because of my experiences.*

Some of the most powerful impacts that young people reported with regard to their feelings of self-confidence and self-esteem had to do with the sense that they had "made a difference" in other people's lives and in their communities. This theme was one we heard over and over again in our interviews with young volunteers, across several studies. One of the youth we interviewed, for example, had worked as a literacy tutor with young children and described her experience as follows:

> *Just the fact that I was getting involved outside of the high-school community...that was I was actually within my community where I am from and I could actually see what I was doing was making a difference...that was a big deal.*

The feeling that one can "make a difference" is at the core of a number of important concepts in psychology—concepts such as empowerment, self-efficacy, and agency—and is seen as a powerful force in motivating individuals to behave in ways that will produce positive changes in their own lives and in the lives of others.

Closely related to individuals' self-esteem is the concept of identity. Identity has to do with one's sense of who one is, and how one relates to others and to society. The first detailed exploration of identity was undertaken by developmental psychologist Erik Erikson, in his book *Childhood and Society* (Erikson, 1968). Erikson saw the teenage years as a critical period for the development of a sense of identity. He suggested that during this period, young people are particularly concerned with exploring who they are, how they fit in with others and society, and where they are going in life. According to a later development of Erikson's theory by James Marcia (1966), young people who have engaged in a process of exploration about who they are, and have committed themselves to a set of beliefs and goals for the future, show the most developed sense of identity, a state that Marcia refers to as "identity achievement."

In our study of high school students' civic involvements described earlier (Pancer et al., 2007), we had students complete a measure of identity development called the Objective Measure of Ego Identity Status (OM-EIS—Adams, Shea, & Fitch, 1979). The OM-EIS asks young people to indicate their agreement or disagreement with statements such as, "I've gone through a period of serious questioning about faith and can now say I understand what I believe in as an individual." Youth who agree with such statements are more "identity achieved," in that they have explored different beliefs and then settled upon their own. We found that young people who were civically engaged were significantly more likely to demonstrate "identity achievement," and had a more developed sense of who they were, than were young people who were not civically engaged.

Several other studies, using different methodologies, confirm the link between civic engagement and identity development (Busseri et al., 2011; Dworkin, Larson, & Hansen, 2003; Hardy et al., 2011; Larson et al., 2006; Yates & Youniss, 1996; Youniss, McLellan, & Yates, 1997; Zeldin, 2004). One aspect of identity that seems to be particularly influenced by involvement in civic activities has to do with the way in which one relates to others and to society in general. My own research with young people has led me to believe that civic involvements lead to an identity of social responsibility, in which individuals see themselves as connected to others in society and responsible for their well-being (Pancer & Pratt, 1999). Jim Youniss and Miranda Yates (Yates & Youniss, 1996; Youniss, McLellan, & Yates, 1997; Youniss & Yates, 1997) see civic engagement as having an even broader and more profound impact on young people's identity. They suggest that when young people are involved in their communities by doing community service, they are confronted with the fact that there are those in society who are suffering and in need. In grappling with why such things happen, young people begin to develop a sense of what their role in society is and the responsibility that they themselves have and society has to help people who are in need.

It comes as no surprise that youth who become involved with their schools and communities are generally more satisfied with their lives (Albanesi et al., 2007;

Jimenez et al., 2009; Magen et al., 1992). In a study of Italian youth, Jimenez and her colleagues had research participants complete a measure of community participation in which they indicated their agreement or disagreement with statements such as, "I participate—alone, with my family or with friends—in organizations and associations in my community." In addition, the research participants completed a measure that assessed their satisfaction with their lives (the "Satisfaction with Life Scale," Diener et al., 1985). Results indicated that the more youth had participated in their communities, the more satisfied they were with their lives. Other research (Magen et al., 1992) suggests that young people who participate in their communities through activities such as community service feel a stronger sense of purpose and coherence in their lives and experience positive events in their lives more intensely.

Connection

Another major "capacity" that is characteristic of young people who are thriving is their connection with their peers, family, school, and community. Research suggests that civic engagement, in the form of community service, membership in school organizations, participation in community groups, and other activities, helps young people establish all of these connections.

Several studies show that young people who are involved in their communities experience better relationships with friends and family members (Jimenez et al., 2009; Pancer et al., 2007; Rose-Krasnor et al., 2006). Rose-Krasnor and her colleagues (2006), for example, in a survey of Canadian high school youth, found that young people who were involved in a broad range of activities in their schools and communities reported better relationships with their peers and best friends and stronger relationships with their parents. They also had larger "social support networks"—people they could go to if they needed help or support. These improved relations with peers and family members may be at least in part the result of the improved social skills that young people develop when they participate in their communities—skills such as being able to communicate more clearly and effectively or "regulate" their emotions when they disagree with others (for example, by not losing their temper in an argument) (Dworkin et al., 2003; Hansen, Larson, & Dworkin, 2003; Mahoney et al., 2003).

Being involved in the community, as one would expect, also serves to strengthen young people's connection to their communities. This connection is manifested in many ways. One way is in the expanded social networks that civic participation produces. Through their participation, young people develop new connections, not only with peers, but with individuals who represent a diverse array of ages, cultures, and backgrounds (Dworkin, Larson, & Hansen, 2003). This was demonstrated in several of the interviews we conducted with young people as part of our study of high school mandatory service programs

(Henderson, Pancer, & Brown, 2014). One of the students we interviewed, who had served as a member of a municipal committee in her home town to fulfill her community service requirement, had this to say about her experience:

> *There was a lot of networking... it was just like meeting people in the community so now I know the head of the chamber of commerce... so now when I go back to [my home town] I run into them, the mayor or the head councilor... and we'll sit and talk for a bit and it's just like now that I am in co-op I'm planning to go back and look for a job and the first thing that I am doing is calling up the head guy at Zehrs [a grocery chain] because he's involved with all these volunteer things and in the community so it's really nice.*

Another way in which young people's connection to their community is manifested is in terms of their sense of belonging to their community. The term used to refer to this feeling of belonging is "sense of community." Albanesi and colleagues (Albanesi, Cicognani, & Zani, 2007), in a study of Italian high-school students, found that students who belonged to one or more community groups involving sports, culture, or the arts had a significantly stronger sense of community than did students who didn't belong to any groups.

Young people who participate in community life also manifest their enhanced connection to their communities through their increased commitment to working toward community and societal improvement (Astin & Sax, 1998; Johnson et al., 1998; Magen, Birenbaum, & Ilovich, 1992). Astin and Sax (1998), in a study of American college students, found that students who were involved in activities such as community service and politics were more likely to have future plans that involved doing volunteer work, participating in community action programs, or working for a nonprofit organization. Johnson and colleagues (1998) found similar results in a study of volunteering in American high school students. Students involved in the study completed a survey that asked them whether they had done any volunteering and, if so, how many hours of volunteering they had done. They also responded to a question asking, "How important do you think each of the following things will be to you when you are an adult?" This question was followed by a list that included marriage, friendships, and "participation as a citizen in my community." The results showed that the importance of participating in the community was rated significantly higher by students who had volunteered than it was by students who had not volunteered. Magen and colleagues (1992) found similar results in a study of Israeli young people (14 to 17 years of age). In their study, they asked youth who had or had not been active volunteers, "What is the best thing you would like to do with your life?" Those students who had volunteered were significantly more likely to give answers that indicated that when they became adults they wanted to contribute to the welfare of others in society:

> *The best thing I'd like to do with my life is to contribute to others. Lots of things in this country bother me, like traffic accidents and the treatment of the elderly, but the solution is not to run away but rather to try and change things.* (Magen et al., 1992, p. 52)

Longitudinal research shows that these commitments made during one's youth are not just idle musings. Individuals who participate in their schools and communities as youth are much more likely to participate in community life as adults (Astin, Sax, & Avalos, 1999; Ladewig & Thomas, 1987; Obradovic & Masten, 2007; Youniss, McLellan, & Yates, 1997; Zaff et al., 2003). This was demonstrated in a study by Obradovic and Masten (2007), who surveyed a sample of youth when they were 14 to 19 years of age, asking them to indicate which of 41 extracurricular activities they had been involved in since the beginning of high school. The list included belonging to a student organization, working on a school newspaper, performing community service, and being a member of a club or team. These same individuals were surveyed again more than 15 years later, when they were young adults of 28 to 36 years of age. The later survey asked about participants' involvement in a wide variety of civic activities, including volunteering, voting, doing jury duty, and participating in a community organization. The study's results indicated that individuals' civic involvements as young adults could be predicted from their extracurricular involvements in their teens. Individuals who had participated in extracurricular activities in their teens were significantly more likely, as adults, to volunteer, join community organizations, and, in general, participate in the life of their communities. A study by Ladewig and Thomas (1987) found that individuals who had been members of youth organizations such as 4H when they were in their teens were two or three times more likely to belong to community organizations in adulthood compared to individuals who had not participated in these kinds of organizations.

Another kind of connection that can be fostered by extracurricular involvement is that formed with one's country and society. This connection is demonstrated through individuals' participation in political activities and their concern with prominent social issues, both national and global. People participate in the political life of their countries in many ways. They stay informed about national events by reading newspapers and watching the news on TV, they vote in elections, they join political parties, they write letters to the newspapers and elected officials, and they become involved in political action groups such as Amnesty International. Research tells us that young people who participate in extracurricular groups and activities are significantly more likely to become adults who show a connection to their country and society through political participation. Individuals who participated in extracurricular activities as youth are more likely to contribute money or time to a political campaign, attend a political gathering, participate in a demonstration or protest march, and vote in local or national elections when they reach adulthood (Glanville, 1999; Jennings, 2002; McFarland & Thomas, 2006; Sherkat & Blocker, 1997; Smith, 1999; Zaff et al., 2003). Community involvement has immediate impacts on young people, as well. Involved young people are more knowledgeable about government, politics, and national issues (Schmidt et al., 2007), and they believe that their actions can make a difference in the world (Roker et al., 1999). These impacts were powerfully demonstrated in some of the responses that British psychologists Debi Roker, Katie Player, and John Coleman got from young people in their study of volunteering and social activism in British youth. One young woman in their study, for example, a 15-year-old who had written letters to free political prisoners as a member of Amnesty International, said:

> *My activities with Amnesty International had a big effect on me. I felt good being with a group of people who were all working for the same thing, who were all caring about others. But it made me feel that I mattered too, like how many people my age have had to write to the King of Indonesia and ask him about political prisoners?* (Roker et al., 1999, p. 193).

Caring

The connections that young people establish with others through their participation in their school and community helps them see that the individuals they meet and interact with can have very different needs, ideas, and backgrounds from their own. This new understanding leads to greater empathy for others (especially those who are suffering), an enhanced respect for diversity, and a greater sense of social responsibility (Dworkin, Larson, & Hansen, 2003; Henderson, Pancer, & Brown, 2014; Roker et al., 1999). We saw considerable evidence of the empathy that young people developed in our study of students who had been part of a mandatory service program in Canadian high schools (Henderson, Pancer, & Brown, 2014). For example, one youth who had volunteered in a retirement home described her experience as follows:

> *I just got to see the different aspect of elderly people ... like you always think of old people, and I have my grandma at home ... but I actually got to see what it's like in a retirement home, and what they are experiencing and what they are feeling and the struggles they go through ... it was really sad to see a lot of them kind of suffering and in pain and alone, so it just kind of made me appreciate the fact that I have a lot of people that care about me and that I have a family, and I know that my grandma lives at home, like we would never put her in a retirement home, but all those people were just like kind of forgotten, and no one is visiting them or anything.*

Connecting with others from diverse backgrounds also helps build an appreciation for diversity, as well as break down stereotypes that individuals have of different groups (Astin et al., 1999; Yates & Youniss, 1998). This was demonstrated in a study of high school students who had participated in a year-long service-learning program in which they worked in a downtown soup kitchen during the school year (Yates & Youniss, 1998). Students worked a total of 20 hours at the soup kitchen, over the course of four visits. After each visit, they wrote an essay describing their experience and how they felt about it. Another component of the study involved contacting individuals who had graduated from the high school, and asking them to write essays about how their experience working in the soup kitchen had influenced them. Many of the students involved in the study talked about how their experience had broken down stereotypes they had held. For example, one student talked about how her view of homeless people had changed:

> *Working at [the soup kitchen] taught me there are people who are less fortunate than me. Before going there, I always thought of homeless people as being dumb, uneducated, dirty individuals. After meeting with some of them, I realized that most of them did not want to be homeless or come to a soup kitchen. Most of them I talked with were college graduates, young mothers, and everyday people just like everybody else.* (Yates & Youniss, 1998, p. 508)

A study by Astin and colleagues (1999) suggests that, as well as breaking down stereotypes, involvement in civic activities such as volunteering can produce more frequent interactions with people from diverse backgrounds. They found that university students who had volunteered in their communities while they were undergraduates were significantly more likely to have socialized with people from different racial and ethnic groups more than 9 years after they had graduated.

These kinds of experiences that young people have through their involvement in their schools and communities help create a sense of social responsibility in young people—a feeling that they have a responsibility to help those who are less fortunate than themselves. We have seen evidence of this sense of social responsibility in several of the studies we have conducted. In one of studies (Pancer et al., 2007), described in earlier chapters, we had students from several high schools complete the Youth Inventory of Involvement, a measure that assessed their involvement in a wide range of school and community groups and activities. We also had these students complete a scale we entitled the "Youth Social Responsibility Scale," in which they indicated their agreement or disagreement with items such as, "People have a responsibility to help those who are less well off than themselves," and "It's important for people to speak out when an injustice has occurred." Our results showed that students who were more engaged in their schools and neighborhoods had a significantly greater sense of social responsibility than students who were not engaged. A young volunteer that we interviewed in another of our studies (Pancer & Pratt, 1999) described this sense of social responsibility in this way:

> *A lot of times, the... reason that you're in a position to help is just luck, you know, nothing that you've done to deserve to be... in a different position... and you know, things could change... in the blink of an eye and something could be different, and definitely people have a responsibility to be volunteering and doing things in their community. It's what makes it a community.* (p. 52)

Competence

Civic involvement, in the form of participation in groups and activities in school or in the community, helps build a wide range of skills and capacities. Young people who participated in several of our own studies of volunteering and other forms of civic activities often talked about the many things they learned and skills they developed. For example, one person we interviewed in our first study of youth volunteers (Pancer & Pratt, 1999) said:

> *There's just innumerable things that I've learned, little things about working with people and... even how people think and how people work and how people will respond and what's the best way for me to respond when things happen.* (p. 51)

The young people who participated in our interviews mentioned many skills they had acquired through their involvement. They talked about learning how to work in teams, solve conflicts, communicate clearly and effectively, manage their time, and lead activities. Other studies confirm the notion that civic involvement helps build skills (Astin & Sax, 1998; Dworkin et al., 2003; Hamilton & Fenzel, 1988; Hansen et al., 2003; Larson et al., 2006; Zeldin, 2004). Astin and Sax (1998), for example, used results from a survey of undergraduate students from 42 American universities to examine differences in skill acquisition between students who had been involved in community service activities and those who had not. They found that involved students rated their leadership ability, conflict resolution skills, ability to work cooperatively, and ability to get along with people of different races and cultures significantly more highly than uninvolved students had. Dworkin and colleagues (2003), in their study of teens who had been involved in school and community organizations, found that young people involved in these organizations had developed "initiative"—which they defined as "the capacity to direct attention and effort over time toward a challenging goal" (p. 21). This was demonstrated by their ability to set realistic goals, persevere at a task, and manage their time.

Young people who have acquired these kinds of skills through their civic involvements can be expected to achieve success in important endeavors in their lives. This is certainly true of their school achievements. Youth who are involved in the life of their school and community have more positive attitudes toward school, study more, and get better grades compared to youth who are uninvolved (Anderson-Butcher et al., 2003; Astin & Sax, 1998; Bartko & Eccles, 2003; Denault et al., 2009; Eccles et al., 2003; Fredricks & Eccles, 2008; Harrison & Naryan, 2003; Marsh, 1992; Marsh & Kleitman, 2002; Schmidt et al., 2007). They also have higher educational aspirations, are more likely to attend university, and complete more years of education (Astin et al., 1999; Barber et al., 2001; Eccles & Barber, 1999; Eccles et al., 2003; Fredricks & Eccles, 2006; Mahoney et al., 2003; Marsh, 1992; Marsh & Kleitman, 2002; Zaff et al., 2003). When they do get to university, civically engaged students do extra work for their courses, have more contact with their professors, and are more likely to graduate (Astin & Sax, 1998; Barber et al., 2001; Eccles et al., 2003; Marsh & Kleitman, 2002).

The interests, connections, and skills that young people acquire through their school and civic involvements can also help them in deciding what kinds of careers to choose, and lead to improved employment prospects and career success. Several of the youth whom we interviewed about their volunteer activities talked about how their volunteer experiences had influenced their choice of career. One young person, for example, who worked as a volunteer with disabled children, said:

> *It's been one of the most draining volunteer work that I've done but I loved it the most, I've learned so much...and working with them [disabled children] is actually what helped me decide on what I want to do for the rest of my life.* (Pancer & Pratt, 1999, p. 51)

The impact that civic engagements such as community service can have on people's careers was demonstrated in another study that my former graduate student, Trevor Taylor, and I conducted with students from my own university (Taylor & Pancer, 2007). In this study, we had undergraduate students who performed community service as part of their psychology course requirements complete a scale that assessed how positive their service experience was. We also asked them to complete measures that assessed various aspects of their decision making about their future careers. We found that students who had more positive community service experiences were more decided about what kinds of career they wanted to choose and had more information about the careers they were considering.

Civic participation can also help young people secure jobs, often through the connections that they make in their civic activities. Zeldin (2004) found evidence of this in an interview study he did with young people who had served on governing boards and committees of service organizations. These youth had been offered internships, references for employment applications, and even jobs as a result of their involvement in these organizations. One young woman described how she had benefitted from her experience by saying "doors that I didn't even know existed are now open" (Zeldin, 2004, p. 83).

Character

Another of the major capacities that develop in young people as a result of their civic involvements and commitments is "character." Lerner (Lerner et al., 2005) defines character as behaving with integrity and having a sense of morality and respect for societal and cultural rules. As discussed in earlier chapters, research and theory in developmental psychology suggests that children develop a sense of morality—of what is right and wrong—by observing the behavior of others. Early in life, these "others" are the child's parents. By the time an individual reaches adolescence, the "others" who influence one's sense of morality include one's peers and significant adult role models. Individuals observe what their parents, peers, and others do, and from their observations, begin to fashion a sense of what is right and wrong and what is considered "correct" or normative in their society. Young people who are involved in extracurricular school and outside-of-school activities have the opportunity to observe people who, for the most part, are behaving in a positive way. As members of teams and clubs, they observe people working in concert to achieve group goals. In doing community service, they observe others who are attempting to help those in need. As members of social or environmental action organizations, they observe others who are trying to build a more equitable and sustainable society. Out of these observations, young people begin to see a "norm of social responsibility" operating in society—a societal rule or standard that says that people should help others in need, and work toward making their community and their world a better place. They then begin to "internalize" this norm, adopting it as part of their own moral philosophy. We certainly saw evidence of this in our interviews with young people about their volunteer experiences while in high school. For example, one of the high school students we interviewed in our study of mandatory volunteering (Henderson, Pancer, & Brown, 2014) described her own moral philosophy in this way:

> *We are so blessed to be in such a rich country and we have so many resources, and if you just think, we are the 1 per cent of the world and other people in the world don't have what we have, it's kind of our responsibility to be able to give what we have. By giving some of your time and money it's not going to make you bankrupt. It's not going to take anything away from you, but it could change their lives.*

The organizations and institutions that young people become involved with—their schools, churches, youth organizations, cultural groups, and others—carry with them their own norms and ideologies. Yates and Youniss and their colleagues refer to these kinds of organizations as "ideology-bearing" or "norm-bearing" institutions (Yates & Youniss, 1996; Youniss, McLellan, & Yates, 1997). For example, as mentioned in chapter 4, almost every major religious faith has a set of beliefs that include behaving with integrity, showing concern for others, and working to improve their communities and the world around them. These organizations, then, provide young people, who are searching for their own ideology or philosophy, with one that emphasizes moral behavior and a concern for the well-being of others.

Who Is Most Affected by Civic Participation?

Young people who grow up in adverse circumstances, such as poverty or dysfunctional families, are significantly more likely to suffer from a wide range of social, emotional, and behavior problems and are said to be "at-risk" (Bradford, Vaughn., & Barber, 2008; Bradley & Corwin, 2002; Masten, 2011). Moreover, when these at-risk children and youth develop problems, they are often the most difficult to help. But not all young people are affected by adversity in this way. Young people who are resilient have assets and capacities that protect them from the effects of these circumstances and allow them to thrive and develop into emotionally healthy adults, even under difficult conditions (Fergus & Zimmerman, 2005). Research shows that civic engagement helps young people become more resilient. Fredricks and Eccles (2008), for example, used results from a longitudinal survey of American youth to examine the relationship between students' involvements and their "psychological resiliency." Resiliency was measured by a scale that asked the research participants to indicate how often they were "very good at" things such as "bouncing back quickly from bad experiences" and "learning from your mistakes." The results showed that youth who had participated in school clubs when they were in grade 8 had significantly higher levels of psychological resilience than youth who had not participated in clubs. They continued to show higher resilience three years later, when they were in grade 11.

Several studies show, further, that it is the more at-risk youth who benefit the most from civic engagement (Kinney, 1993; Mahoney, 2000; Mahoney & Cairns, 1997; Mahoney et al., 2003; Marsh & Kleitman, 2002). In one of these studies, Joseph Mahoney and Robert Cairns (1997) compiled a record of students' extracurricular involvements by examining descriptions of each of the students in their high school yearbooks. Using other information, they employed a statistical procedure called "cluster analysis" to place the students into three groups: an "at-risk" group, consisting of students who came from poor families, had demonstrated aggressive behavior at school, were performing poorly at their academic work, and were unpopular with their peers; a "marginal competence" group, consisting of students who demonstrated some of the attributes of the at-risk group, but not all; and a "high competence" group of students who were from families that were at least reasonably well-off financially, were popular with their peers, and were doing well at school. In addition, the researchers examined school records to determine whether a student had dropped out before completing high school. What they found was that participating in extracurricular activities had a much greater impact on the at-risk students than it had on the marginal and high-competence students. At-risk students who were not involved in any activities were two or three times more likely to drop out of school than were marginal or high-competence students who also were not involved in activities. But at-risk students who were involved in even one activity were much less likely to drop out—and their rate of drop-out wasn't any different from the marginal and high-competence students (see Figure 6.1, taken from Mahoney & Cairns, p. 249). Other studies by Mahoney and his colleagues (Mahoney, 2000; Mahoney et al., 2003), and other investigators (Kinney, 1993; Marsh & Kleitman, 2003) show that at-risk young people benefit more from extracurricular involvements than youth who aren't at risk in terms of criminal behavior, educational aspirations, and educational achievement.

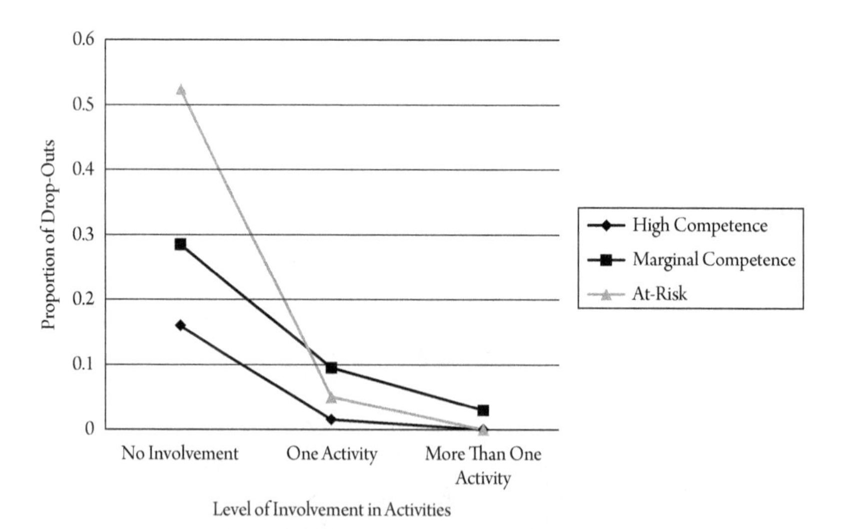

Figure 6.1 Drop-Out as a Function of Extracurricular Activity and Risk Status.
From Mahoney, J. L. & Cairns, R. B. (1997). Do extracurricular activities protect against early school dropout? *Developmental Psychology,* 33(2), 241–253. Reprinted with permission from APA.

How Long Do the Effects of Civic Participation Last?

There is strong evidence that civic engagement, in the form of participation in school clubs, youth organizations, community service, social activism, religious organizations, and other activities, helps reduce problems in young people and promotes positive youth development. But how long do the effects of this kind of participation last? There are now several studies that have looked at the impacts of civic participation years after it has taken place. The results of these studies consistently show that the effects of civic engagement can last for many years and, quite possibly, for a lifetime. Beane and colleagues (1981), for example, examined individuals who had participated in an intensive school-based community service project when they were in high school between 1945 and 1949. The involved students had participated in creating a development plan for their city in the northeastern United States. Among other things, they conducted a citizen survey, studied land use and traffic patterns, made recommendations concerning the development of parks and other recreational facilities, and gave presentations to local government. These individuals, along with a comparison group of students who had not participated in the project, were surveyed more than 30 years later, in 1979. The study showed that individuals who had participated in the community service project 30 years earlier had participated in four times as many organizations and had served in leadership positions in twice as many organizations over the intervening years as had students from the same high school who had not been involved in the project.

Sociologist Doug McAdam found similar long-term effects in individuals who had participated in the civil rights movement in the United States in the summer of 1964 (McAdam, 1988, 1989). During that summer, as participants in what was called the Freedom Summer project, hundreds of students from universities in the northern United States travelled to Mississippi to help register black voters and fight for their civil rights. Twenty years later, in 1983 and 1984, McAdam contacted as many of these individuals as he could find, as well as individuals who had signed up to participate but were unable to, and had them complete a questionnaire that asked them about their current involvements. He found that, compared to the individuals who hadn't participated in Freedom Summer, individuals who had participated were significantly more likely to be involved in a social movement and to belong to political organizations. Another study, by Jennings (2002), found similar differences between individuals who had engaged in protests in the early 1970s and those who had not. When they were surveyed again nearly 25 years later, the protesters were more likely to have been involved in political activities such as contacting a public official, attending a political rally, or taking part in a demonstration.

Studies of other kinds of involvement during one's youth also show long-term effects. A number of studies found that that individuals who had participated in extracurricular groups and activities as high school students were significantly more likely than nonparticipating youth to be involved in civic organizations and activities years later, when they were adults (Hanks & Eckland, 1978; Ladewig & Thomas, 1987; Obradovic & Masten, 2007). Hanks and Eckland (1978), for example, found that people who belonged to youth organizations such as 4H when they were adolescents were twice as likely to be active in community organizations as adults, compared to individuals who had not been involved.

What Causes What?

In this chapter, I have described many studies that show a link between young people's civic engagements and a wide range of positive outcomes. Young people who participate in school and community groups experience fewer problems and greater well-being than those who do not. But it is important to note that the existence of a link or correlation between involvement and well-being does not mean that one causes the other. It is certainly possible that involvement produces well-being, but it is also possible that well-being produces greater involvement. For example, young people who are doing well at school have more time to do things such as extracurricular activities. So it may be that school competence leads to greater involvement in activities such as clubs and youth groups. In other words, school achievement may lead to greater extracurricular involvement rather than extracurricular involvement producing greater academic achievement. Or it may be the case that neither of these things leads to the other, but it is some other variable, such as financial resources, that produce both greater involvement and higher school competence. Families that are well off are better able to pay the fees required to enroll their children in extracurricular activities, so their children engage in more activities; they can also provide them with resources (such as books and learning materials) that will allow them to do better at school. Once again, this would mean that it is not involvement that is producing better school achievement but some other factor, such as family financial status, that leads to both involvement and achievement. Well-designed studies attempt to address this issue of what causes what. For example, almost all the longitudinal studies by Mahoney and Eccles and their colleagues described in this chapter attempted to account or control for any variables, such as young people's academic performance before beginning their extracurricular involvements or their family's financial status, so that they could be more certain that it is indeed young people's involvements that lead to or cause things such as improved academic performance.

The most rigorous way to establish a causal link between engagement and well-being is to develop a program that is designed to engage young people in community activities, randomly assign youth to participate in either the program or in a control group that doesn't get the program, and then look at differences between the program group and the control group. The study by Allen and colleagues (1997), described earlier in the chapter, demonstrates this approach. In this study, young people were randomly assigned to participate in a program (Teen Outreach) that had a community service component or to a control group in which no community service was required. They found that youth who participated in the program were significantly less likely to fail at school than were youth who were in the control group. In this study, we can be quite confident that it was involvement in community service that produced better school achievement, rather than school achievement (or something like intelligence, which is related to school achievement) producing greater community involvement.

Summary

Civic engagement for young people may take the form of joining clubs and teams at school, doing volunteer work, participating in a youth group at church or synagogue, or becoming a member of a youth organization such as Girl Scouts, among other activities. Research tells us that youth who participate in these kinds of civic activities are much less likely to get into trouble. They are less likely to abuse drugs and alcohol, smoke, engage in delinquent acts, and fail at or drop out of school. They are also less likely to become pregnant, get a sexually transmitted disease, or experience mental health problems. On the contrary, engaged youth experience many benefits. They have higher self-esteem, a more developed sense of identity, and greater life-satisfaction. They develop better relationships with their parents, peers, schools, and communities. They also demonstrate more caring for others, a greater sense of social responsibility, and an appreciation and respect for diversity. They acquire a wide range of skills and capacities, do well at school, and have higher aspirations for their future. Research tells us, further, that it is young people who are at-risk for developing problems, because they are living in poverty or dysfunctional family environments, who benefit the most from being civically engaged. Studies indicate, too, that the effects of civic participation can last for many years and, quite possibly, for a lifetime.

7

Impacts of Civic Engagement on Adults

More than 20 years ago, I became involved with an initiative called Better Beginnings, Better Futures (described briefly in chapter 3). Better Beginnings, the name that we came to use in referring to the project, is a prevention program. It was designed to prevent children who were living in poor communities from developing social, emotional, and learning problems by providing the children—and their families and communities—with programs and supports when the children were very young (under the age of 8). Each of the eight communities selected as Better Beginnings sites provided a range of programs and services to parents and children living in those communities, including home visits, classroom enrichment, before- and after-school activities, nutritious snacks and lunches, parent and child drop-in centers, play groups, toy lending libraries, parenting classes, and much more.

These kinds of programs and activities are by no means unique to Better Beginnings; they are found in many other communities around the world. What was distinctive about Better Beginnings, particularly when it first began in the early 1990s, was the role that parents and other community residents had in the way the program was implemented. Rather than just receiving program services, residents took an active role in every aspect of the project's development. They sat on the steering committees that oversaw the projects (in fact, it was required that residents make up at least 51% of these committees). They were involved in hiring the project staff, including the project director or coordinator. In partnership with local health and social service professionals, they developed budgets and planned future programs. They acted as advocates for the project, and they helped reach out to other residents to get them involved in project programs. They provided services such as preparing snacks and lunches, facilitating parent groups, running toy lending libraries, and a multitude of other tasks. The Better Beginnings project, then, was designed not only to promote healthy development in children, but to encourage active citizenship among parents and other residents living in the community, as well.

Our research team, which has studied the Better Beginnings project since its inception, conducted extensive quantitative and qualitative research on the impact the project has had on children, their parents, and other community residents (see Peters et al., 2010, and www.bbbf.ca). One of the studies we undertook to assess the project's impact used a narrative approach, a qualitative methodology that is becoming increasingly common and accepted in psychological investigation. This approach involves asking research participants to tell their life story, recounting events of significance and the feelings associated with those events. In our narrative study, we did interviews with 81 individuals who had had significant involvement with the Better Beginnings project as a program participant, staff member, or volunteer. We asked them to tell us the story of their involvement with the Better Beginnings project in their community, guiding them with questions such as, "What was it like before you got involved with Better Beginnings? How did you first get involved? What difference has Better Beginnings made in your life?"

The stories that residents told formed the basis of a report that we called the "Stories" report (Pancer & Foxall, 1998). The most striking impression one has when reading this report is how much residents benefitted from their active partnership in guiding the development of the Better Beginnings project. In the "Stories" report, we included the complete narratives of several of the individuals we interviewed. The following is an excerpt from the story told by one of these individuals (whom I will refer to by the pseudonym Anna), illustrating some of the benefits that individuals can derive from this kind of active citizenship:

> *When I first got involved with Better Beginnings, I was a stay-at-home mom with two young children—my youngest was just a baby. Being home alone I felt very bored, very isolated, nothing to do. I just sat around and watched a lot of TV. I first heard about Better Beginnings from one of the parents I knew from the school. She went on and on about it—the Better Beginnings drop in—and so I started coming. Really liking it. Just sitting around with parents and letting the kids play and meeting people.*
>
> *And then I joined the parents group. One of the people from the parents group asked me to come to a meeting. The first meeting was in this empty portable at the school and we sat around and talked about what we thought the community needs, what we would like to see in the school, what we thought the kids needed. From there it just grew. The very first committee after that meeting was either the nutrition committee or in-school committee. Then I was doing outreach with the community development worker as well. Even before the committees I was asked to sit on the hiring committee—to help hire the project coordinator!*

The first few months with the project felt amazing—very exciting. Very empowering, which was a word I didn't know back then, but I do now. I loved it—I still do. Breaking the isolation was a big factor for me. It changed my personality drastically. I never really pictured myself as a shy person but I think when I came out around other people I was kind of shy and laid back, and unless you spoke to me first, I wouldn't speak to you first. Just being able to talk to other parents made a difference—coming out and talking to other parents, and getting involved and getting your ideas on paper. Having what I had to say in the Newsletter was a big to-do for me. Being accessible to the principal and to the teachers, being known by the vice-principal. Being known and feeling important that way has been really good.

I've learned a lot of skills, too. The coordinator encouraged me to take an assertiveness training course, and that impacted my life a lot. I also got some training on how to run a committee. That was helpful not only with committee work, but on a personal level. Being able to balance time and what's important and what's not important, being able to communicate.

About three years ago, my husband and I separated, and I became a single parent. The kids were so young and they were so upset and withdrawn and quiet for a while. The project helped. Some of my friends in the project came up to me shortly after the separation and said "you need to get away from the kids, we're going for this Christmas celebration. We've put together $50 and it will pay everything, you have to come." That kind of thing goes on all the time. I think if it hadn't been for the project, going to people and saying "this is what I think, give me some advice, tell me what to do," if I hadn't had those close relationships, I wouldn't have said anything. That helped a lot and I think it definitely benefitted the kids.

I can't imagine my life without Better Beginnings. Being at the school all the time. Feeling so needed. Being able to plug in where you're needed. Having the school trustee write me letters, call me on the phone. I think it's important for the kids, for the future, and for the community.

In many ways, Anna's story is similar to many others that we heard from residents who, through Better Beginnings, became more active citizens in their communities. In her story Anna talks about the many benefits she received through her involvement: a sense of empowerment, reduced isolation, the skills that she acquired, the support she had from others when she went through her separation, and so on. These kinds of benefits were mentioned over and over again by almost everyone we interviewed.

When one looks at the research literature on the kinds of impacts that people experience from getting involved in their communities, the overwhelming impression one gets is that good things almost always happen when individuals become active citizens. In what follows, I describe what research tells us about the kinds of benefits that adults experience when they become active citizens.

Self-Esteem, Self-Efficacy, and Empowerment

One of the things that we heard in our many interviews with people who were involved in the Better Beginnings, Better Futures project was that their participation had made them feel greater confidence and have more self-esteem. One resident who had been involved in a number of project committees described it this way:

> *At the beginning, I was not hoping to get anything. It was just an outlet. I didn't think about getting a job out of it or anything like that... it's just a place to go that I didn't have to take a bus... But then, sitting on various committees and actually having people seeming like they were listening to me... I got my confidence, 'cause I thought, I always knew I had a brain but it was dormant there for a while. It's true... and I started getting respect for the first time in a long time... people were actually listening to me.* (Pancer & Cameron, 1993, p. 70)

Many studies, using a wide range of qualitative and quantitative methodologies, find similarly positive impacts of civic engagement on self-esteem (Attree et al., 2011; Brown et al., 2012; Pancer & Cameron, 1993). Australian researchers Brown, Hoye, and Nicholson (2012), for example, conducted a survey of a random sample of adults in the state of Victoria, Australia, asking them if they "currently volunteer with any formal organized group." They also had those participating in the survey complete a popular measure of self-esteem—the Rosenberg Self-Esteem Scale (Rosenberg, 1965)—which asked participants to indicate their agreement or disagreement with statements such as, "I feel that I have a number of good qualities." The results showed that individuals who were currently volunteering had significantly higher levels of self-esteem than those who were not.

Participants in this study also completed a measure of self-efficacy—the belief that one can succeed in achieving important goals in life. In completing this measure, individuals read a series of statements, such as, "I can always manage to solve difficult problems if I try hard enough," and indicated how true each of the statements was of them. The results showed that those currently volunteering had greater self-efficacy—a stronger sense that they could achieve desired goals—than those not currently volunteering.

Closely related to the notion of self-efficacy is the concept of empowerment. *Empowerment* is a term that is now very widely used, and has come to be seen as an important process in enhancing the lives of both individuals and communities. Community psychologist Julian Rappaport was one of the first social scientists to define the term, develop theories about how it develops, and determine the impact it has on individuals and communities. In one of his earlier essays on the subject, Rappaport talked about empowerment as the development of the sense that one has the power to determine the course of one's own life, and that one has the right to exert this power to achieve positive change in both oneself and the community (Rappaport, 1987). Research suggests that civic participation, through membership in community organizations, the performance of community service, and other activities, produces empowerment. Zimmerman and Rappaport (1988), for example, administered measures that assessed various aspects of empowerment to two groups of people—university students and community residents. They also asked these individuals how many groups or organizations, such as political groups, service organizations, and church groups, they belonged to. They found that individuals who were more civically active, in that they belonged to more of these groups, were more empowered in almost every way than were those who were less or not at all civically active. The more active individuals felt they had more control over their lives, more skills and capacity to achieve their goals, and greater power to effect changes in their lives and their communities.

We certainly found evidence of enhanced empowerment in our research on the Better Beginnings, Better Futures project. As part of our "Stories" report on the project, we asked individuals who served as volunteers and members of project committees how their involvement had affected them. Many of those we interviewed talked about how their participation had helped them realize that they had a "voice" and a role to play in shaping their future:

> *Before I was involved in Better Beginnings, you would have to give me a hint if you asked me who the Prime Minister was, I mean I was just so uninvolved... nothing that was happening in the government was affecting me. But through them it kind of opened my eyes and it helped me realize that I can participate in the outcome of my future... have control in that. I don't have to just let things happen to me. I can help change things and... even if things don't necessarily change, at least I'll know that I didn't sit by and let people walk all over me or let the government walk all over me. At least... I've got a voice. I think having a voice is really important, and when people listen to you, it feels really good.* (Pancer & Foxall, 1998, p. 43)

Relationships and Sense of Community

One thing that almost all civic activities have in common is that they bring people into contact with one another. As we saw in the last chapter with regard to young people, getting involved in community groups and activities brings people into contact with others, and fosters the development of new friendships and social contacts. Prestby and her colleagues (1990) demonstrated this in their study of social contacts among people who were members of neighborhood organizations in New York City. They found that individuals who were active members of these organizations had more social contacts than individuals who were only nominally involved, and never attended meetings of the organization. Having friends and social contacts can be especially important for older people, who may be more socially isolated and at greater risk for health and other problems. Rook and Sorkin (2003), in a study of older individuals (60 to 92 years of age), found that those who helped look after a developmentally delayed child as part of a foster grandparent program formed significantly more new relationships over the course of the study than had individuals who had not participated in the program. Over 70% of the new relationships they formed were with people they had met through the program.

Many benefits derive from these kinds of social connections. One of the most significant benefits is the sense of support that people get from their networks of friends and social contacts. We certainly found this to be the case in our research on the Better Beginnings project. This is what one of the women who had participated as a volunteer with the project said of the relationships she formed through Better Beginnings:

> *It has made a difference because I have made a lot of very good friends that I could really depend on... that if I'm not there one day and something should happen to my kids, I could easily call the people here to take care of my kids before I get there... We have... made friends to the point that we're more like a family, like we're beyond friendship... we're like family... we work very closely together... whatever problems we have, there's someone that we can talk to.* (Pancer & Foxall, 1998, p. 44)

The relationship between civic engagement and social support is corroborated by other studies via a variety of methodologies. Australian researchers Helen Berry and Jennifer Welsh (2010), for example, assessed this relationship by examining data from the Household Labor Dynamics and Income Survey, administered to a random sample of Australian adults over the age of 15. Respondents to the survey answered questions about their civic participation, indicating how often they had been involved in volunteering, attending community events, or working on the boards or committees of clubs. They also completed a measure of social support, indicating their agreement or disagreement with statements such as, "When I need someone to help me out, I can usually find someone." The results of the study showed that individuals who were more civically active had greater social support than individuals who were less civically engaged.

Individuals who participate in community life, through activities such as volunteering and community organizational work, often come into contact with individuals who have backgrounds very different from their own. In the previous chapter, I talked about how the connections that youth make with people from different backgrounds can help break down stereotypes and create empathy and an appreciation for diversity. Research suggests that civic participation can have the same impact on adults. In one of my own studies, conducted with my colleagues Mark Baetz and Evelina Rog (Pancer, Baetz, & Rog, 2002), we interviewed employees of the Ford Motor Company of Canada who had been involved in their company's corporate volunteer program. Company employees who participated in the program were given time off from work to volunteer in the community with a group of fellow employees. One of the outcomes that we observed in employees' descriptions of their volunteer experience was that they showed greater empathy and appreciation for individuals who had different life experiences from their own. For example, one employee who worked at a food bank offered this description of the impact his volunteer work had had on him:

> *It really did open my eyes... I honestly would... have the idea that maybe these people really don't need the Food Bank because they can't manage their money or they didn't study well enough in school... and they got themselves into their own mess and then we went to the Food Bank and the woman was telling us about... the fact that we had large industries in our area where they just closed down and then you would have these families where they had jobs and kids in schools... and suddenly they don't have any income any more.* (Pancer, Baetz, & Rog, 2002, p. 15)

Participation in civic life also gives people a "sense of community"—a feeling of belonging and relatedness to other community members (Chavis & Wandersman, 1990; Ohmer, 2007; Talo, Mannarini, & Rochira, 2014). Social work researcher Mary Ohmer provided evidence of this relationship in a study she conducted with members of neighborhood organizations in four poor neighborhoods in Pittsburgh, Pennsylvania (Ohmer, 2007). She sent questionnaires to members of all of the neighborhood organizations in these areas, asking them about how much they had participated in different organizational activities and functions; she also asked them to complete a scale that measured sense of community. The scale they completed—a short form of the Sense of Community Index (Perkins et al., 1990)—contained statements such as, "It is very important to me to live in this neighborhood," to which respondents indicated their agreement or disagreement. The results showed that individuals who were more involved in their neighborhood organizations had a greater sense of community than individuals who were less involved. In a recent meta-analysis of 34 studies that had examined the link between civic participation and sense of community, Talo and colleagues (2014) found a significant and sizeable relationship between civic participation and people's sense of community across all of the studies. This relationship held for a wide variety of civic activities, including participation in protests, voting, political campaigning, and volunteering.

Health

Several studies have shown a relationship between civic participation and people's overall health (Berry & Welsh, 2010; Borgonovi, 2008; Helliwell & Putnam, 2004; Kim & Kawachi, 2006; Oman et al., 1999; Poortinga, 2006; Thoits & Hewitt, 2001). In the study by Berry and Welsh (2010), discussed earlier in this chapter, the investigators looked at Australian adults' participation in various civic activities, such as attendance at community events, participation in clubs or community groups, or working for a political cause, and how their participation in these activities related to their physical health, as assessed by a popular measure of health and mental health—the Short Form 36 Health Survey (Ware et al., 1993). They found that individuals who were more civically engaged had better health than individuals who were less engaged. Borgonovi (2008) found similar effects when she looked at the relationship between volunteering and health in a survey of American adults. Participants in the survey were asked if they had done volunteer work within the last 12 months, and they were also asked to indicate if they felt that their overall state of health was poor, fair, good, very good, or excellent. She found that individuals who had performed volunteer work reported significantly better health than individuals who had not volunteered.

One of the most interesting studies of health and civic participation was conducted by Phyllis Moen and her colleagues (1992), using data from interviews that had been conducted with 313 women in 1956. One of the questions the women were asked at that time was whether they were members of clubs or organizations. A large percentage of the women (70%) reported having been involved in organizations, such as Parent Teacher Associations, church groups, hospital auxiliaries, and Brownie troops. Thirty years later, in 1986, the women were interviewed again and asked about the state of their health. The results of this study showed that women who had reported being civically active in 1956 were significantly healthier 30 years later than women who had not been civically active. They were less likely to have become seriously ill in the intervening 30 years, and they were better able to perform activities like walking up and down stairs or doing heavy work around the house.

Individuals who are civically engaged not only experience better health, but they also act in ways that serve to enhance their health and reduce the likelihood that they will become ill. Poortinga (2006), using data from the Health Survey of England, an annual survey of English adults, found that civic participation in the form of belonging to clubs and organizations was related to smoking and eating habits. Those who were members of clubs and organizations were less likely to smoke and were more likely to eat five or more portions of fruit and vegetables each day than were nonmembers. Oman and colleagues (1999), in a study of older adults (55 years of age and older) in Marin County, California, also found that individuals who had been active as volunteers were less likely to smoke than individuals who didn't volunteer; in addition, they found that volunteers exercised more frequently. A study of injection drug users attending methadone clinics in New York City found that users who were civically engaged, in that they were registered to vote and identified with a political party, were less likely to share needles, placing them at lower risk for HIV infection (Mino et al., 2011).

Perhaps the ultimate indicator of one's health is how long one lives. There have been a number of studies that show that people who are engaged in their communities through activities such as volunteering and membership in community organizations live substantially longer than those who are not (Harris & Thoresen, 2005; Moen et al., 1989; Musick et al., 1999; Oman et al., 1999). Harris and Thoresen (2005) used data from an American longitudinal study of aging in their examination of community service and mortality. The individuals involved in this study were 70 years of age and older when they were first interviewed in 1984. In the interview, the study participants were asked if they were currently involved in any volunteer activities, such as doing community work, volunteering with a nonprofit organization, or working in a hospital or nursing home. They were also asked how often they had done this kind of work over the previous 12 months (never, rarely, sometimes, or frequently). Eight years later, in 1992, the researchers consulted the National Death Index, a database of all deaths that had occurred in the United States, to determine who among those who were interviewed in 1984 had died in the intervening years. It turned out that nearly 40% of the sample died during that interval. It also turned out that substantially fewer of the people who had been active volunteers in 1984 had died compared to those who had not been volunteers. Those who reported volunteering only "rarely" or "sometimes" in 1984 showed more than a 40% reduction in mortality over the next 8 years, while those who had reported volunteering "frequently" showed an astonishing 53% reduction in mortality, compared to those who had reported doing no volunteer work. Other studies have shown even greater reductions in mortality in those who volunteer. Oman and colleagues (1999) found a 63% reduction in mortality among older individuals who volunteered with community organizations compared to nonvolunteers.

The study by Moen and colleagues (1989), described earlier in the chapter, found a similar relationship between civic engagement and mortality in their examination of women who had participated in a longitudinal study of women's roles. When the researchers attempted to recontact these women to participate in a follow-up interview 30 years after their initial interview in 1956, they found that, of the women who were interviewed in 1956, 76% were still alive and 19% had died (5% of the original group could not be located). When they compared women who had been involved in community organizations in 1956 with women who had not, they found that civically involved women were significantly less likely to have died during the 30 years after the initial interview.

Another noteworthy study demonstrating a link between civic participation and mortality was conducted by Semenza and colleagues during a heat wave in Chicago in the summer of 1995 (Semenza et al., 1996). In July of that year, over 700 people died of heat-related causes when the temperature in the city hit record levels over a four-day period. The researchers compared a sample of individuals who died of heat-related causes over that interval to a sample of control individuals, matched for age and place of residence, who survived the heat wave. A key factor that distinguished those who survived from those who died was their involvement in their communities. Those who survived the heat wave were significantly more likely to have been participating in clubs, support groups, or church activities than were those who perished from the heat.

Mental Health

Research indicates that civic participation is associated with mental, as well as physical, health (Berry & Welsh, 2010; Brown et al., 2012; Musick & Wilson, 2003; Thoits & Hewitt, 2001). The study by Brown and colleagues (2012), mentioned earlier in this chapter, examined the relationship between civic engagement (in the form of doing volunteer work) and mental health, using data from a survey of adults in the state of Victoria, Australia. Participants in the survey, in addition to reporting whether they currently volunteered, completed a measure of mental health that asked them questions such as "During the past 4 weeks, how much of the time have you accomplished less than you would like in relation to your work or other regular activities as a result of any emotional problems (such as feeling depressed or anxious)?" The results indicated that volunteers had better mental health than nonvolunteers. Berry and Welsh (2010), also using Australian survey data, looked at a somewhat broader index of civic participation and how it related to mental health. Participants in this survey indicated how frequently they had participated in a range of civic activities (e.g., working on boards or committees, attending community events, attending services at a place of worship, as well as volunteering), in addition to completing a standardized measure of mental health. The results showed that individuals who were more civically engaged reported better mental health than those who were less engaged. Similar results have been found in American studies of civic participation. Musick and Wilson (2003), for example, using data from a survey of American adults, found that individuals who had attended meetings of groups or clubs, or who had volunteered with community organizations, were less likely to experience symptoms of depression.

Well-Being and Quality of Life

All of the attributes that have been associated with civic participation—self-esteem, social support, a sense of belonging, health, and mental health—can be seen as important elements of a person's overall quality of life. It is not surprising, then, that research consistently shows a link between civic engagement and quality of life (Borgonovi, 2008; Brown et al., 2012; Meier & Stutzer, 2008; Piliavin & Siegl, 2007; Thoits & Hewitt, 2001). Individuals who are involved in a wide variety of civic activities, whether it be volunteering, participating in community organizations, or engaging in advocacy or social activism, tend to experience greater satisfaction with their lives than do individuals who aren't involved in these kinds of activities. Thoits and Hewitt (2001) demonstrate this link between civic engagement and life satisfaction using data from a longitudinal study of American adults, conducted through the University of Michigan's Survey Research Center. Participants in the survey were asked whether, within the previous 12 months, they had done volunteer work with organizations such as their church, their children's school, a political group or labor union, or a senior citizens group, and how many hours they had spent doing this work. They also responded to a statement about their quality of life that read, "Think about your life as a whole. How satisfied are you with it? Are you completely satisfied, very satisfied, somewhat satisfied, or not at all satisfied?" The study's results indicated that the more volunteer work participants had engaged in, the higher their quality of life. Other questions that survey respondents were asked had to do with how often they attended religious services or participated in meetings of organizations, clubs, or groups in their community. The results showed that these forms of civic participation were also related to quality of life; individuals who participated more frequently in their church and in community organizations were more satisfied with their lives.

One of the most interesting studies of civic participation and quality of life was an investigation undertaken by Stephan Meier and Alois Stutzer, using data from a longitudinal survey of German citizens. The survey was first administered to citizens of (then) West Germany in 1985, and it was then administered annually until 1999, the time at which Meier and Stutzer did their analysis. Beginning in 1990, after the fall of the Berlin wall but before re-unification of East and West Germany, the survey was also administered to citizens of East Germany, also annually, until 1999. Each of the annual surveys contained measures of volunteering and life satisfaction. The measure of volunteering asked survey participants how frequently they had performed volunteer work (weekly, monthly, less frequently, or never), and the measure of life satisfaction asked, "How satisfied are you with your life, all things considered?" The results showed a consistent correlation between volunteering and life satisfaction; the more individuals had volunteered, the more satisfied they were with their lives. This relationship held for individuals from both East and West Germany. The most interesting finding of the study was that both volunteering and life satisfaction dropped precipitously for East Germans between 1990 (before re-unification) and after 1990, when re-unification of the two parts of Germany had taken place. Why did this happen? The study's authors attribute the drop in life satisfaction to the fact that when the two countries were brought together, a sizeable proportion of East German volunteers (more that 37%) stopped their volunteer work, many of them because the groups and organizations with whom they had previously volunteered had ceased to exist in the new, reunified Germany. The researchers make a compelling case that it was this reduction in volunteering, at least in part, that caused the drop in life satisfaction. They found, for example, that East Germans who were able to continue their volunteer work after reunification didn't show as much of a decline in quality of life as did East Germans who were unable to continue volunteering.

Other forms of civic engagement have also shown to be related to greater life satisfaction. Malte Klar and Tim Kasser (2009) demonstrated this link in a study they conducted with social activists living in the United States. They obtained the participants for their study by e-mailing individuals registered with CampusActivism.org, an online network of groups and individuals involved in social activism. In addition to participants they solicited in this manner, they used a survey agency to find individuals who matched the activist group with regard to age, gender, and education level and who could serve as a comparison group, in that they were not as likely to be involved in social activism. The activists and comparison group participants completed a number of measures that assessed their activism and their quality of life. With regard to activism, the research participants indicated their agreement or disagreement with statements such as, "Being an activist is central to who I am." They also responded to a question asking them how much they had engaged in a variety of activities, such as organizing a protest march. Quality of life was assessed by having participants indicate their agreement or disagreement with statements such as, "I have a sense of direction and purpose in life," and, "In general, I feel confident and positive about myself." The results showed that the activists were significantly more satisfied with their lives than were the nonactivists. In a second study, using university students as research participants, Klar and Kasser determined that students who were involved in social activism were three times as likely as nonactivists to experience a psychological state that the researchers considered to be "flourishing."

Skills and Resources

In the last chapter, I talked about the many skills and capacities that young people developed as a result of their participation in civic life through school and outside-of-school activities. Adults who are involved in community life also develop these kinds of skills. Civic engagement through activities like volunteering, community organizational work, and social activism provides people with opportunities to do many things that they may not have the chance to do in their normal family and work life. Verba, Scholzman, and Brady (1995), in their study of civic voluntarism in the United States, asked individuals if within the last 6 months they had gone to a meeting where they took part in making decisions, planned or chaired a meeting, or gave a presentation or speech. Nearly 40% of those belonging to community organizations, and 32% of those belonging to religious organizations, had attended a meeting where decisions were made. Nearly 20% of those belonging to a church or community organization had made a speech or presentation. These opportunities almost certainly serve to improve skills in the areas of communication, decision making, and leadership. The skill-enhancing effects of civic engagement were demonstrated in Mary Ohmer's (2007) study of individuals who had been involved in neighborhood organizations in Pittsburgh, Pennsylvania. In this study, Ohmer had individuals who were members of these organizations indicate, on a scale from 1 to 5, how frequently they had participated in different organizational activities, such as attending meetings, serving as a committee member, or recruiting new members. Study participants also rated their skills in leadership, decision making, and planning and their knowledge of policies affecting their neighborhood. The study results showed that individuals who were more involved in their neighborhood organizations rated themselves as being more proficient in all of these skills than individuals who were less involved in the organizations. Prestby and colleagues (1990) found similar results in their study of individuals belonging to neighborhood organizations in New York City. Those individuals who were most active in the neighborhood associations reported the greatest benefits in terms of learning new skills. They also indicated that they had benefited by being more informed about their community.

We have found similar benefits of neighborhood involvement in our studies of the Better Beginnings, Better Futures project. When we asked individuals who were involved in the project how it had affected them, many of them talked about the skills they had learned through their participation:

> *It's like going to college. It's hands-on experience. Most people who go to college can get the theory part of it, you know, just theory, but... hands-on is just, just so different, and, to me, I received a college degree in terms of the skills I learned, you know: chairing committees, writing letters, going to events and meetings and actually making presentations, so it improves your speaking skills, takes away your fear to talk to a large crowd, and knowing, regardless of how many people are sitting out there looking at you, you can handle this... I don't think I would have learned all I learned had I gone to college for that four years... And also,*

> *the more you learn, the more you feel capable, because I went back and took many workshops.* (Pancer & Foxall, 1998, p. 41)

Participation in Better Beginnings also gave involved residents greater access to information and resources that they could use to enhance their own lives and the lives of their children and families:

> *Through working at Better Beginnings, I found a lot of resources that I never knew of before, like I found Big Sisters...I also found [a camp program] for my son to go camping every summer...I am finding out different agencies and stuff through Better Beginnings. I find now there are a lot more people using the programs.* (Pancer & Foxall, 1998, p. 42)

Not surprising, adults' participation in community activities, because it enhances their skills and gives them greater access to resources, has been shown to produce benefits for their children, as well as for themselves. Mahoney and Magnusson (2001), in a study of Swedish boys and their parents, found that the sons of fathers who were involved in community organizations such as church groups, labor unions, political parties, or nonprofits were less likely to have been involved in criminal activity than sons of fathers who were not involved in community organizations.

By working with professionals from their local schools, housing authorities, and welfare agencies, not as recipients of services, but as equals while serving on boards and committees, residents who were involved in the Better Beginnings, Better Futures project also forged new, more equal relationships with these professionals:

> *We've got better relations with agencies and there's been a whole lot of difference in the neighborhood now people know there's places they can go, there's people they can talk to and then those people can put them where they need to go or who they have to talk to ... When they see somebody from welfare sitting at the same table with you, they've proven that they're ordinary people. They're just like you and I and they have a job to do.* (Pancer & Foxall, 1998, p. 43)

Negative Impacts

The overwhelming weight of research evidence indicates that the effects of civic engagement are almost always positive. Those who are involved in the life of their communities are healthier, happier, more confident, and less emotionally distressed than those who are not. There are, however, occasional costs to individuals who participate in community activities and organizations. Pamela Attree and her colleagues (2011), in their review of 22 studies of individuals' subjective experience of community engagement found that "community engagement was not inevitably a positive experience for participants in all circumstances" (p. 252). Some of the negative experiences mentioned in the studies they reviewed included the feeling of "consultation fatigue," when participants were overwhelmed by the amount of work they were expected to do in their organizational roles, and instances in which community residents felt that their participation was only tokenistic. Prestby and colleagues (1990) assessed some of the costs associated with civic engagement in their study of neighborhood organizations in New York City. These costs included the time required for participation, as well as financial costs for child care and transportation. Participants in the Better Beginnings, Better Futures project talked about some of these costs, as well. For example, when the project began, a relatively small number of community residents were serving on several different committees and taking on a great deal of administrative work, which began to lead to a feeling of stress and burnout:

> *I'm even feeling pressure now, just on a daily basis. Today I decided, well, this [focus group interview] was probably more important than the program, but then everybody who usually goes to the program said why aren't you coming to the program any more, so you're feeling like, oh geez, I should go to that, but wait, should I go to this, and you have to decide for yourself what you can do, because, sometimes, some days, you can do it all and some days you just can't* (Pancer & Cameron, 1994, p. 207)

Who Benefits the Most from Civic Participation?

Some people have a greater risk of developing health and other kinds of problems than others. One of the factors that places individuals at-risk for health and social problems is their income level. Those living in poverty have a much greater risk of developing a wide range of health and social problems and of dying earlier. Another factor that places people at-risk is their age. The older one is, the greater one's risk of experiencing health problems. In the last chapter, we saw that it was often the young people who were at greatest risk who benefitted the most from participating in civic life. The same appears to be true of adults. Studies demonstrate that adults who are at-risk because of factors such as low income or age are the ones who show the greatest benefits from civic participation (Borgonovi, 2008; Lancee & ter Hoeven, 2010; Musick et al., 1999; Oman et al., 1999). Oman and colleagues (1999), for example, studied older adults (55 to over 85 years of age) in Marin County, California. Participants in the study were interviewed in 1990 and 1991 and were asked how many voluntary organizations they were involved with at that time. Five years later,

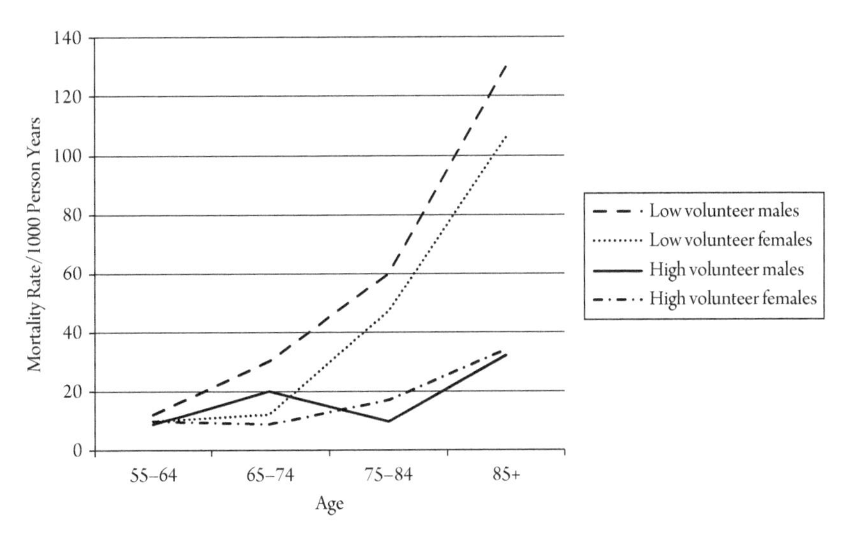

Figure 7.1 Mortality Rates for Low and High Volunteers.
From Oman, D., Thoresen, C. E. & McMahon, K. (1999). Volunteerism and mortality among the community-dwelling elderly. *Journal of Health Psychology, 4*(3), 301–316. © 1999 by SAGE. Reprinted by permission of SAGE.

the researchers attempted to contact study participants to schedule a follow-up interview. Over the five-year interval, a number of the participants had died; as one might expect, older individuals were more likely to have died than were younger individuals. The researchers also found, as mentioned earlier in the chapter, that those who had been involved in volunteering were less likely to have died during the five-year interval than those who had not volunteered. The most striking finding of this study was that the biggest differences in mortality between volunteers and nonvolunteers occurred among the oldest individuals, who were at greatest risk. In the youngest age category (55 to 64 years of age), there was no difference in mortality between active volunteers and less active or nonvolunteers, but the difference in mortality between volunteers and nonvolunteers increased substantially with age. For individuals in the oldest age group (over 85 years of age), mortality rates among low or nonvolunteers were more than three times higher than they were among active volunteers (see Figure 7.1).

Summary

Adults who are civically active experience considerable benefits. They have higher self-esteem and a sense that they can overcome difficulties and achieve their goals in life. They have larger social networks and greater social support, as well as having a greater appreciation of the diversity in their communities and a greater sense of belonging. Civically engaged adults also experience better physical and mental health and a better quality of life. They have fewer illnesses, are able to perform their daily activities more easily, have healthier life-styles, experience lower levels of depression, and even live longer. Through their civic activities, individuals also gain skills in communication, planning, decision making, leadership, and other areas. Research shows that it is often those who are at-risk for developing problems because of their age or social circumstances (such as living in poverty) who experience the greatest benefits from civic participation. Although civically engaged adults mostly derive benefits from their involvements, there are instances in which they can feel overworked and overwhelmed.

8

Impacts of Civic Engagement on Programs, Organizations, Neighborhoods, and Society

I began the last chapter with something called a "life narrative"—a story that one woman told about her life and how her involvement in shaping a community program had influenced the course her life had taken. These stories tell us a great deal more than simply what has happened during a person's lifetime. They reveal the essence of a person's identity and the way in which that person has made sense of the events that have taken place (McAdams et al., 2006). But life narratives are not only about individuals. Life stories can be told about organizations, neighborhoods, communities, and even entire societies (Rappaport, 1995, 1998, 2000). These kinds of narratives are often shared among the individuals who live in a community, and they reveal things that define that community for its members, just as individuals' life narratives help us understand how those individuals define themselves. One of the defining elements of the Better Beginnings, Better Futures project, the prevention initiative that I described in previous chapters, was the participation of community residents in every aspect of the project's development. This participation and the feelings of connection and trust that participation engendered among those who worked together as volunteers with the project were clearly evident in the interviews we conducted with residents throughout the project's existence. In many of the interviews, residents talked about how Better Beginnings had become like a "family" to them; this shared sense of the Better Beginnings project as a family was most certainly a core element of the project's life narrative:

> *I would fight tooth and nail to keep Better Beginnings. It's my family. It's my extended family. I don't have anyone in the city. I don't have anyone here. I have lots of friends but no family. They have become my extended family.* (volunteer resident, Better Beginnings, Better Futures: Pancer & Foxall, 1998, p. 44)

Statements like this, which were echoed in the stories of many individuals who participated as volunteers in the Better Beginnings project, suggest that civic engagement affects not just the individuals who are involved but also the whole community in which these individuals live. In what follows, I will be describing what research tells us about the effects that civic participation has beyond its impact on individuals—how it affects programs, organizations, neighborhoods, and society at large.

Impacts on Programs and Organizations

In planning for and administering almost any community program, it has become expected—and often mandatory—to involve citizens of the community affected by the program in key decisions about what that program will look like and how it will be implemented. In the area of health promotion, for example, the World Health Organization has spearheaded a movement known as Healthy Cities and Communities, a key principle of which is that citizens should be involved in the development of any health promotion initiative undertaken in their community (Kegler et al., 2009). In the field of mental health, it has long been recognized that community members should be involved in the development of mental health services. Over 30 years ago, community psychologist Bernard Bloom stated that

> *the mental health professional is not the sole source of data as to the mental health-related needs of the community or the best ways to meet those needs. Rather, the staff of a community mental health clinic should join with the community or its representatives to identify needs, propose and evaluate programs to meet those needs, and plan for future program development.* (Bloom, 1973, p. 2)

The need to involve citizens is also recognized in the field of urban planning. Raymond Burby, a professor of City and Regional Planning at the University of North Carolina at Chapel Hill, states that

> *planners can produce better plans and increase the potential for government action on issues that initially lack publics if they succeed in involving a broad spectrum of stakeholders in the plan-making process. The reasons are not complex...citizen involvement can generate information, understanding, and agreement on problems and ways of solving them. It can give stakeholders a sense of ownership of planning proposals and ease the formation of coalitions who will work hard for their realization.* (Burby, 2003, p. 34)

Indeed, the desirability of citizen involvement in decision making has been acknowledged in almost every kind of community-based program and organization, from educational institutions to housing authorities to police services. In a survey of over 1,200 local affiliates of national health and social service organizations in the United States, nearly two-thirds of those responding to the survey indicated that they thought that it was advantageous or essential to have citizens or consumers of their services sitting on their board of directors (Blair, LaFrance, & Murray, 1999).

What impact has the active involvement of citizens had on these programs and organizations? While there is almost universal recognition that citizen involvement is necessary for the effective functioning of organizations, there has been relatively little research on the actual effects that citizen participation has had at the organizational level. Much of the research that is available consists of case studies of organizations' experience with citizen involvement; few systematic studies have been undertaken that look at citizen participation across multiple organizations and how it has affected organizational functioning (Crawford et al., 2002). The research that is available, however, suggests that the active involvement of citizens can have a profound influence on the way community-based organizations operate and their impact on the communities that they have been established to serve.

More Appropriate, Accessible, and Better Utilized Services

In a systematic review of research that assessed the results of involving citizens in the planning of health services, Michael Crawford and colleagues (2002) found evidence of a number of positive impacts. One of these impacts had to do with the accessibility of services to community members. Several factors can serve as barriers to individuals attempting to gain access to health services. These include the cost of services, the location of facilities, inconvenient hours of operation, and the lack of amenities for individuals with disabilities. Several of the studies that Crawford and colleagues reviewed described ways in which citizen participation in decision making had resulted in a reduction of these kinds of barriers and enhanced access to health services through changes such as extending opening hours and improving transport to health facilities.

Another positive outcome of citizen participation that this review identified was the development of new programs and services that met community needs. Because of their intimate knowledge about life in their communities, residents are particularly knowledgeable about services that they and their neighbors need that are not currently being provided. Many of the studies examined in the review by Crawford and colleagues identified new services, such as fertility treatment and crisis services, that would not have been provided without citizen input. In general, the provision of more accessible and needed services that citizen participation has stimulated has resulted in programs and organizations that are more responsive to community needs. In a survey of health service planning bodies from across the United States (Checkoway, 1982), 88% of those responding indicated that the participation of citizens had made health planning more responsive to community needs.

The development of programs and services that are accessible and responsive to community needs can have a strong impact on program utilization and attendance. Zeldin and his colleagues (Zeldin, 2004; Zeldin et al., 2000) found this to be true in their studies of organizations that had youth on their boards of directors and other decision-making bodies. Young people are rarely involved as members of boards of community organizations. According to one study, only 3% of board members of nonprofit organizations are under the age of 29 (Moyers & Enright, 1997). Even organizations whose major function is to serve youth have few, if any, young people on their boards or in other key decision-making roles. This has begun to change, however, and there are now several youth-serving organizations that include young people on boards and key committees. Zeldin and colleagues' study was the first to examine the impact of this kind of youth participation on organizations. They interviewed youth and adults who had worked together as board and committee members in a wide range of youth-serving organizations, asking them what impact the inclusion of youth had had on organizational practices and functioning. One of the things they discovered was that the presence of young people on boards and committees had resulted in new programs and activities that were more appealing to youth, and yielded greater youth participation; these activities included things such as increasing the effort to reach out to youth in the community, distributing safe sex packets to young people, and sponsoring community celebrations. As a consequence, enrollment in the organizations' programs and activities increased.

We found similar effects in our research on the Better Beginnings, Better Futures project (Pancer & Cameron, 1994). In Better Beginnings communities, residents served on the project's board of directors and program development committees and were active in reaching out to other residents in the community. Because community residents, who had an intimate understanding of their communities, were the ones who helped decide what kinds of programs would be offered, and because they reached out to their neighbors to inform them about and encourage them to attend these programs, enrollment and attendance was almost always healthy. As a social service provider at one of the Better Beginnings sites said:

> *They [volunteer residents] feel a little more for the project than people who are just working there... It's probably moved a lot faster... The home visitors wouldn't have anywhere to go if parents weren't involved... The project would*

> *flop because the parents [i.e., other parents in the community] wouldn't have anything to do with it.* (Pancer & Cameron, 1994, pp. 204–205)

I and my colleagues have seen similar effects in our research on the inREACH gang prevention project mentioned in chapter 6 (Pancer et al., 2013). As I described in that chapter, the inREACH program attempted to reduce gang involvement in young people living in poor, high-risk communities by providing them with activities that would serve as a positive alternative to gang involvement. The idea of providing youth with positive alternatives to gang activity was not something that began with the inREACH project. Before the project started, community centers in these neighborhoods had on a number of occasions attempted to establish programs for youth, but they were always poorly attended. What was different with the inREACH project was that it involved young people in deciding what activities they wanted, rather than adults in the community centers making that decision for them. The result was that the new programs, which youth had a voice in selecting, were very popular, and on program evenings it was not uncommon to have 30 or 40 youths attending a program that had previously only attracted a handful of young people. One youth involved in the project described it this way:

> *It's gonna be for us, run by us, and gonna involve all of us right?... we had some say in what was gonna happen with it... it's like hey—what do you guys want to do... what do you want to see in your community, and what are your personal talents or anything that is special to you that you kind of want to show everybody else, and maybe [other] people might like it too, right? It's not just to keep kids off drugs but for under-privileged kids, kids who may have never had a chance to be part of something... discover their love of art or anything like that, so it's giving everybody a chance to actually do those kind of things, do the things they want to do, so that's why I started coming.* (Pancer et al., 2013, p. 42)

More Effective Organizations

There are very few studies that have examined the impact of citizen participation on organizational effectiveness. The studies that have been undertaken, however, indicate that the presence of citizens on decision-making bodies can significantly enhance organizational performance (Burby, 2003; Checkoway, 1982; Zeldin, 2004; Zeldin et al., 2000). Burby (2003), for example, looked at the effects of citizen involvement on the effectiveness of planning organizations in 60 cities and counties in the states of Washington and Florida. Planning effectiveness was assessed by counting the number of proposals that these organizations made in their plans concerning the protecting the community from the effects of natural hazards (a process known as hazard mitigation). Burby also looked at the number of proposals in these plan that were actually implemented. Citizen involvement was determined by counting the number of citizen and other stakeholder groups that participated in the planning process. The results showed that when the number of stakeholder groups involved in making the plan increased from fewer than 5 to 10 or more, the number of hazard mitigation proposals in the plan increased 72%, and the number of proposals that were implemented more than doubled. Burby claimed that this increase in implementation indicated that greater participation of citizens produced stronger plans that stood a better chance of being implemented.

The study of youth participation on the boards and committees of youth-serving organizations conducted by Zeldin and colleagues (Zeldin, 2004; Zeldin et al., 2000), mentioned earlier in the chapter, also showed evidence of enhanced organizational effectiveness as a result of involving citizens—in this case, young citizens—in decision making. According to adults who worked in partnership with these young people, the youth participants contributed to the organizations' effectiveness in several ways. They brought a fresh perspective to deliberations, one that was grounded in an intimate knowledge of young people and their needs. They were more willing to challenge current ways of doing things, and they sparked greater acceptance of organizational change and innovation. Their presence also changed the way discussions occurred, making them less formal and more dynamic and productive.

More Representative, Inclusive, and Accountable Organizations

It appears, then, that having citizens participate in the governance of community organizations by sitting on boards and key committees has the potential to make those organizations more responsive and effective and their programs and services better utilized. But it may have even more profound effects than that. Research suggests that the presence of citizens on committees and boards of directors can produce fundamental changes in the way the bodies that govern these organizations are constituted. According to a 1997 report from the National Center for Non-Profit Boards (*A Snapshot of America's Non-Profit Boards*, Moyers & Enright, 1997), the governing boards of nonprofit organizations in the United States at the time the report was published consisted primarily of older, white men and women. Eighty-five percent of the boards were white, and nearly two-thirds were between 40 and 64 years of age. It is clear that these boards did not reflect the diversity of the populations they served. Research suggests that having citizens participating in decision-making roles makes organizations much more representative of their client population. Blair and colleagues' 1999 survey of national health and social service organizations in the United States indicated that organizations that had citizens on their boards were significantly more likely than organizations whose boards did not include citizens to reflect the demographic make-up of their communities in terms of socio-economic status, ethnicity, and geography. Checkoway and colleagues (1984), using data from a survey of health planning agencies in the United States, determined that agencies that had more effective and higher quality citizen participation had members that were more representative of the citizenry in the communities for which they planned; they had significantly more women, ethnic minorities, and seniors than did agencies that had less effective citizen participation. Zeldin and colleagues (Zeldin et al., 2000), in their study of organizations that had youth on boards of directors and key committees, found that after having positive experiences with youth serving on these bodies, organizations began to consider the inclusion of members of other diverse populations, such as the elderly and ethnic minority groups, on their boards and committees.

When the governing bodies of organizations become more representative of their communities, they also become more accountable to those communities. This was demonstrated in a study of school boards of governors in the United Kingdom by Ranson and colleagues (2005). Between 1986 and 1988, the United Kingdom enacted legislation that drastically changed the way schools were governed. Prior to this legislation, schools were regulated by local government; after the legislation, schools were deregulated and each school was managed by a board of governors that consisted largely of volunteer citizens. As a result, hundreds of thousands of citizen volunteers became involved in the management of their children's schools, participating in things such as the hiring of school administrators, decisions about class size, and overseeing the school's budget. In their examination of the impact that enhanced citizen involvement had had on schools, Ranson and colleagues found that the involvement of citizens in school government had increased the scrutiny of the way schools were being managed; school governors were now setting standards and performance targets and monitoring how the school was performing with regard to these standards. Citizen participation in school government had increased the accountability of schools to the citizens whose children attended those schools.

Greater Access to Resources

Citizens provide a huge resource to community organizations through their work as volunteers. But they also help leverage other kinds of resources for these organizations. Ranson and colleagues, in their study of school boards of governors in the United Kingdom, found evidence that the presence of residents on boards helped schools lobby more successfully for greater financial resources from their local government authorities. Zeldin and colleagues (2000) found that the presence of youth on the boards of directors of youth-serving organizations helped those organizations obtain funding from charitable foundations. Indeed, it was often the foundations themselves that raised the issue of youth board participation before the issue was even broached by the organizations seeking funding. Zeldin and colleagues also found that youth were very effective as representatives and spokespersons when organizations made presentations to prospective funders. One of the staff members of a national youth organization in the United States talked about how much of an impact the involvement of youth had had on her organization's ability to obtain funding:

> *I can't tell you how many people I had say 'the only reason I am giving you this is because I have never gotten a letter from a 14-year-old before.'* (Zeldin et al., 2000, p. 42)

Impacts on Neighborhoods and Communities

The research that I have reviewed so far in this chapter suggests that when citizens participate as decision makers in community organizations, those organizations become more inclusive, accountable, and effective. But what of the communities in which those organizations operate? How are they influenced by the participation of their citizens in community life? Are communities whose citizens participate actively in community affairs and organizations better off than those whose citizens do not? My own research and that of others suggests that they are, in a number of ways.

Sense of Community

In the last chapter, I talked about sense of community as a feeling of belonging and connection that individuals have with regard to their community. But sense of community can be more than just a feeling that individuals have; it can also be used to describe entire communities. Whole neighborhoods in which residents feel a sense of belonging and attachment, and where neighbors know and trust one another, can be said to have a sense of community. Our own research on the Better Beginnings, Better Futures project has shown that the involvement of large numbers of residents in a project such as Better Beginnings can effect changes in the entire community, creating a neighborhood that has a sense of community. One of the residents we interviewed described the transformation her neighborhood had undergone in this way:

> *I really think that before [Better Beginnings] was in place, it was pockets of people…I think the neighborhood is now starting to think of itself as a community, and I don't think it was doing that before.* (Pancer & Cameron, 1994, p. 205)

Another resident of a Better Beginnings community expressed her sense of belonging to her neighborhood in terms of the connections she had formed with her neighbors:

> *It's a lot quieter and people are pretty respectful. And we know each other, like I know a fair amount of people around here. If they need stuff, they can come here or if they need help they can go to X... there's a connection. If people have problems they can phone and have people to talk to... You'll drive by a house for sale and you'll think, that's a nice house for sale and then I'll go, but it's not in the Better Beginnings neighborhood and I really don't want to leave, because it's working so well here.* (Pancer & Foxall, 1998, p. 65)

Another indication of residents' developing sense of community was that people in Better Beginnings neighborhoods began to take steps to make their community cleaner and more attractive:

> *I think one of the things that is evident almost immediately is the recognition that this is our home. We, as members of the community, live here... this is our home. Respect for the physical community, the fact we've planted gardens, flowers and that we've been able to renovate [the local park] by putting in walkways, trees and that kind of thing is the first evidence that people feel at home... People have gotten together and raised issues... to preserve green space in the community...* (Pancer & Foxall, 1998, p. 56)

We found other evidence of residents' sense of community from the questionnaires we administered in Better Beginnings communities and in comparison communities that were similar in ethnic and socioeconomic make-up but did not have a Better Beginnings project. The sense of community measure in the questionnaires we administered included statements such as, "I feel like I belong to this neighborhood," and, "I feel I am important to this neighborhood," to which respondents indicated their agreement or disagreement. Our results showed that Better Beginnings communities had a significantly greater sense of community than the comparison communities had (Peters et al., 2010).

Community Leadership and Action

When large numbers of individuals become involved in community life, it is almost inevitable that some of these individuals will recognize that they have talents in organizing and working with people, and become leaders in their community. This has certainly been the case in all of the Better Beginnings, Better

Futures communities. I witnessed this process myself in one of the communities that I worked with very closely in my 20-year involvement with the project. The first meeting I ever attended in this community was held in a local high school. Several individuals came together at this meeting—the first meeting of the project's steering committee—to begin to plan what the project would look like. At the meeting was the high school principal, a senior manager from the local branch of a child welfare organization, a school superintendent, the principal of the local elementary school, a professor of psychology (me),... and three young mothers who lived in the neighborhood. It was a very lively discussion, with everyone contributing their ideas about the project... except for the young women, who never uttered a word. It became clear later that they were intimidated by the presence of all the senior officials present at the meeting. But as more and more community members became involved over the years, residents took a much more active role in the project. They began to find their voice, and a number began to take on leadership roles in the project and in other groups and organizations operating in the neighborhood. A recent steering committee meeting that I attended—nearly 20 years after the first—was chaired by a community resident who demonstrated considerable skill in leading committee members (many of whom were also residents) through a packed agenda. And everyone contributed ideas during the meeting.

The leadership and organizational skills that residents acquired through their participation in Better Beginnings were used not only to guide the project, but also to enhance their neighborhoods through social and community action. In one Better Beginnings community, for example, residents organized to lobby for a flashing stop-sign to be installed at an intersection where a neighborhood child had been killed in a car accident. In another Better Beginnings community, residents worked together to clean up a local park and to obtain better lighting for the park, which had been closed due to a lack of security. This park subsequently became a much used hub of activity for the whole neighborhood. This kind of community activism not only helped improve life for everyone in the neighborhood, but also allowed residents to learn how to advocate for needed programs and services.

Safety, Security, and Crime

When neighbors come to know each other through their involvement in community programs and organizations such as Better Beginnings, Better Futures, research evidence suggests that they become safer places in which to live. Several residents whom we interviewed in our evaluation of the project talked about how they felt safer in their neighborhood and how crime had decreased, because of the enhanced connections among neighbors brought about by their involvement in Better Beginnings:

> *When I taught ballet years ago, kids would come and smash the windows, throw things at my students. Now you've got the Neighbourhood Watch and so on. But the people are learning to speak up . . . Even if they don't do it directly, at least they will speak to someone on the issue and handle it. I find you can walk the streets more . . . I'm on the court community committee for the Youth diversion program, and we have kids coming in there and the majority of them are in detention in other communities, not here.* (Pancer & Foxall, 1998, p. 54)

We also found evidence of a reduction in criminal or antisocial activity in a recent study involving young people who had grown up in Better Beginnings communities. In questionnaires we administered to youth from Better Beginnings and comparison communities, we found that youth from Better Beginnings communities rated their neighborhoods as having significantly fewer individuals engaging in "deviant" behavior such as drug use or violence than did youth from comparison communities (Pancer et al., 2013).

Other studies have also shown that civic engagement, particularly among young people, can have a marked effect on crime levels in a neighborhood. This was demonstrated in an impressive study conducted by Jones and Offord in two neighborhoods in Ottawa, Canada (Jones & Offord, 1989). Both of these neighborhoods had attributes that would place them at-risk for high levels of crime; almost all residents were either on social welfare or could be considered working poor and required public assistance to be able to afford housing. In one of these neighborhoods, the researchers started a program called PALS (for "participate and learn skills"); over a period of 32 months, youth in that community were offered 40 programs and activities in which they could take part, from scouting to hockey to playing music. A large proportion of the youth in this neighborhood participated in the project; in the first year, more than 70% of the 322 young people in the neighborhood took part in at least one activity. In the comparison community, no additional activities, other than those already present, were offered. The researchers tracked police charges against youth over the two years prior to the introduction of the PALS program, during the PALS program, and for 16 months after the program ended. The results showed that criminal charges against youth were about the same in the two communities before the PALS program began, but that the number of charges in the PALS community dropped to less than one quarter the number in the comparison community while the program operated, and it remained at less than half that of the comparison community after the program had ended (see Figure 8.1). These results suggest that neighborhood crime levels can be reduced substantially by increasing young people's civic involvements.

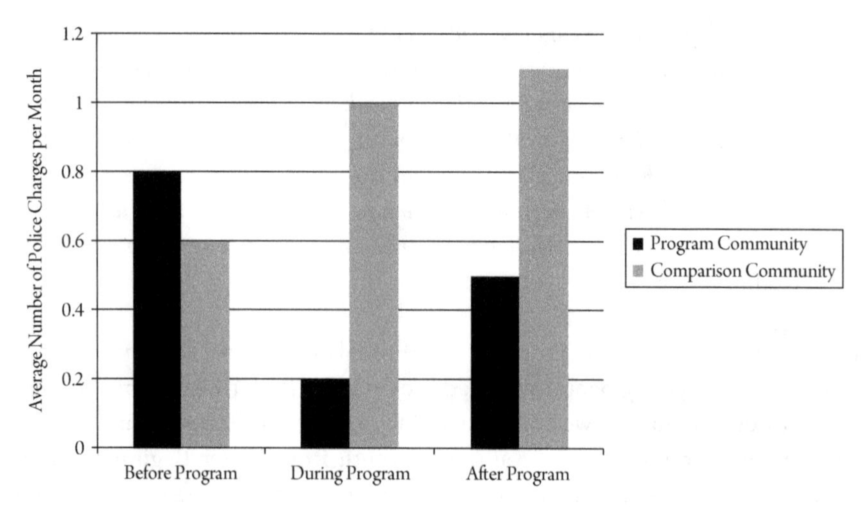

Figure 8.1 The PALS Program: Police Charges per Month Against Youth.
From Jones, M. B., & Offord, D. R. (1989). Reduction of antisocial-behavior in poor children by nonschool skill-development. *Journal of Child Psychology and Psychiatry and Allied Disciplines, 30*(5), 737–750. Reprinted with permission from John Wiley & Sons.

Health and Well-Being

There are relatively few studies of civic engagement and its impact on the health and well-being of neighborhoods or small communities, but the studies that do exist indicate that the involvement of individuals in community life can affect the health and well-being of all community members. One of these studies, by Miller and colleagues, examined the relationship between social capital and health in a study of over 300 communities in Indonesia (Miller et al., 2006). To assess social capital, they counted the number of civic organizations (such as senior citizens groups, youth groups, and community gardening groups) in each community, assuming that the more of these groups there were, the more individuals there would be who participate in them. They then used data from a family life survey that asked residents about various aspects of their health to examine the link between civic participation and health. They found that levels of self-reported health were significantly higher in communities with more civic groups (and presumably greater civic participation), compared to those with fewer groups. Citizens in communities with many groups and organizations also reported having less pain and fatigue and being better able to carry on their daily living activities. They demonstrated better mental health, as well, reporting lower levels of symptoms such as sadness, anxiety, insomnia, and short temper.

Another study, by Weitzman and Kawachi (2000), examined university communities across the United States. One of the problems affecting those attending university in the United States is alcohol abuse. Weitzman and

Kawachi used data from a survey administered to students in colleges across the United States to assess binge drinking (defined as consuming 5 or more drinks in a drinking session) at each of these colleges. They found that nearly half of the students in these colleges had engaged in binge drinking over the two weeks prior to completing the survey. The researchers also looked at civic engagement at each of the campuses, in terms of the amount of volunteering that students did. They found that universities with high levels of volunteering had significantly fewer problems with alcohol abuse among students; students at universities with high levels of volunteering were 26% less likely to engage in binge drinking than were students at universities with low levels of volunteering.

In another study that examined the way in which health and well-being at a community or neighborhood level relate to civic engagement, Lochner and colleagues (2003) examined mortality rates for individuals between 45 and 64 years of age across 342 neighborhoods in Chicago, Illinois. The researchers assessed levels of civic participation using data from a survey in which residents of these neighborhoods were asked to indicate their membership in community organizations such as neighborhood associations, ethnic or nationality clubs, places of worship, and local political organizations. This information was used to compute the average number of associations to which individuals in each neighborhood belonged. To determine the mortality rates of individuals between 45 and 64 years of age, the researchers consulted records kept by the state Department of Public Health. This midlife age group was selected because mortality at this relatively young age could be considered premature death. The results showed that in neighborhoods with high rates of civic participation, mortality rates in the midlife age group were significantly lower than in neighborhoods with low rates of civic participation.

Impacts on Society

We have seen, then, that civic participation can have an impact on programs, organizations, and even entire neighborhoods and communities. But research over the last 20 years or so tells us that civic engagement can have an even broader impact, affecting the well-being of entire states and countries. Many of these impacts are documented in Robert Putnam's seminal book, *Bowling Alone: The Collapse and Revival of American Community* (Putnam, 2000). In the book, Putnam provides compelling evidence of the link between levels of civic engagement in American states and the overall health of those states in terms of violent crime, economic well-being, and even the quality of schooling. Other researchers have added substantially to this body of knowledge, demonstrating links between social capital and societal levels of attributes such as physical and mental health.

Health and Well-Being

One of the researchers who has contributed the most to our understanding of the relationship between civic involvement and health at a societal level is Ichiro Kawachi, a professor in Harvard University's School of Public Health. In one study, Kawachi and his colleagues (1999) classified American states in terms of how healthy their citizens were, using data from a telephone survey that asked respondents, "Would you say in general that your health is excellent, very good, good, fair, or poor?" They used another survey to determine how much social capital each state had. States with higher social capital had citizens who were involved in community organizations such as political groups, churches, and sports associations, and who expressed high levels of trust in their fellow citizens. When they looked at the relationship between social capital and health, they found that states with high levels of civic participation and social capital had substantially healthier citizens than states with low levels of social capital. Indeed, Kawachi and colleagues determined that moving from a low to a high social capital state could increase a person's chances of having good health by as much as 73%, an increase that would be comparable to the effects of quitting smoking.

Other studies show that societies characterized by greater civic participation are healthier in terms of having lower rates of disease and health problems among their citizens. One study, by Scheffler and colleagues (2008), involved individuals in several counties in California who had experienced acute coronary syndrome. The researchers were interested in the proportion of these individuals who later had a recurrence of their heart problems and how that related to the level of civic participation in the counties in which they lived. Civic participation was assessed by determining the number of individuals (per 1,000 population) in each county who worked for voluntary organizations. This presumably reflected the number of residents in the county who participated in these organizations. The study's results showed that individuals who lived in counties with high levels of civic participation were less likely to have a recurrence of their heart problems than those who lived in counties with low levels of civic involvement. Civic participation at a county or state level has been linked to other health problems, as well. Holtgrave and Crosby (2003) found that American states with higher levels of civic engagement, assessed in terms of volunteering and membership in community organizations, had significantly lower rates of sexually transmitted diseases such as gonorrhea, syphilis, and AIDS. Kim and colleagues (2006) found that states with higher levels of civic engagement showed lower rates of obesity. Kawachi and colleagues (1997) determined that states with higher levels of civic engagement, indicated by greater per capita membership in community groups and associations, had lower rates of coronary heart disease, cancer, and infant mortality, as well as lower overall mortality rates.

Recent research evidence suggests that civic engagement at a state and country level can influence rates of mental as well as physical health. Richard Layte, a sociologist with the Economic and Social Research Institute in Ireland, recently conducted a study in which he examined the relationship between income inequality and mental health in 31 European countries, using results from the European Quality of Life Survey (Layte, 2012). Mental health was assessed on the survey by means of the "WHO5," a World Health Organization measure widely used to assess mental well-being. It consists of five statements, such as, "I have felt cheerful and in good spirits," and, "I have felt calm and relaxed"; respondents indicate how much they have felt this way over the previous two weeks. Individuals completing the survey also responded to a three-item measure that assessed their civic participation, asking them whether in the last year they had, "Attended a meeting of a trade union, a political party, or political action group," "Attended a protest or demonstration, or signed a petition, including an e-mail petition," or "Contacted a politician or public official." The results showed a substantial correlation between civic participation and mental health. Citizens of countries with higher levels of civic participation demonstrated significantly better mental health than citizens of countries with lower levels of civic participation.

The link between civic participation and mental health is also evident when one looks at rates of suicide across states and countries (Cutlip et al., 2010; Helliwell, 2007). Canadian economist John Helliwell examined the relationship between suicide rates and civic participation in 50 countries that had participated in the World Values Survey and European Values Survey (Helliwell, 2007). There were large differences in suicide rates among these countries at the time the surveys were administered (between 1980 and 2000); countries such as Peru, the Dominican Republic, and Turkey had fewer than 5 suicides per 100,000 population annually, while countries such as Russia, Hungary, and Lithuania had nearly 10 times that many, with suicide rates approaching 40 per 100,000. Helliwell assessed civic engagement in each of these countries by calculating the average membership in nonreligious voluntary associations. The results showed a significant relationship between civic engagement and suicide rates; in countries with greater civic participation, suicide rates were substantially lower than in countries with less civic participation.

Crime

Counties, states, and countries with high levels of civic participation are not only healthier physically and mentally, they also show significantly lower levels of crime (Lee, 2008; Kennedy et al., 1998; Layte, 2012; Rosenfeld, Messner, & Baumer, 2001). This was demonstrated in a study by Bruce Kennedy and colleagues from Harvard University's School of Public Health (1998). The types of crime they focused on in their study were those that involved the use of firearms. Kennedy and colleagues, using statistics available from the American National Center for Health Statistics and the Federal Bureau of Investigation, determined the number of firearm-related assaults, robberies, and homicides that occurred in every American state over a period of 3 to 5 years. They also calculated the amount of civic engagement in each state, using results from a national survey to determine the average number of community groups and associations to which state residents belonged. They found a substantial correlation between all types of firearm crimes and civic participation; states with higher levels of civic engagement had significantly lower levels of firearm-related assaults, robberies, and homicides compared to states with lower levels of civic engagement. Putnam (2000) found a similar relationship between homicides and civic engagement across states in the United States. These differences in homicide rates between states with high and low civic engagement could not be explained by the fact that states with high civic engagement also tended to be higher in terms of things such as residents' income and education. Differences in homicide rates between states with high and low levels of civic engagement remained even when factors such as income and education were accounted for in statistical analyses. In fact, these analyses showed that civic engagement was a better predictor of homicide rates than either income inequality or education over the period examined.

Other research shows that civic engagement is related to differences in crime rates across countries, as well as states or provinces. Richard Layte's (2012) study of health and well-being across 31 European countries, mentioned earlier, included an examination of homicide rates and citizens' feelings about crime, violence, and vandalism in their country. His analysis showed a substantial relationship between crime and civic engagement across countries; those countries with higher levels of civic participation had lower homicide rates, and their citizens tended to feel that crime was less of a problem, compared to countries with less civic participation.

Economic Prosperity

There is some evidence that regions and countries can also benefit economically from the participation of their citizens in community life. In his analysis of European countries, Layte (2012) examined per capita Gross Domestic Product, a commonly used indicator of a country's economic health and standard of living and how it related to civic engagement. He found a very high correlation between countries' civic engagement levels and their economic health, in terms of GDP. Robert Putnam found a similar relationship in his examination of regions in Italy (Putnam, 1993). The northern regions of Italy had, for centuries, been richer than the southern regions. Putnam found that these differences in economic prosperity were matched by the level of civic participation in these regions. The wealthier northern regions had much higher levels of civic engagement than did the southern regions.

Naryan and Pritchett, researchers formerly with the World Bank, looked at civic engagement in villages in rural Tanzania, one of the poorest countries in the world, and how it related to income levels in those villages (Narayan & Pritchett, 1999). The level of civic engagement in each of the villages was determined from the results of a national survey, in which village residents were asked how many groups and organizations, such as religious groups and political organizations, they belonged to. On average, village residents belonged to 1.5 of these groups. When they looked at per capita income levels in the villages, they found that residents of villages with higher levels of civic engagement had significantly higher incomes than residents of villages with less civic participation. Indeed, their analyses indicated that if half the residents of a village belonged to just one more group, this would boost incomes by 20 to 50%. The researchers determined that an equivalent increase in education levels (estimated at 3 additional years of education) would only raise income levels by 3 to 5%.

Education and Child Welfare

In chapter 6, I discussed the many ways in which young people's involvement in their school and neighborhood communities was linked to their well-being on a number of dimensions. This link, between civic involvement and children's well-being, is present at a societal, as well as an individual level. This was demonstrated by Robert Putnam (2000), in his analysis of child welfare and education across American States. Putnam used a state-level measure of child well-being—the Kids Count Index—published annually by the Annie E. Casey Foundation, to assess children's welfare on a state-by-state basis. The Kids Count Index uses a wide variety of statistics, such as infant and child death rates, numbers of high school dropouts, juvenile arrest rates, and percentage of children living in poverty, to determine a ranking for each state in terms of the welfare of its children. Putnam examined states' Kids Count ranking in relation to the state-level index he developed to measure civic participation in each state. This Social Capital Index reflects levels of volunteering, voting, and joining community organizations, as well as informally connecting with friends and neighbors within each state. Putnam found an astonishingly high correlation between statewide levels of civic participation and the welfare of children in a state. States with high levels of civic engagement, such as North Dakota and Vermont, had children who were much healthier and better-adjusted than states with low levels of civic engagement, such as Georgia and Mississippi.

Putnam found a similarly high correlation when he looked at the relationships between statewide civic engagement and educational outcomes for children and youth. Children and youth who lived in high civic engagement states performed significantly better on standardized tests taken at the elementary, junior high, and high school levels. Indeed, analyses showed that civic engagement was a much more important determinant of educational achievement than factors such as race and income. Richard Layte's (2012) study of countries in Europe also shows a link between civic engagement and education. He found that countries with greater civic participation spent a higher proportion of their GDP on education than did countries with less civic participation.

Good Government

When citizens participate actively in community organizations and hold those organizations to account for their operations and impacts, those organizations become more effective. The same appears to be true when those organizations are the ones responsible for governing the community. States and countries whose citizens participate in civic affairs tend to have more effective government. This has been demonstrated in a number of studies (Helliwell & Putnam, 2000; Knack, 2002; Layte, 2012; Putnam, 1993). In one of these studies, Stephen Knack, an economist with the World Bank, used ratings of governmental performance for each of the 50 American States, produced by a group known as the "Government Performance Project." In arriving at their ratings, the group considered factors such as how effectively the state government had managed its finances and human resources and the extent to which it had used performance information for making policy. Knack looked at government performance in relation to different indices of civic participation, such as the rate of volunteering in a state and attendance at club meetings. He found that a number of these indicators of civic engagement were related to the effectiveness of state governments. States with high levels of volunteering, for example, tended to have more effective governments than states with low levels of volunteering. Layte (2012) also found evidence of a link between civic participation and government effectiveness in his study of civic engagement in European countries. He found that citizens of countries with higher levels of civic participation had greater trust in government and other civic institutions.

Summary

Civic engagement can have effects not just on individuals, but on the community organizations that provide services to those individuals, as well. Research indicates that when citizens participate as decision makers in community organizations, those organizations provide services that are more appropriate, accessible, and better utilized. Organizations in which citizens are involved also tend to be more inclusive and representative of the populations they serve. Ultimately, such organizations are more accountable and effective. The research evidence suggests, further, that the civic participation can influence the health and well-being of entire neighborhoods, states, and even countries. Neighborhoods with higher levels of civic participation have a greater sense of community, and they have more community leaders with better skills. These neighborhoods have lower levels of crime, and their citizens are healthier and happier. States and countries with high levels of civic participation experience better health and mental health, with lower rates of disease, mental illness, and suicide. They, too, have lower crime rates. Research evidence indicates that they are also more prosperous economically, have healthier and better-educated children, and are better governed.

9

The Why's and Wherefore's of Civic Engagement

Why does civic engagement have such consistently positive effects on individuals, communities, and societies? What kinds of civic involvement are most likely to produce positive outcomes? These are important questions to address, particularly for those who are concerned with building civic participation through programs and policies. If we understand the mechanisms through which civic engagement influences well-being and have a sense of the kinds of civic participation that are most likely to have a positive impact, this helps us create the circumstances in which it will be most beneficial.

Mechanisms through Which Civic Engagement Has Its Impacts

How Civic Engagement Affects Individuals

In chapters 6 and 7, I discussed the many positive outcomes that people, young and old, experience when they participate in civic life by joining community groups and organizations, volunteering, and getting involved in social activism or traditional political activities. Engaged young people do better at school, have more confidence in themselves, relate better to their friends and families, and are less likely to experience problems with alcohol and drug use, delinquency, and mental illness. Civically engaged adults also experience many benefits; research indicates that they are healthier, happier, and even live longer. What is it about civic participation that makes it so beneficial for individuals?

Social Support. One of the things that happens when individuals join a neighborhood organization, do volunteer work, or become members of a club or team, is that they meet other people. These individuals become part of the individual's "social network," the group of friends and acquaintances that can serve as a source of help and support when needed. This social support, provided by members of one's social network, can be manifested in many ways. Individuals in one's network can provide material help, such as lending money, providing transport to a doctor's appointment, or assisting with a move. They can give emotional support by listening to a person's problems and offering sympathy and encouragement. Simply being a member of social network can give a sense of belonging and identity. Members of one's social network can also serve as an important source of guidance and information. It comes as no surprise, then, that social support has been found to be a significant factor in determining a person's well-being. Individuals with greater social support experience better physical and mental health, are better able to withstand stressful events and circumstances in their lives, and even live longer than individuals who lack such support (Berkman & Glass, 2000; Cohen & Wills, 1985; Cutrona & Russell, 1990).

A number of studies suggest that it is through its effects on social support that civic participation affects health and well-being. This is especially true for young people (see Crean, 2012; Dworkin et al., 2003; Eccles et al., 2003; Mahoney et al., 2002). Dworkin, Larson, and Hansen (2003), in their study of high school youth who were involved in extracurricular groups, asked the young people to describe how their participation in these youth organizations had enabled them to grow as individuals. The youth they interviewed frequently talked about how their involvement had led to new friendships with peers in the organization. They said that these relationships gave them a sense of support and intimacy, helped them develop empathy and understanding, and broadened their horizons by giving them the chance to make friends with peers from different backgrounds. The youth also talked about the relationships they formed with their adult leaders and how important these leaders were as a source of advice and support. Relationships with adults outside of one's family are particularly important for young people. These adults not only serve as a source of support and information, but they act as positive role models, as well (Crean, 2012; Rhodes, 2004). A recent study by Hugh Crean (2012) found that young people who were involved in a broad range of extracurricular activities had better decision-making skills and were less likely to be involved in delinquent behavior compared to uninvolved young people. The critical factor through which their involvements influenced their behavior was their relationships with adults. Involved youth felt greater support from adults in their neighborhood than did uninvolved young people, and it was this adult support that was the critical factor in improving decision-making skills and reducing delinquent behavior. A study of Swedish youth by Mahoney, Schweder, and Stattin (2002) similarly found that young people who were involved in after-school activities such as scouting or sports were less likely to experience depression and that, among involved youth, it was those who felt they had supportive relationships with their activity leaders who reported the lowest levels of depression.

Norms of Behavior. The people with whom we associate as members of community organizations also serve to establish norms or standards of behavior. This is particularly true of young people, who are strongly influenced by the kinds of behaviors in which they see their peers engaged. If their peers are concerned about doing well in school, they are likely to be concerned with school achievement, as well. If their friends are involved in delinquent acts, they are more likely to get involved in these kinds of activities themselves. Most organized groups that young people get involved in are populated by peers who are engaged in positive behaviors, and this sets the standard of behavior for group members. Studies by Jacquelynne Eccles and her colleagues, for example, found that high school students who were involved in extracurricular activity groups had a higher proportion of friends who were doing well in school and who planned to attend college or university compared to students not involved in these kinds of groups. Their friends were also less likely to skip school or use drugs or alcohol. Students belonging to sports teams constituted an exception to this latter finding, however, as their fellow team members tended to drink alcohol more than other students (Eccles & Barber, 1999; Eccles et al., 2003; Fredricks & Eccles, 2008).

Adults are influenced in the same ways by the members of civic groups to which they belong. Doug McAdam (1989) found this in his study of individuals involved in the American civil rights movement, working to register Black voters as part of the 1964 Freedom Summer project. Volunteers with the project found themselves embedded in a network of relationships with individuals who valued social justice and who believed that they had a responsibility to work for a more just and equal society. McAdam claimed that these individuals had become part of an activist subculture and that their involvement in this subculture, with its strong beliefs in using action to promote social justice, sustained their civic involvements for years after their participation in Freedom Summer. Evidence for this claim came from the fact that the more people that volunteers maintained contact with from their Freedom Summer years, the more likely they were to have remained involved in activist movements over the years following the Freedom Summer.

Identity and a Sense of Purpose. Almost all civic and community organizations are established with a purpose in mind. They bring people together to create something more than their individual members can create on their own. Cultural, ethnic, and religious groups create a sense of identity. Activist groups work to achieve social change and social justice. Arts groups such as choirs and amateur theater companies come together to create performances that enhance community life. Youth groups help young people develop skills and learn to work together toward a common goal. When people become involved in these organizations and their activities, they often come to adopt the organization's goals and purpose as part of their own purpose in life. This gives them a sense of identity and provides meaning and direction for their own lives. I have seen evidence of this sense of purpose in the many interviews that I and my colleagues have conducted with young volunteers, who frequently talked with great passion about how they had "made a difference" in someone's life through their volunteer activities. Sociologists Jane Piliavin and Erica Siegl (2007) refer to this sense of purpose as "mattering": "the perception that, to some degree, we are a significant part of the world around us—that people notice us, care that we exist, and value us" (Piliavin & Siegl, 2007, p. 452). They claim that by engaging in other-oriented activities such as volunteering, people develop the sense that they "matter," and begin to feel not just good, but also good about themselves. Piliavin and Siegl found support for their claims in a study they conducted on adult volunteers. They measured volunteering by asking study participants about their involvement in civic groups such as parent-teacher associations and neighborhood organizations. They also assessed participants' feelings that they "mattered" by asking them how much they agreed with statements such as, "People tend to rely on me for support." Well-being was measured via standardized questionnaires that assessed purpose in life, self-acceptance, and health. The results showed a strong link between volunteering and well-being—the more people volunteered, the greater their health and well-being. But Piliavin and Siegl's analyses also showed that it was largely through its effects on mattering that volunteering affected well-being. Volunteers were healthier, physically and psychologically, because they felt that what they did mattered and that their existence was important to others and to society.

In addition to helping people feel that they matter, participating in civic life also leads people to think about how they fit into the organizations in which they participate and the role they play in society. Reinders and Youniss (2006), for example, found that young people who had had direct contact with people in need in the course of fulfilling their school's community service requirement had reflected more about their beliefs and attitudes than students who had not had these kinds of experiences. This increased reflection led to greater intentions to be civically involved in the future by voting, working on a political campaign, or boycotting a product or service. Youniss and his colleagues suggest that when young people attempt to understand what they have witnessed through volunteering and other civic activities, they begin to see themselves in a social and historical context—not just as individuals, but also as members of organizations, communities, and a society that espouse certain beliefs and that often have long-standing problems that need to be addressed (Youniss et al., 1997). They also see themselves as having "agency"—the ability to change the course of events through their own actions. This sense of agency, coupled with their awareness of social problems, leads to the feeling that they have a responsibility to work toward seeking a resolution to these problems.

Ultimately, people's civic engagement experiences, and their reflection on them, can fundamentally shape their sense of identity. Civically engaged individuals come to see themselves not just as individuals, but also as part of a community, with the ability to contribute to that community and a responsibility to work toward its welfare. They have developed what has been referred to as a "civic" identity, one that is inextricably bound to their community (or communities) and to society (Youniss et al., 1997). It is this civic aspect of one's identity that leads to continuous and life-long involvement in community and to the benefits that this involvement can yield in terms of health and well-being.

Skills and Initiative. In chapters 6 and 7, I talked about the skills and knowledge that individuals acquire through their participation in civic life. Civically engaged individuals learn how to organize their time, work with others, resolve conflicts, make decisions, and communicate their ideas. In young people, these skills help them perform better in school, get along better with their peers and family members, gain access to programs and services, and avoid situations that could get them into trouble (Crean, 2012; Dworkin et al., 2003; McFarland & Thomas, 2006; Obradovic & Masten, 2007; Wood et al., 2009). Crean (2012), for example, in his study of delinquent behavior in adolescents, found that young people who participated in a broad range of extracurricular activities showed better decision-making skills than youth who did not participate in these activities. Decision-making skills were assessed by asking youth about things such as their ability to say "no" when someone wanted to do things that were wrong or dangerous or their ability think about the possible consequences of their actions before making decisions. It was because of these improved decision-making skills that they were less likely to get involved in delinquent activities such as stealing or damaging property. In adults, the skills acquired through civic involvement lead to many of the same positive outcomes. The social, organizational, and daily living skills that they learn lead to better relationships, greater success and fulfillment in their careers, and a greater sense of confidence and well-being.

For young people, particularly, involvement in civic life allows them to experience a diversity of social contacts, activities, and settings that can lead them to discover what they are truly interested in and passionate about. Developmental psychologists Peter Benson and Peter Scales refer to these core passions in a person's life as "sparks" (Benson & Scales, 2009). These sparks can be anything from doing volunteer work with children to playing a musical instrument to working on car engines. What all sparks have in common is that they are pursued for their own sake and that they energize and excite the individual who has them. When these sparks are combined with an environment that encourages their expression, a young person develops a sense of purpose and direction in life and is more likely to become a thriving, contributing member of society. Recent research by Scales, Benson, and Roehlkepartain (2011) supports these notions about "sparks" and "thriving" in young people. They asked American 15-year-olds if they had a "spark" in their life—something that they "are passionate about" and "gives them real purpose." They also asked these youth about the kinds of resources and relationships that they had that supported their passions and interests. These included the presence of youth programs (e.g., the YMCA or Boys and Girls Clubs) in their neighborhoods, or adults such as youth group leaders or teachers who provided help and encouragement in developing their interests. The results of the study showed that young people who had "sparks" and resources that supported their development (e.g., youth programs, adult leaders) experienced greater thriving, demonstrated by school achievement and having a sense of purpose in life. Participation in extracurricular clubs, youth groups, and community organizations, then, can lead to the healthy development of young people by providing them with opportunities to discover their sparks and an environment that supports the development of their interests and passions. Also, when young people spend their time pursuing activities that interest and excite them, this leaves less time for them to get involved in problem behaviors such as using drugs and alcohol or engaging in delinquent acts.

How Civic Engagement Affects Communities and Society

In the last chapter, I talked about the ways in which civic engagement can influence the well-being of whole communities and even entire states and countries. Communities and societies with an engaged, active citizenry have lower rates of disease and mortality, less crime, greater economic prosperity, and more effective governments, among many other benefits. While part of this can be explained by the fact that there are more individuals in those countries who are civically engaged and who derive benefits from that engagement, this is not the whole story. Even those who do not participate in community life derive benefits from the fact that most other people do. How does this happen?

Collective Action. One way in which this happens is through the collective action of engaged citizens. When a significant number of citizens work together to create and lobby for policies, programs, and services, such as universal health insurance, then these programs and services are more likely to be implemented. The new services then benefit all of society, not just those who worked toward their development. In their study of civic engagement in rural Tanzanian villages, for example, Narayan and Pritchett (1999) found that villages with more engaged citizens had better schools, because parents participated in school meetings and activities. They also found that in villages with high levels of civic involvement there was more road-building activity, because residents participated in efforts to build and repair roads. The ultimate impact of efforts such as better roads and schools was increased economic prosperity for villages whose citizens were civically engaged. Similarly, when there are many individuals who work with community organizations to deliver meals to shut-ins, organize a community event, or clear snow from sidewalks, this benefits everyone in the community.

Norms and Diffusion of Information. When individuals are connected with one another through their participation in civic life, important information is more readily diffused among citizens. In Naryan and Pritchett's study of Tanzanian villages, for example, they found that villages with higher levels of civic participation used more advanced agricultural practices than did villages with little civic participation. The study's authors claim that this kind of innovation occurs quickly because information about innovative practices spreads easily among citizens who know one another through their membership in community organizations. The rapid and extensive spread of information is particularly important in the area of health promotion. Information about practices such as immunization, smoking, exercise, and nutritious eating can affect the health of entire communities (Kawachi et al., 1999; Kim et al., 2006). The rapid spread of information in communities with extensive citizen participation also provides for the establishment of social norms, which can have an impact on health and well-being. For example, norms relating to the importance of physical activity or the harmful effects of smoking can be quickly transmitted among individuals connected through membership in community groups and organizations.

Accountability. In the last chapter, I talked about a study by World Bank economist Stephen Knack (2002), which found that American states with more engaged citizens had better and more effective governments than states whose citizens were less engaged. Knack suggests a number of reasons that an involved citizenry might result in more effective government. Engaged citizens will hold their governments to account by staying informed about the actions of their politicians and public officials and by making it known, through voting, protest, or communication with officials, when they think their government is heading in the wrong direction or is demonstrating incompetence or malfeasance. Involved citizens also help inform government about their interests so that government officials can more easily create policies that align with the public interest. Knack also argues that when large numbers of citizens from across the political spectrum stay informed about what their governments are doing and participate in political life, those with extreme political views will be less likely to dominate the political agenda. This results in greater compromise, less partisan bickering, and better policymaking. Knack attributes the kind of gridlock currently experienced in political decision-making in the United States to the fact that participation in political life has been declining, particularly among political moderates, leaving those at the extremes to fight with one another for dominance.

Social Trust and Reciprocity. When citizens have frequent contact with one another through their participation in community organizations, they begin to develop a sense of "social trust"—the feeling that most people in their community can be trusted. This sense of social trust is a key element of social capital. Social trust, in turn, is critical to the development of strong norms of reciprocity—the feeling that citizens have that they should reciprocate when other individuals in their community do things that benefit them. This norm of reciprocity can even take a more generalized form, in which community members think, "I'll do this for you now, without expecting anything immediately in return and perhaps without even knowing you, confident that down the road you or someone else will return the favor" (Putnam, 2000, p. 134). Communities that are characterized by high levels of trust and feelings of reciprocity do better in terms of economic prosperity because citizens feel they can trust one another when they make financial transactions with one another and with community businesses and organizations. They also do better in terms of the health and well-being of their citizens because community members are more willing to help one another, thinking that this is normal, appropriate behavior and that the help they provide to others will be reciprocated.

What Types of Civic Engagement Are Most Beneficial?

We know, then, that civic engagement can yield significant long-term benefits for both individuals and communities. We also know something about the ways in which civic involvement produces these benefits. But not all types of civic participation yield the same benefits. What kinds of civic activity produce the most positive outcomes?

High-Quality Civic Activities

The integrative theory of civic engagement that I presented in chapter 1 suggests that activities that occur in a supportive social milieu and produce short-term positive outcomes will lead to continuing involvement in the community and long-term benefits in health and well-being. A supportive social milieu is present if civic involvements are supported by family and friends and are appreciated and recognized by the clubs, groups, and other community organizations in which individuals are involved. Positive short-term outcomes of engagement might include enhanced social networks and social support, the feeling that one is engaged in something that "matters," the sense of competence and accomplishment one derives from developing new skills and abilities, and the enjoyment of engaging in interesting activities with friendly and like-minded individuals. Activities that are supported by family and friends, occur in organizations that recognize and appreciate those who are involved, and provide opportunities to develop skills, discover new interests, form relationships, and do things that matter and are enjoyable can be said to be of high quality. In turn, high-quality activities should lead to continuing involvement and long-term benefits.

Trevor Taylor and I conducted a study in which we attempted to confirm these notions about high-quality civic involvements and their long-term impacts (Taylor & Pancer, 2007). Our research participants were students who were required to do a community service field placement as part of their undergraduate course in psychology. The students worked in schools, nursing homes, multicultural centers, community justice settings, and other organizations, spending 2 hours a week at their placement for 10 weeks of the 12-week fall term. One week before the end of term, we had students complete a scale we had developed—the Inventory of Service Experience, or ISE—to assess the quality of students' community service experiences during the term. This 49-item questionnaire had 7 groups of statements, each group of statements reflecting one of the characteristics one would expect of a high-quality activity. Students indicated their agreement or disagreement with each statement, and responses were totaled for the entire scale to give an overall quality score. A score was also computed for the set of statements relating to each of the 7 aspects of quality, resulting in 7 subscale scores. Table 9.1 describes each of the subscales of the measure and provides a sample statement from that subscale.

In addition to completing the ISE, students completed questionnaires assessing identity development and how decided they were in terms of the kind of career they planned to pursue in the future. Approximately 10 weeks after they had completed their community service requirement, well into their next term of study, we contacted the research participants to see if they had continued on as volunteers with the organization in which they had performed their required service. We found that individuals who had continued as volunteers with their placement organizations had significantly higher total scores on the ISE, and on all of its subscales, with the exception of the "Relations with Others" subscale. Individuals who had higher-quality placements also showed more advanced identity development and were more decided about the kinds of careers they wanted to follow. These results indicate that activities that had the desired characteristics were more likely to lead to positive outcomes and to a long-term commitment to community service. In later research, my colleagues Ailsa Henderson, Steve Brown, and I used the ISE to assess the impact of high school students' community service experiences on civic participation 15 months after they had completed their high school studies (Henderson, Brown & Pancer, 2012). We found that students who had had a positive experience doing community service during high school, as determined by their responses to a shortened version of the ISE, were significantly more likely to have been involved in school and community organizations, social activism, and political activity after graduating from high school.

In another study of what constitutes a quality experience in civic activities, Thanh-Thanh Tieu and I had first-year university students make a list of all the activities they had been involved in over the previous year, outside of schoolwork and paid employment (Tieu & Pancer, 2009). The resultant lists of activities included community service, involvement in arts and cultural groups, and membership in religious groups and community organizations. We then had

Table 9.1 **Inventory of Service Experience**

Quality Assessed	*Name of Subscale*	*Sample Item*
Enhanced social networks and social support	Relations with Others	"I have met a lot of nice people through my community service work"
Support from family and friends	Family and Friends	"My family is very supportive of my community service involvement"
Support and recognition from the organization served	Organizational Support	"I feel a part of the organization with which I perform my community service"
Opportunity to do things that "matter"	Making a Difference	"I feel that my community service work helps to make a difference"
Opportunity to learn skills	Learning Skills	"Doing community service helps me learn skills that will be useful in my career and work life"
Opportunity to explore career possibilities	Exposure to Career Possibilities	"My community service experience is providing me with information about possible careers"
Enjoyability of activities	Enjoyable Activities	"I have a lot of fun doing my community service"

From Taylor, T. P., & Pancer, S. M. (2007). Community service experiences and commitment to volunteering. *Journal of Applied Social Psychology*, 37(2), 320–345. Reprinted with permission from John Wiley & Sons.

them select the most important activity on their list and indicate their agreement or disagreement with a number of statements that related to the quality of their experience while engaging in that activity. The qualities to which the statements related had to do with how meaningful or important the activity seemed to them (e.g., "Participation in this activity is very meaningful to me"), how positively participation in the activity made them feel (e.g., "Participating in this activity makes me happy"), and their sense of belonging and connection with others through participating in the activity (e.g., "I feel a sense of connection to others that also participate in this activity"). We found that students whose involvements had been of higher quality, as indicated by their responses to our scale (which we called the Quality of Involvement Scale) adjusted better to life at university, experienced greater social support, had higher self-esteem, felt less stressed, and reported greater social skills than students involved in lower-quality activities.

Structured Activities

One of the ways in which civic activities differ is in how structured they are. Some are relatively unstructured. For example, participating in an ethnic club or organization may involve simply socializing with members of one's ethnic group. Others are more structured. For example, participating in an environmental action group may involve working together with others, assigning roles and responsibilities to group members, and exerting effort toward the attainment of a specific goal, such as a reduction in a community's energy use. Developmental psychologists Joseph Mahoney and Hakan Stattin (2000) suggest that activities are structured to the extent that they occur on a regular schedule, are directed or organized by a leader, require effort and the development of skills, are guided by rules, demand sustained attention, and are aimed at the achievement of a goal or objective. They conducted a study in which they looked at differences in Swedish youth who participated in more structured activities such as church groups or scouting and those who participated in Youth Recreation Centers, in which youth engaged primarily in unstructured activities such as playing pool and video games. They found that youth who participated in structured groups did better in school and were less likely to be involved in antisocial behavior such as fighting, stealing, or vandalizing property. Other studies show that young people who are involved in structured activities such as school government and community youth organizations are more likely to develop a sense of social responsibility and to be engaged in the political process as adults by voting in local and national elections, attending political rallies, and working on political campaigns (Glanville, 1999; Wood, Larson, & Brown, 2009).

My own research, with Thanh Tieu and other colleagues, lends support to the idea that structured civic activities are more likely to produce positive impacts than are unstructured activities (Tieu et al., 2010). In one of our studies, we had undergraduate students make a list of all the activities in which they'd engaged over the previous year, outside of schoolwork and paid employment. We then asked them to answer yes or no to six statements relating to how structured each activity was. The statements were: "This activity is led/organized by a senior student, faculty member or school administrator," "Participation in this activity occurs regularly," "Participation in this activity is directed at a goal, aim, or objective," "Participation in this activity may lead to the development of at least one particular skill," "Participation in this activity requires effort and attention," and "I receive feedback on how well I perform this activity." Each activity received a score indicating how structured it was, by summing the number of "yes" responses to the six statements. We found that compared to students who participated in activities with little structure, those who took part in activities with more structure had higher self-esteem, more social support, lower levels of stress, and generally showed better adjustment to life at university.

Voice and Ownership

In 1969, a woman named Sherry Arnstein, who at the time worked as director of community studies with a nonprofit research institute called The Commons, published an article entitled "A Ladder of Citizen Participation" (Arnstein, 1969). In the article, she discussed civic engagement in terms of citizens' power and influence in making decisions about the programs, organizations, and policies that affected their lives. She envisioned citizen power in terms of a ladder. At the lowest rungs of the ladder, citizens have no say in how programs and policies are designed and implemented. At the middle rungs, citizens are "informed" and "consulted" when decisions are being made about programs and policies, but they have no real influence on the final decisions that result. At the highest rungs of the ladder, citizens work in partnership with program developers, policymakers, and others in making decisions, and they may even assume a leadership role in this process. This article, published in an obscure journal, has been reprinted many times and has had a profound impact on current thinking about how citizens should be involved in community organizations. It is now considered accepted practice that citizens who have a stake in the community organizations that affect their lives should be involved in key decisions that those bodies make. We saw in the last chapter that when citizens do have power and participate in making decisions, more effective community organizations and better programs result.

Research evidence suggests that when individuals have a voice in making decisions about the community programs and organizations in which they participate, they derive more benefits from their involvement (Larson & Walker, 2010; Morgan & Streb, 2001; Ohmer 2007; Wood et al., 2009; Zeldin, 2004). Social work researcher Mary Ohmer, in her study of individuals who belonged to neighborhood organizations in Pittsburgh, asked her research participants to indicate how much they participated in decision making in the organizations they belonged to by checking one of the following six statements: (1) "I take no part at all"; (2) "I play a passive role"; (3) "I participate in relaying information"; (4) "I carry out various tasks at the instruction of the staff and/or board"; (5) "I participate partially in planning and decision making and implementation"; (6) "I am a full partner in planning, decision making, and implementation." She found that individuals who played an active role in decision making felt they had gained more knowledge and skill from their participation, developed greater leadership capacity, and experienced a greater sense of community than did individuals who played a more passive role. Those active in decision making also developed a greater sense of empowerment; they felt that they themselves, and the organizations to which they belonged, exerted more influence on the policies that affected life in their neighborhood.

Studies of young people's involvements have produced similar findings. Political scientists Morgan and Streb examined "student voice" in a study they conducted with students involved in a service-learning program in Indiana schools (Morgan & Streb, 2001). Student voice in the service projects in which they participated was assessed by asking them how much they agreed with statements such as, "I helped plan the project" and "I made all important decisions." The results indicated that students who felt they had a voice in decision making experienced greater gains in self-confidence, self-efficacy, social responsibility, and interest in community and political affairs during the course of their project participation, compared to students who felt they were less involved in decision-making. Shepherd Zeldin's (2004) study of young people who served on boards of directors of youth-serving organizations demonstrated a similar impact on self-confidence among youth who are involved in organizational decision making. A young board member who was interviewed as part of the study described the experience in this way:

> *I have never been in a situation before where my voice had any meaning or power, or where my opinions and ideas were really wanted. I felt empowered to change my personal life for the better.* (Zeldin, 2004, p. 81)

Contact with the "Other"

Many people have only limited contacts with individuals who are different from themselves. They live, work, and socialize with people who are similar in socioeconomic level, education, values, and upbringing. Individuals living in such situations can easily come to view those from different backgrounds in stereotypical ways. They see individuals who are poor as lazy and irresponsible. They view young people as rebellious and self-centered. They feel uncomfortable with individuals from different religious or ethnic backgrounds. In previous chapters, I described research showing that civic participation can help break down these stereotypes by giving people the opportunity to get to know the "other"—those who may differ in socioeconomic status, education, religion, race, or ethnicity—in a more face-to-face, personal way. These kinds of contacts provide additional benefits, as well. They increase people's knowledge about their community and their world. They help build skills in understanding other people's perspectives, and working effectively with them. They can also serve to make individuals reflect on their own lives in terms of how privileged or underprivileged their lives may be, and in terms of the social conditions that may have given rise to differences in wealth and opportunity.

The kinds of civic activities that are most likely to allow people to get to know the "other" are those in which individuals have direct contact with those from other backgrounds. Yates and Youniss (1997), for example, in their study of young people who worked at a soup kitchen as part of their school's community service requirement, found that the youths got to know those who came for meals as individuals, rather than as "the poor" or "the homeless." In a recent article that looked back on this study, Youniss and Reinders claim that "on repeated encounters with them at the kitchen, youth realized that homeless people were simply people, albeit people with problems which brought them to their present state" (Youniss & Reinders, 2010, p. 242). Zeldin, in his study of young people and adults who served together on boards of directors of youth-serving organizations, found that working in close partnership with youths profoundly changed the way adults looked at young people. As one of the adult board members said:

> *I find working with young people to be surprising and enlightening. I did not have much exposure to young people …I had low expectations for what they could do. I'm embarrassed to say that after 4 years of working with young people, how they continue to surprise me and my stereotypes keep coming out. But really, they are so committed. I just got completely turned around.* (Zeldin, 2004, p. 84)

Other studies show findings that are consistent with the idea that direct contact with others who are different from oneself can produce more substantial benefits. Educational psychologists Jennifer Schmidt, Lee Shumow, and Hayal Kackar (2007), using data from an American national education survey, compared young people who had performed community service that involved direct contact with individuals from other backgrounds (e.g., working directly with homeless or elderly individuals) with those who had performed service that did not involve this kind of contact (e.g., working on a political campaign, helping to raise funds for a hospital). They found that youth who worked directly with those in need showed better school achievement than those who did not. Reinders and Youniss (2006) found similar results in their study of youth who performed community service as part of their high school requirements. They found that service that put youth in direct contact with individuals in need, such as providing entertainment to elderly individuals in a seniors residence, led to more self-awareness, and subsequently to greater civic engagement, than service that did not involve direct contact.

Breadth, Intensity, and Continuity of Involvement

People can be involved in civic groups and activities in many different ways. Some will devote all their time to one organization, often to one specific set of tasks within that organization. Others will become involved in a number of organizations and activities that may be very different from one another. Researchers have talked about the former kind of involvement in terms of its "intensity." They typically measure intensity by determining how much time individuals devote to their civic activities or how frequently they engage in these activities.

Researchers refer to the latter kind of involvement in terms of its "breadth" or "diversity"; they assess breadth by looking at the number of different kinds of organizations or activities in which individuals are involved. But which pattern of involvement is better? Research suggests that both intensity and breadth of involvement are related to greater benefits for engaged individuals. But studies that have compared both types suggest that breadth of involvement produces more positive outcomes than intensity of involvement, particularly when looking at young people's civic activities (Busseri et al., 2006, 2011; Metzger & Smetana, 2009; Rose-Krasnor et al., 2006). In one of these studies (Busseri et al., 2006), young people, approximately 15 years of age, completed a survey in which they were given a list of activities (e.g., played school sports, gone to school clubs, gone to clubs outside of school, done volunteer work) and were asked to indicate which of the listed activities they were involved in, and how frequently they were involved in each activity. The researchers computed an intensity score for each youth by averaging the frequency of involvement for those activities in which the youth had been engaged. They computed a breadth score by simply summing the number of different activities in which the youth had been involved—so if a young woman indicated that she had been involved in three of the activities on the list, she would receive a score of 3 for breadth of involvement, regardless of how frequently she engaged in each of the three activities. In addition to assessing young people's involvements, the youth completed measures that assessed their adjustment in terms of their well-being, school achievement, relationships, and risk behavior (e.g., alcohol and drug use, gang membership). The results of the study showed that both intensity and breadth of involvement were related to better adjustment and well-being, but that breadth was more strongly related. When Busseri and colleagues assessed adjustment in these young people again, two years later, when they were about 17 years of age, they found that the more kinds of activities the youth had been involved in over the two intervening years, the better their adjustment. Other studies, with both young people and adults, have also found that breadth of involvement is related to greater benefits (Crean 2012; Piliavin & Siegl, 2007; Simpkin, Eccles & Becnel, 2008). Piliavin and Siegl (2007), for example, found that the more organizations for which adults volunteered, the better their perceived health. Individuals who worked with three organizations experienced better health than those that worked with only two, and those who worked with two organizations had better health than those who volunteered with only one organization.

Why does being involved in a diverse range of activities produce greater benefits? One possible reason is that it brings individuals into contact with more people, allowing them the opportunity to improve their social skills and expand their network of social contacts and social support. It can also increase the diversity of individuals with whom one comes into contact, helping to break down stereotypes. For young people, in particular, it gives them more opportunities to find caring adults who can provide support and guidance and serve as role models. Crean (2012) found that young people who were involved in a broad range of organized activities, compared to those involved in a narrower range of activities, experienced greater adult support, and it was through this adult support that they developed improved decision-making skills and were less involved in delinquent behavior. Involvement in a diverse set of activities also allows individuals to discover their "sparks"—the interests and passions that lead to thriving and an enhanced sense of well-being (Benson & Scales, 2009). Each activity also requires a different skill set, so being involved in a broad range of civic activities serves to build an individual's skills and capacities.

Another aspect of individuals' pattern of civic involvements that is related to the amount of benefit they experience is the continuity or regularity of their involvement. Several studies show that those who are regularly involved in civic activities, over an extended period of time, experience greater benefits than those involved on a more sporadic basis, over a shorter time (Horn, 2012; Henderson et al., 2012; Musick & Wilson, 2003; Piliavin & Siegl, 2007; Zaff et al., 2003). Piliavin and Siegl (2007), for example, in their longitudinal study of adult volunteers, found that the longer the period of time over which study participants had performed volunteer work, the better their health and well-being. In my own research, with colleagues Ailsa Henderson and Steve Brown (Henderson, Brown & Pancer, 2012), we found that young people who had performed regular community service for a year or longer while in high school showed significantly greater civic involvement and were more politically active two years after high school compared to young people who had done service for less than a year. It is likely that these kinds of effects occur because over time people develop a habit of civic participation and are more likely to develop a civic identity (Pancer & Pratt, 1999; Piliavin & Callero, 1991; Youniss et al., 1997).

Although for the most part, a broad range of involvements over a longer period appear to produce the most benefits for individuals, there are instances in which a relatively brief but intense civic experience can stimulate long-term civic engagement and associated benefits. Developmental psychologist Linda Rose-Krasnor (2008) refers to these kinds of involvements as "high-density" or "turning point" experiences. For example, the young people who spent a single summer helping to register black voters as part of the Freedom Summer project in 1964 continued to be civically engaged when they were interviewed more than 20 years after their Freedom Summer experience. Linda Rose-Krasnor, Lisa Loiselle, and I (Pancer, Rose-Krasnor, & Loiselle, 2002) found that specialized week-long youth conferences, in which young people from across the country were brought together to develop social action programs for youth in their home communities, had a similar transformative effect on youth. A key element of such experiences seems to be that they connect people with something larger than themselves such as a social or religious movement that provides them with the sense that, working together with others, they can accomplish something that "matters."

Type of Activity

Several studies of young people's involvements have placed these involvements into distinct categories and compared these categories in terms of the kinds of impacts they have (Barber et al., 2001; Denault, Poulin, & Pedersen, 2009; Eccles & Barber, 1999; Hansen, Larson, & Dworkin, 2003; Horn, 2012; Larson et al., 2006; McFarland & Thomas, 2006; Metz et al., 2003; Rose-Krasnor et al., 2006). Eccles and Barber (1999), for example, categorized young people's extracurricular activities into five types—pro-social activities (e.g., community service, church attendance), performance activities (e.g., theater groups, school orchestra), team sports, school involvement (e.g., student government, cheerleading), and academic clubs (e.g., math club, debating club). Others, like Reed Larson and his colleagues, have put faith-based activities and community service in different categories and have added community-based youth organizations to the list of the kinds of activities in which young people can be involved. While these studies have found that almost all of the activities have positive impacts on young people, different activities were often associated with different kinds of benefits. Denault and colleagues (2009), for example, found that young people involved youth clubs did better at school and were less likely to abuse alcohol, while those involved in performance and fine arts were less likely to experience depression. Among all these studies, however, the activity that stood out in terms of its positive effects was volunteering or community service. Young people engaged in community service did better at school, had fewer emotional problems, were less likely to abuse drugs and alcohol, and were more likely to develop into well-adjusted healthy adults. What is it about community service that makes it so beneficial? If one thinks of the attributes that characterize highly impactful involvements, community service has almost all of them. When performed under the direction of a community organization, it is a structured and organized activity. It puts young people into contact with other young people and adults who can provide social support, convey positive social norms, and serve as positive role models. It allows them to experience the "other"—what life is like for those who are in need or who come from different backgrounds. It gives them a chance to develop skills, discover their passions, and engage in something that "matters." Certain kinds of community service—the kind that Youniss (2011) describes as "justice-oriented"—can also serve to connect young people with something larger than themselves, making them feel that they are part of a history and tradition of seeking to change social conditions that have produced suffering and disadvantage.

Summary

Civic engagement affects the health and positive development of both individuals, and the communities and societies in which they live. It does this in many ways. For individuals, it increases their social networks and social support, brings them together with people and organizations that convey positive norms or standards of behavior, and provides them with the feeling that they are doing things that "matter." All of these benefits contribute to positive health and development. Civic participation also provides individuals with the opportunities to find their passions and to develop skills, thus providing a sense of direction in life.

Civic engagement, on a state or country level, enhances the well-being of all citizens, even those who are not civically active. This happens through the collective action of engaged citizens, which helps establish programs, policies, and resources that benefit all community residents. Civic participation also serves to establish positive norms of behavior and allows for the rapid spread of information about things such as the dangers of smoking, thereby further enhancing health at a population level. When citizens are involved in civic life by voting, protesting, or contacting public officials, they make their leaders and officials more accountable and effective. Civic involvement also creates social trust, which further contributes to community well-being.

Research that has compared various types of civic engagement tells us that high-quality activities—those that help develop new skills, are enjoyable, provide the opportunity to do things that matter, and are supported by family, friends, and the organizations with whom one works—yield the greatest benefits. Civic activities that are structured, in that they are performed regularly, under supervision, and are aimed at achieving a goal or objective, also produce greater benefits. When individuals engage in a wide variety of civic activities with individuals from a range of backgrounds and have a voice in the activities they undertake, these activities will have a greater impact. Volunteering, in particular, seems to have all the attributes that make a civic activity particularly beneficial.

10

Building Citizenship through Research, Programs, and Policy

The last 15 years or so have seen a burgeoning of research on every aspect of civic engagement, from volunteering to participation in community organizations to working with social justice and environmental groups. A significant proportion of this research has been fuelled by studies that have shown a marked decline in many forms of civic participation over the last 40 years. This decline is evident in the steadily decreasing turnout of voters in national elections, particularly among young people, but in many other kinds of civic involvement, as well (Putnam, 2000). Research on civic engagement tells us that we should be concerned about this decline, because it shows that those who do not participate in civic or community life are at risk for a host of health and social problems. But this body of research holds promise, as well, because it identifies the key factors and mechanisms that influence civic participation, and it can inform the development of programs and policies that can enhance it. In this chapter, I discuss what we have learned about citizenship and civic engagement through research, what we still need to find out, and how research findings can be translated into programs and policies that can help build citizenship.

Research

What Have We Learned?

The Impacts of Civic Engagement. First and foremost, we have learned that those who are civically engaged almost always experience substantial benefits and rarely show any problems as a result of their participation. Young people who are civically engaged through their involvement in things such as extracurricular activities, youth organizations, and church groups are less likely to fail at school, abuse drugs or alcohol, perform delinquent acts, or suffer from depression. They are more likely to be self-confident, form meaningful relationships, be socially responsible, do well at school, have a strong moral sense, and be involved in their communities throughout their lives. Civically engaged adults experience many of the same benefits. They have greater self-esteem, an enhanced sense of empowerment, better physical and mental health, more social support, more skills and resources, and greater quality of life. The research suggests that they are even likely to live longer! A number of studies indicate, also, that it is those who are at greatest risk for developing problems that benefit the most from being involved in their communities.

Research tells us, moreover, that entire organizations, communities, and even countries can be affected by the active participation of their members or citizens in civic life. When citizens play a prominent decision-making role in community organizations, those organizations are more representative of and accountable to their members and communities, they provide services that are more accessible and better utilized, and they are more effective in achieving their goals. When residents are actively involved in neighborhood organizations, those neighborhoods tend to experience less crime and fewer health and social problems. States and countries that have high levels of civic participation show lower levels of illness and disease, reduced incidence of mental health problems, lower crime levels, greater economic prosperity, and more effective government.

The Factors Influencing Civic Engagement. We have also learned much about the factors that influence civic participation. We have learned that parents exert a strong influence on the civic activities of their children by serving as role models and by talking about social issues and events. Parents also serve as links to the community through their own involvements and act as vehicles through which norms and values relating to community participation are transmitted. Friends exert a similarly strong influence on civic engagement at every age level through many of the same mechanisms. They, too, transmit norms and values and can serve as models of civic participation. Both family and friends exert a strong direct influence on civic participation. It is through their exhortation and encouragement that most individuals first become involved in things such as volunteering and community activities.

Individuals are part of many "communities" throughout their lives—their school, their neighborhood, their church, their workplace—and the nature of these communities has a great deal of influence on civic participation. We have learned, for example, that schools that provide high-quality service learning programs, offer students a wide range of extracurricular activities, and encourage students to express their views freely and openly produce young people who are more civically involved. Neighborhoods that have a sense of community and in which many community organizations are located show higher levels of civic participation. Churches and other religious organizations encourage civic participation through the values they convey about the importance of service and through their connection to the community. They also serve as settings in which members can discuss social problems and recruit one another to perform civic activities such as volunteer work. Workplaces can influence civic involvement through corporate volunteer programs and by giving employees the opportunity to learn skills that can be transferred to their work with community organizations. The largest community to which people belong is the state, region, or country in which they live. Countries that have high levels of income inequality, whose governments are characterized by rampant, vicious partisanship, where electoral processes make people feel that their needs and wishes do not matter, and whose people aspire to have material goods rather than good relationships tend to have citizens who are less civically involved.

How Civic Engagement Produces Benefit. We have also learned a great deal about how active citizenship may produce the many benefits associated with it and what kinds of civic participation are the most beneficial. Civic engagement appears to benefit the health and well-being of individuals by enhancing their networks of social support, giving them a sense of identity and purpose, exposing them to positive social norms, and giving them the opportunity to build their skills and capacities. On a community or state level, those who are civically engaged improve the well-being of their fellow citizens by making governments and civic organizations more accountable, spreading information about beneficial health and social practices, taking collective action, and creating a sense of social trust. Through research, we also have a good idea about what kinds of civic participation are most beneficial. We have learned that civic activities that are supported by family, friends, and the organizations with which individuals are involved; that give individuals the opportunity to discover their passions and do things that they feel "matter"; that allow those involved to develop skills; and that bring people into contact with others from different backgrounds are all particularly likely to produce benefits. We have also learned that individuals derive the greatest benefit when they participate in activities that are structured and that give them a voice in decision making and a sense of ownership. We know also that when individuals engage in a broad range of civic activities, they are more likely to experience the benefits of civic participation. Of all the civic activities in which a person can be involved, volunteering appears to be most likely to have these various attributes and produce the greatest benefits.

What Do We Still Need to Learn and What Research Methods Should We Employ in Acquiring This New Knowledge?

Civic Engagement in Marginalized and At-Risk Populations. It has been well established that those who are involved in and connected with their communities experience substantial benefits. Studies suggest, further, that those who are at greatest risk are least engaged in civic life but show the greatest benefits when they do participate in civic activities (Mahoney & Cairns, 1997; Marsh & Kleitman, 2003; Oman et al., 1999; Lancee & ter Hoeven, 2010). However, there are very few studies that have looked at the ways in which different groups and populations are affected by civic participation. More research needs to be done, in particular, to examine civic participation in groups that are at risk because of factors such as poverty or race. We know that individuals living in poverty and who belong to certain racial and ethnic groups are less likely to be involved in civic life. Why is this so? Do individuals from these less involved groups experience the same kinds of benefits from civic participation as do those from the mainstream? Do they engage in different kinds of civic activities compared to others? What kinds of programs are needed to boost participation levels and what kinds of changes do civic and political organizations need to undergo to promote greater involvement of disadvantaged and marginalized groups (Watts & Flanagan, 2007)? What impact will it have when these groups participate more fully in civil society?

The Interface between Individuals and Social Systems. Research that compares countries in terms of civic participation tells us that individual civic behavior is strongly influenced by social systems. But this influence moves in two directions. When many individuals within a society participate in civic life, this can affect social systems and through these social systems, the health and well-being of entire nations. This interface between individuals and social systems requires greater examination. More research needs to be undertaken to examine how social systems—the qualities of governments and government policies, the nature of economies, the policies that govern community organizations such as schools and labor unions, the paucity or abundance of civic groups and organizations in a region or municipality—influence individual civic behavior. At the same time, greater attention needs to be focused on how individuals, through civic behavior such as collective action or simply through the expression of public opinion, influence social systems. An excellent example of research that examines the interface of individuals and social systems is the work of social psychologist Tim Kasser and his colleagues (Kasser et al., 2007; Kasser, 2011). In a recent study, Kasser (2011) compared 20 countries in terms of the extent to which individuals in those countries expressed values that were "egalitarian" (the belief that everyone in society needed to be cared for and that individuals should work together to promote social welfare) or "hierarchical" (the belief that inequalities among citizens in terms of wealth and power were acceptable). He found that the values of individuals within a country were highly related to the policies and practices enacted by the social systems in their country. Countries populated by individuals who had more egalitarian values were more likely to have policies in place (such as parental leave to care for newborn or ailing children) that promoted child welfare.

Multidisciplinary Research. This kind of research would benefit from the collaboration of individuals from different disciplines. Although behavior is considered the domain of psychologists, when researchers begin to look at factors such as the interface between behavior and social systems, the expertise of individuals from other social science disciplines such as sociology and political science, who specialize in looking at systems, would be tremendously beneficial. When I began this book, my notion was to look at citizenship-related research in the different subdisciplines of psychology: social psychology, developmental psychology, community psychology, and so on. I ended up reading articles and books from a wide range of disciplines (sociology, political science, public health, education, social work, and economics, among others) because the subject matter they addressed—civic behavior—was the same. This suggests to me that it would be extremely worthwhile for the study of civic participation if individuals from different disciplines, but with a common interest in citizenship and civic engagement, worked together. An effective way to initiate such interdisciplinary work would be to convene a conference on citizenship to which researchers from every area of social science with an interest in the topic would be invited. Another way would be to have a journal that focused on the topic of citizenship to which individuals from different disciplines would be invited to contribute.

Civic Engagement as a Process. When I conducted my first studies on volunteering by young people, I discovered that the things that got them started doing volunteer work were not necessarily the same as the things that kept them doing it. Many had started volunteering because their parents or teachers had suggested it to them or because they thought they might be more likely to get a job or a scholarship if they volunteered. As they got involved, their motivation changed. They continued in their volunteer work because they began to feel that what they did mattered, that they were making a difference in people's lives. They were proud of the skills they learned and interested in the people they met. More research needs to be undertaken to document the process that individuals go through as they become involved in their communities. What kinds of changes do people experience as they become more involved in civic life? How do these changes affect the likelihood of their continuing to engage in civic activities? Why do some people reduce their involvements over time while others increase them? The kind of research that is best suited to answering these questions is qualitative research, in which individuals are interviewed at several points in their "career" as volunteers, political and social activists, and members of community organizations.

Qualitative and Mixed Methods Research. Qualitative methods are useful not just for examining the process individuals go through as they become engaged in their communities but also for understanding the impact that civic engagement has on individuals, the barriers that people confront that may deter them from becoming more involved, and the factors that promote or inhibit their involvement. It is one thing to say, on the basis of quantitative survey results, that young people are not engaged in political life because their rate of voting is so low relative to the voting rates of older individuals. One gains a different and equally rich understanding of young people's behavior by asking those who did not go to the polls on election day, "Why didn't you vote?" Qualitative methods are also useful in generating ideas for new programs to promote civic participation and for evaluating programs that are already in operation (Patton, 2002). Social science researchers are coming to the realization that the best way to come to a full understanding of a phenomenon is to use both qualitative and quantitative methods in combination (Tashakkori & Teddlie, 2003), but there are relatively few examples of this approach in the study of civic engagement. More qualitative and mixed-methods research needs to be undertaken.

Social Media and the Internet. The development of the Internet has transformed the world in many ways. It has given people access to a vast array of information undreamed of before its advent, and it has also given individuals a voice with which to express their opinions about social issues and world affairs. A single blogger, sitting at a computer anywhere around the globe, can register dissatisfaction with government policy, inform people about the location of a mass protest, or recruit others to a social cause. The power of the Internet and social media can be seen in the events that took place during the "Arab Spring" of 2011, when thousands of individuals participated in mass protests in an attempt to overthrow autocratic rulers. Social media such as Facebook were critical in informing individuals about the timing and location of the protests, as well as telling the world what was happening by uploading photographs and videos of the demonstrations onto social media pages that could be widely viewed (Tufekci & Wilson, 2012).

In its early days, it was hoped that the Internet would democratize civic affairs and encourage civic engagement in all citizens by giving individuals formerly without a voice the opportunity to express their views and be widely heard. Has it achieved its promise? Results of a survey conducted by the Pew Research Center suggest that it has not (Smith et al., 2009). The survey results showed that Americans with higher incomes and more education were more likely to be engaged in online political and civic activities, to the same degree that they are more likely to be engaged in traditional, offline civic activities. For example, while 35% of those with over $100,000 annual incomes participated in online political activities, such as contacting a government official or signing a petition, only 8% of those with incomes of less than $20,000 did so. While these findings may partly be explained by the fact that those with lower incomes have less access to computers, smartphones, and other information and communication technologies (a phenomenon known as the "digital divide"), differences among socioeconomic groups were still present among those who did have access to these technologies. These differences are less pronounced among young people, however, suggesting the possibility that, in future, the Internet and social media may indeed become a force for promoting democracy.

One of the concerns that have been expressed about spending time on the Internet is that it would crowd out or displace the amount of time that individuals have to spend interacting face-to-face with one another as members of civic organizations (Kraut et al., 1998; Putnam, 2000). Research suggests that a more nuanced view of the relationship between Internet use and civic participation is necessary. Communications researchers Dhavan Shah, Nojin Kwak, and Lance Holbert (2001), for example, found that Internet use did affect civic engagement but that its effects depended on the purpose for which the Internet was used. Those who used the Internet for more recreational purposes, such as playing games and chatting with others, were less likely to be involved in civic activities such as such as volunteering or working on a community project, while those who used the Internet to seek out and exchange information were more likely to be civically engaged.

Researchers will need to continue to monitor the impact of the Internet, social media, and other information and communication technologies as they develop. Research suggests that these new technologies have the potential to both enhance and displace civic participation. More research is necessary to determine the conditions under which it will have these very different kinds of effects.

Dissemination of Research Results. A considerable amount of information about citizenship and civic engagement has been amassed by social scientists—more than any one book could hope to describe. How much of this knowledge is getting into the hands of those who can use it to develop programs and policies, and to the general public? It has become increasingly recognized that the transfer of knowledge and information from researchers to those who develop and promote programs and public policy does not happen automatically and that greater attention needs to be given to how this transfer occurs (Davies & Powell, 2012). Researchers must be much more involved in this process.

In the research that I and my colleagues have done, we have attempted to accomplish this in a number of ways. For example, we have taken the findings from our evaluation of the Better Beginnings, Better Futures project (a program designed to prevent children from developing social and emotional problems, discussed in chapters 3, 7, and 8), and used them in the development of a "toolkit" for those working with young children in schools and community organizations (Hayward et al., 2011). The toolkit outlines how our research results could inform the development of similar programs in other settings, describing strategies that can be used to involve community residents in the process of program development and how partnerships among child-serving organizations can be cultivated. In addition, we developed a brief video to accompany each section of the toolkit, and we made both the toolkit and videos available online at no charge (see www.bbbf.ca). We are currently in the process of conducting workshops for community program workers and policymakers to discuss ways in which our findings and approach can be used in different communities around the country.

Research findings concerning citizenship and civic participation need to be made available to the general public, as well. An informed public is a strong impetus for the development of an engaged public. Academics and other researchers need to write more books, op-ed pieces, and blogs designed for popular consumption, so that they can describe their research results and talk about how their research can be used to enhance the health and well-being of communities. Box 10.1 presents an illustration of this kind of writing; it is an op-ed article that I wrote for my local newspaper (the *Kitchener-Waterloo Record*) on youth volunteering (Pancer, 2005).

Box 10.1 **Op-Ed on Youth Civic Engagement, *Kitchener-Waterloo Record*, May 26, 2005**

Young People a Powerful Source for Good

By Mark Pancer
For *The Record*

Rebels. Delinquents. Potheads. Gang members. These are the images that many adults have of young people. This is not surprising, given some of the things we read in the newspapers, and see on television. Adults tend to see youth as a period of "sturm und drang"—storm and stress—during which young people argue constantly with their elders, flaunt their sexuality, and engage in a variety of risky behaviours such as using alcohol and drugs.

While we are right to be concerned about our children's behaviour, the stereotypes that we have of young people can do a great deal of harm. Rather than viewing youth as a community resource, and making us want to take advantage of their energy and creativity, such stereotypes make us, instead, view young people as a problem.

Research tells us, furthermore, that stereotypes of young people are just plain wrong. A recent review of psychological research on adolescence showed that the "sturm und drang" view of adolescence is overblown. While adolescents do tend to be somewhat moodier, and more likely to engage in risky behaviour, they are not the alienated and rebellious individuals they are sometimes portrayed to be.

On the contrary, research shows that young people are a powerful force for good. Every few years, Statistics Canada surveys Canadians from across the country to ask them about their volunteer work. The most recent survey, conducted in the year 2000, showed that 37% of young people between the ages of 15 and 19 volunteered over the previous year, a rate which was higher than that of any other age group. And their volunteering efforts were not one-shot, short-term affairs; on average, youth volunteers gave a whopping 136 hours of their time during the year.

The benefits of volunteering, for both our communities and for the youth themselves, are substantial. Research shows that young people who volunteer are less likely to use drugs and alcohol, get pregnant, be involved in any kind of criminal activity, or drop out of school. Youth who volunteer are more likely to go on to college or university, develop a sense of civic and social responsibility, and volunteer as adults.

Our own research substantiates these findings. Over the last several months, I and my colleagues Steve Brown, Ailsa Henderson, and Kimberly Ellis-Hale from Wilfrid Laurier University conducted surveys with nearly 1,500 young people, and in-depth interviews with 100 of them, to ask about their experiences volunteering. Half of these individuals had been part of the "younger cohort" of students who had been required to perform 40 hours of community service in order to obtain their high school diploma. The other half were from the "older cohort" of students, who did not have to fulfill such a requirement.

The experiences these students had, whether their community service was required or not, were overwhelmingly positive. Consider the experience of one young person who worked with disabled children in order to fulfill her 40 hour volunteer requirement: "It was one of the most positive experiences of my life. It was just amazing to see the difference you could make in someone's life . . . just being there, just giving them a hug or just making them smile is just big, and the people there are so devoted to each other. It's just amazing to see that."

Some have suggested that making community service mandatory undermines any "intrinsic" or natural motivation that young people have to volunteer. Our research did not support this view. Youth who volunteered because they had to were no different from those whose community service was not mandated in terms of their attitudes toward volunteering and their intentions to volunteer in the future. The overwhelming majority of both groups had a positive attitude towards volunteering.

The factor that was most significant in shaping young people's view of volunteering was the quality of their experience. Youth who felt they had made a difference in the lives of those they worked with, who were made to feel valued and appreciated by the organizations with which they volunteered, and who learned valuable skills through their service, were much more positive about their experience and had much stronger intentions to volunteer in the future. For those of us who work with young volunteers, this means that we have to ensure that we give our young people meaningful work to do and that we let them know how much we appreciate what they are doing. If we are successful, we will have young people who become life-long volunteers and active, engaged members of the community.

And then, perhaps, our stereotypes of youth will change. We will begin to view them, not as rebels and delinquents, but as peer tutors, coaches, child-care providers, hospital workers, and, ultimately, as valued partners in building a better community.

Evaluation Research. The kind of research that is probably most urgently needed is evaluation research. Evaluation research

> *involves the application of a broad range of social research methods to answer questions about the need for social programs, the way in which such programs are designed and implemented, and their effectiveness in producing desired changes or outcomes at a reasonable cost.* (Pancer, 1997, p. 49)

We have accumulated a great deal of knowledge about civic engagement. It is now time to use that knowledge to develop programs and policies that have the potential to increase and enhance civic engagement, particularly among those who are disengaged and alienated from community life. By using evaluation research methodologies, we can make decisions about who is most in need of such programs, what kinds of programs should be developed, and how they might best be implemented. Once programs and policies are in place, evaluation research can be used to assess their impact and to suggest modifications, as necessary, to ensure that they are maximally effective (Pancer, 1997; Pancer & Westhues, 1989).

Programs and Policies

While there is a considerable amount of research yet to be done to give us a full understanding of civic engagement, there is a great deal that we have already learned that can guide us in the development of programs and policies that will increase and enhance active citizenship. The following are some recommendations based on research evidence that can help in thinking about the kinds of activities, programs, and policies that are necessary.

Start with the Young

There are a number of reasons for engaging people in civic life when they are young. One reason is that civically engaged youth seem to acquire a habit for participation that can last a lifetime. Those who participate in their communities when they are young are more likely to be involved in community life years later when they become adults. Another reason is that youth is a critical time in the formation of a person's identity. Young people who participate in their communities through volunteering, social activism, and youth organization activities are more likely to develop a civic identity, in which they see themselves not just as individuals, but as part of the community, with a responsibility to contribute to community welfare. Of course, one of the main reasons for engaging people when they are young is that involved young people derive a host of benefits from their participation; they perform better at school, exhibit fewer problem behaviors, and have better physical and mental health.

Provide Quality Programs and Activities

What kinds of programs and activities will be most effective in engaging young people—and adults—in community life and sustaining this involvement over time? Research tells us that the best kinds of activities for engaging people are those in which individuals are given the opportunity to meet a variety of others (both similar to and different from themselves), work with caring adults (for youth), learn skills, explore their interests, and do things that matter or make a difference in the lives of others. To be effective in producing long-term civic engagement, activities should also be structured, in that they occur on a regular schedule, require effort and sustained attention, and are directed toward achieving a goal. Civic activities are further enhanced when individuals are given a voice in deciding that they will be doing and a chance to reflect on the meaning of what they have experienced. The community organizations in which people are involved also play an important role in initiating and sustaining civic engagement. Those organizations need to make people feel that they belong, are appreciated, and have valuable skills to contribute. They also need to convey to their members and volunteers that they are taking part in something that has a history and a set of values, in which contribution to the community is central. Organizations, such as churches, social justice groups, and charities, all of which are built around strong core values regarding service to others and building a better society, can be particularly effective in conveying these kinds of messages.

There are several programs and activities, particularly for young people, that possess many of these attributes. Community service is one such activity. It does not seem to matter whether this service is initiated as part of a service learning program or by a mandatory school requirement. The most important thing is that is has the critical attributes mentioned earlier. Community service has many of these attributes by its very nature; it involves working with caring adults, coming into contact with others, learning skills, and doing things that make a difference in the lives of those served. Youth programs run by organizations such as the

YMCA, Boy and Girl Scouts, and 4H also have many of the critical features that result in life-long civic involvement, as do youth-led and youth-driven organizations such as the International Youth Climate Movement. In-class school programs and curricula, such as CityWorks, where students discuss current issues and problems in their communities and collectively engage in activities to address these problems, also possess many of the critical attributes that promote lasting civic participation (Kahne, Chi, & Middaugh, 2006).

Reach Out to Those Who Are Disengaged

Civic participation will not increase on a population level until individuals and groups who are disengaged from their communities are brought into community life as active and valued participants. But how does one reach out to those who are disengaged or even identify them? Research tells us that by far the most common and effective way in which individuals first become involved in community groups and activities is through personal contact. They are brought into a community group or activity through the urging of a friend, teacher, parent, minister, coworker, or other person in their social network. This knowledge about the importance of personal contact led to the development of a critical component of inREACH, the gang prevention program that I described in earlier chapters (see chapters 6 and 8). The purpose of the project was to have young people living in economically disadvantaged neighborhoods get involved in more positive community activities that would make gangs look less attractive by comparison. Before any programs were developed for youth, project staff (called Youth Outreach Workers, or YOWs), armed with boxes of pizza and money for coffee, went to shopping plazas and other places where young people were known to gather and simply talked with and befriended them. During this time, they asked youth what kinds of activities most interested them. After making these personal contacts over a period of several weeks, the YOWs then worked with local community centers to develop programs that would allow youth to pursue their expressed interests and personally asked each youth to come to the program. They frequently offered to accompany the youth to the program. These youths subsequently attended the programs in large numbers, whereas before the YOWs began their work, hardly any youth had participated in programs offered by the community centers, and some centers had even given up providing youth programs.

The Better Beginnings, Better Futures project—mentioned earlier in this chapter and described in chapters 3, 7, and 8—provides another example of how personal contact can be used to increase the involvement of residents in neighborhood groups and activities. The project was designed to reduce social, emotional, and academic problems in children (aged 4 to 8) by providing in-school assistance to teachers, before- and after-school programs for the children, child management training for the parents, and community development activities for all residents of the community. A key tenet of the approach used was that community residents be involved in every aspect of the project's development. One of the project sites was located in a low-income neighborhood in the west end of Toronto, which formed the catchment area of the local elementary school (Highfield Junior School) that neighborhood children attended. Several strategies involving personal contact were used to get residents involved in the project. Project staff members were present during school registration each fall to introduce themselves and to invite parents to participate in programs. Staff members were also present when parents dropped their children off to school in the morning or picked them up after school, and staff used those opportunities to invite parents to programs. After parents had had some experience as program participants, they were invited to work as volunteers, helping deliver programs or serve on committees. A snowball approach was then used, in which involved parents invited other parents, friends, and neighbors to programs and community events sponsored by the project. As a consequence, over 100 residents came to volunteer with the project each year, and large numbers of residents attended community events sponsored by the project. The research literature, and these examples, tell us that personal contact must be used much more consciously and intentionally to initiate people's first contacts with their community. These kinds of strategies are particularly important to involve individuals who are disengaged from community life.

Provide More Opportunities for Involvement

Research tells us that civic participation is strongly influenced by the opportunities that communities and community organizations offer for individuals to get involved. Schools that provide more extracurricular clubs, teams, and activities have many more students involved in these kinds of activities. Neighborhoods that have many organizations such as YMCAs and community centers also have greater numbers of residents who participate in civic life. Indeed, one of the likeliest explanations for the relative lack of civic participation by residents of economically disadvantaged communities is the scarcity of community organizations and activities in which to get involved (Hart & Atkins, 2002; Watts & Flanagan, 2007). When these opportunities are provided, civic engagement increases. This was demonstrated in the study of the PALS (Participate and Learn Skills) program that I described in chapter 8 (Jones & Offord, 1989). This program provided for a substantial increase in the number of community activities for young people living in a poor neighborhood in the Canadian city of Ottawa. More than 70% of the youth in the community participated in one or more of the newly created activities, and as a consequence the crime rate among youth was cut nearly in half. These studies tell us that by increasing the number of clubs, teams, groups, and organizations in schools and neighborhoods, civic participation will grow, and communities will experience all the benefits that come along with increased civic engagement.

Make Organizations and Social Systems More Inclusive and Participatory

The research that I have reviewed shows that when individuals feel that they are part of something—an organization, a neighborhood, a movement—they derive many benefits. People are most likely to get this feeling through active participation in their community and its organizations. The more actively they participate, the more they benefit. Those who sit on committees, make presentations on behalf of community organizations, and take on leadership roles benefit more than those who are simply members of those organizations. But even those who are simply members of community organizations benefit from their participation. And when significant numbers of individuals in a community participate in civic life, positive outcomes for the entire community result. Research also indicates that community organizations benefit from broad citizen participation in governance and decision making. When citizens are involved in these processes, organizations become more accountable, more accessible, more representative, and more effective. These research findings tell us that to provide for greater civic participation and be maximally effective, community organizations need to be more inclusive and more participatory. One way to do this is by reserving seats on their boards of directors and key committees for community members, particularly those who represent the groups that receive the organization's services. This would mean that parents and students would serve on the governing bodies of schools, youth would sit on the boards of youth-serving organizations, and residents would work together with social service organizations to decide on services for their neighborhoods. This kind of participation can even be mandated through policy and legislation, as it is in the United Kingdom, where at least one-third of the members of the board of governors for each school must be parents of children in the school, and 20% must be residents of the local community.

Overcome Barriers

There are many barriers, both real and perceived, that stand in the way of individuals becoming more involved in community and political life. To be able to volunteer, for example, individuals must have the free time to devote to volunteer work, a means to travel to the setting in which they volunteer, the skills necessary to perform volunteer activities, and some knowledge about the kinds of things they might be asked to do as volunteers. Most individuals start volunteering because someone asks them to, so volunteering also requires that people have connections with others who already volunteer and are trustworthy. Other kinds of civic participation, such as working for a community organization, a social action group, or a political party, require the same kinds of resources and others, as well. Political participation, for example, requires psychological resources in the form of a sense of political efficacy; people must feel that their actions have the potential to influence government decisions and policy. The lack of these resources—financial, human, social, and psychological—constitutes a significant barrier to civic engagement, and these resources are particularly lacking in those who are living in poverty, belong to minority groups, and are less well-educated. The consequence is that individuals from these groups are less civically engaged and are less likely to vote, volunteer, contact public officials, sit on the boards of directors of community organizations, or be involved in more informal community activities (Levinson, 2007; Musick et al., 2000; Verba et al., 1995).

Groups in society that are disengaged from civic life also face substantial systemic barriers to greater civic participation. The poor, minorities, immigrants, and youth have to deal with negative stereotypes that prevent them from being considered as valued partners in helping to build a healthy and prosperous society. Consequently, they are less likely to be asked to do things such as sit on boards and committees or take on decision-making roles in community organizations. They also have fewer settings in their neighborhoods in which they can become involved—fewer recreation centers, YMCAs, and even fewer banks and grocery stores where neighbors can interact informally with one another. Largely because of their limited financial resources, these groups also lack political influence, and there are powerful social forces aligned against them to ensure that they don't achieve greater influence. These forces, comprising primarily those who hold the greatest amount of wealth and power, have introduced and supported policies that help them keep and even increase their power, thereby limiting both the actual and perceived influence that marginalized groups—and even the middle class—have (Bartels, 2008; Hacker & Peirson, 2010; Stiglitz, 2012). And when individuals feel they have no power and no influence, they are less likely to become civically and politically engaged.

What kinds of policies, programs, and activities can be used to overcome these barriers? On an individual level, a number of steps can be taken to reduce or eliminate barriers to civic participation. Individuals can be provided with bus fare and child care to offset the costs required to volunteer or attend the meetings of community groups. Membership fees for joining neighborhood organizations or participating in community activities can be reduced or removed. Those who have experience with civic and political organizations can devote greater effort to reaching out to others in their community who are not yet involved or engaged, and they can teach and mentor those individuals so that they can gain the skills necessary to make meaningful contributions to civic life.

To achieve broader and more significant levels of civic participation, however, changes must be made in the social and political systems that govern civic life. Electoral processes that produce greater political participation, such as proportional representation, must replace those that make people feel that their votes and their voices do not count. Limits need to be set on the extent to which those with power and financial resources can exert a disproportionate influence on government programs and policies. An example of this would be to establish policies that set limits on campaign financing, so that politicians would not be so beholden to their wealthier supporters. But how are these things to be achieved? Political scientists Jacob Hacker and Paul Pierson, commenting on the American political system in their book, *Winner-Take-All Politics,* suggest that these kinds of political reforms will be achieved through "broader participation among those whose voices are currently drowned out" (Hacker & Pierson, 2010, p. 303).

> *Reform will rest on the creation of organized, sustained pressure on legislators to make American politics more responsive and open to citizen engagement.* (p. 303)

They and others suggest that the kinds of social and political changes that are necessary will come when citizens, particularly those who are marginalized because of their social class or minority status, work together in unions, civic and environmental organizations, and social movements to reduce stereotypes, raise political consciousness, and counteract the influence of the wealthy and powerful (Ginwright, 2007; Watts & Flanagan, 2007).

Conclusion

In his classic film, *It's a Wonderful Life,* director Frank Capra tells the story of George Bailey, a man who gives up his dreams of traveling the world to take over the small building and loan association that his father ran, after his father dies of a stroke. As the bank manager, he devotes his life to helping build the homes and businesses in his town and the connections that the townspeople make with one another. When a mistake results in the loss of a large sum of money and threatens to ruin him and his bank, George contemplates suicide. He is rescued by an angel who comes down to earth to show him what his town and the people in it would have been like if he hadn't been around to support them. This town—the one that would have developed without George in it—is an ugly, mean-spirited place, devoid of social capital. When George recognizes what would have happened had he not been alive, he prays to have things in the town brought back to the way they were. In the end, all of the townspeople whom George has helped over the years come together to donate their meager savings to help George through his financial crisis.

To me, this film—shown every Christmas as a parable of faith and fellowship—is all about active citizenship. It shows how active, engaged citizens benefit from their involvement in civic life and how this involvement also benefits the communities in which they live. One of the goals of this book has been to examine the scientific basis for this message about citizenship. The research I have recounted throughout the book provides overwhelming support for the idea that active citizenship benefits both individuals and communities. Another goal of the book has been to examine the research literature to identify the key factors that influence civic engagement and to use the knowledge about these factors to help formulate guidelines for the development of programs and policies that will build and enhance civic participation. My hope is that these goals have been accomplished.

REFERENCES

Adams, G. R., Shea, J., & Fitch, S. A. (1979). Toward the development of an objective assessment of ego-identity status. *Journal of Youth and Adolescence, 8*(2), 223–237.

Adman, P. (2008). Does workplace experience enhance political participation? A critical test of a venerable hypothesis. *Political Behavior, 30*(1), 115–138.

Albanesi, C., Cicognani, E., & Zani, B. (2007). Sense of community, civic engagement and social well-being in Italian adolescents. *Journal of Community & Applied Social Psychology, 17*(5), 387–406.

Allen, J. P., Philliber, S., Herrling, S., & Kuperminc, G. P. (1997). Preventing teen pregnancy and academic failure: Experimental evaluation of a developmentally based approach. *Child Development, 68*(4), 729–742.

Allen, M., & Burrell, N. (2002). The negativity effect in political advertising: A meta-analysis. In J. P. Dillar & M. Pfau (Eds.), *The persuasion handbook: Developments in theory and practice* (pp. 83–96). Thousand Oaks, CA: Sage.

Allport, G. (1985). The historical background of social psychology. In G. Lindzey & E. Aronson (Eds.), *The handbook of social psychology* (3rd ed., Vol. 1, pp. 1–46). New York: Random House.

American National Election Studies (n.d.). *The ANES guide to public opinion and electoral behavior: External political efficacy index 1952–2008.* http://www.electionstudies.org/nesguide/toptable/tab5b_4.htm

Anderson-Butcher, D., Newsome, W. S., & Ferrari, T. M. (2003). Participation in boys and girls clubs and relationships to youth outcomes. *Journal of Community Psychology, 31*(1), 39–55.

Andolina, M. W., Jenkins, K., Zukin, C., & Keeter, S. (2003). Habits from home, lessons from school: Influences on youth civic engagement. *PS-Political Science & Politics, 36*(2), 275–280.

Arnstein, S. R. (1969). A ladder of citizen participation. *Journal of the American Planning Association, 35*(4), 216–224.

Aspy, C. B., Vesely, S. K., Tolma, E. L., Oman, R. F., Rodine, S., Marshall, L., & Fluhr, J. (2010). Youth assets and delayed coitarche across developmental age groups. *Journal of Early Adolescence, 30*(2), 277–304.

Astin, A. W., & Sax, L. J. (1998). How undergraduates are affected by service participation. *Journal of College Student Development, 39*(3), 251–263.

Astin, A. W., Sax, L. J., & Avalos, J. (1999). Long-term effects of volunteerism during the undergraduate years. *Review of Higher Education, 22*(2), 187–202.

Astin, A. W., Vogelsang, L. J., Ikeda, E. K., & Yee, J. A. (2000). *How service learning affects students.* Los Angeles, CA: Higher Education Research Institute, UCLA.

Attree, P., French, B., Milton, B., Povall, S., Whitehead, M., & Popay, J. (2011). The experience of community engagement for individuals: A rapid review of evidence. *Health & Social Care in the Community, 19*(3), 250–260.

Ayala, L. J. (2000). Trained for democracy: The differing effects of voluntary and involuntary organizations on political participation. *Political Research Quarterly, 53*(1), 99–115.

Bandura, A. (1977). *Social learning theory*. Englewood Cliffs, NJ: Prentice-Hall.

Bandura, A. (1986). *Social foundations of thought and action*. Englewood Cliffs, NJ: Prentice-Hall.

Barber, B. L., Eccles, J. S., & Stone, M. R. (2001). Whatever happened to the jock, the brain, and the princess? Young adult pathways linked to adolescent activity involvement and social identity. *Journal of Adolescent Research, 16*(5), 429–455.

Barker, R. G., & Gump, P. V. (1964). *Big school, small school: High school size and student behavior*. Stanford, CA: Stanford University Press.

Bart, C., Baetz, M. C., & Pancer, S. M. (2009). Leveraging human capital through an employee volunteer program: The case of the Ford Motor Company of Canada. *Journal of Intellectual Capital, 10*, 121–134.

Bartels, L. M. (2008). *Unequal democracy: The political economy of the new gilded age*. Princeton, NJ: Princeton University Press.

Bartko, W. T., & Eccles, J. S. (2003). Adolescent participation in structured and unstructured activities: A person-oriented analysis. *Journal of Youth and Adolescence, 32*(4), 233–241.

Baumrind, D. (1991). Effective parenting of adolescents. In P. Cowan & E. M. Hetherington (Eds.), *The effects of transitions on families* (pp. 111–163). Hillsdale, NJ: Erlbaum.

Beane, J., Turner, J., Jones, D., & Lipka, R. (1981). Long-term effects of community-service programs. *Curriculum Inquiry, 11*(2), 143–155.

Beck, P. A. (1991). Voters' intermediation environments in the 1988 presidential contest. *Public Opinion Quarterly, 55*(3), 371–394.

Becker, P. E., & Dhingra, P. H. (2001). Religious involvement and volunteering: Implications for civil society. *Sociology of Religion, 62*(3), 315–335.

Bengtson, V. L. (1975). Generation and family effects in value socialization. *American Sociological Review, 40*(3), 358–371.

Benson, P. L., & Scales, P. C. (2009). The definition and preliminary measurement of thriving in adolescence. *Journal of Positive Psychology, 4*(1), 85–104.

Berkman, L. F., & Glass, T. (2000). Social integration, social networks, social support, and health. In L. F. Berkman & I. Kawachi (Eds.), *Social epidemiology* (pp. 137–173). New York: Oxford University Press.

Berry, H. L., & Welsh, J. A. (2010). Social capital and health in Australia: An overview from the household, income and labour dynamics in Australia survey. *Social Science & Medicine, 70*(4), 588–596.

Beyerlein, K., & Chaves, M. (2003). The political activities of religious congregations in the United States. *Journal for the Scientific Study of Religion, 42*(2), 229–246.

Billig, S., Root, S., & Jesse, D. (2005). *The impact of participation in service-learning on high school students' civic engagement*. Medford, MA: The Center for Information and Research on Civic Learning and Engagement (CIRCLE).

Blair, J., LaFrance, S., & Murray, A. (1999). *Prevalence and perceptions of client/consumer board participation*. Washington, DC: The National Assembly of National Voluntary Health and Social Welfare Organizations.

Blais, A., & Carty, R. K. (1990). Does proportional representation foster voter turnout? *European Journal of Political Research, 18*(2), 167–181.

Blakely, T. A., Kennedy, B. P., & Kawachi, I. (2001). Socioeconomic inequality in voting participation and self-rated health. *American Journal of Public Health, 91*(1), 99–104.

Bloom, B. L. (1973). *Community mental health: A historical and critical analysis*. New York: General Learning Press.

Bohnert, A. M., & Garber, J. (2007). Prospective relations between organized activity participation and psychopathology during adolescence. *Journal of Abnormal Child Psychology, 35*(6), 1021–1033.

Bohnert, A. M., Kane, P., & Garber, J. (2008). Organized activity participation and internalizing and externalizing symptoms: Reciprocal relations during adolescence. *Journal of Youth and Adolescence, 37*(2), 239–250.

Bolland, J. M., & McCallum, D. M. (2002). Neighboring and community mobilization in high-poverty inner-city neighborhoods. *Urban Affairs Review, 38*(1), 42–69.

Borgonovi, F. (2008). Doing well by doing good. The relationship between formal volunteering and self-reported health and happiness. *Social Science & Medicine, 66*(11), 2321–2334.

Bradford, K., Vaughn, L. B., & Barber, B. K. (2008). When there is conflict: Interparental conflict, parent-child conflict, and youth problem behaviors. *Journal of Family Issues, 29*(6), 780–805.

Bradley, R. H., & Corwyn, R. F. (2002). Socioeconomic status and child development. *Annual Review of Psychology, 53*, 371–399.

Brame, R., Turner, M. G., Paternoster, R., & Bushway, S. D. (2012). Cumulative prevalence of arrest from ages 8 to 23 in a national sample. *Pediatrics, 129*(1), 21–27.

Brown, K. M., Hoye, R., & Nicholson, M. (2012). Self-esteem, self-efficacy, and social connectedness as mediators of the relationship between volunteering and well-being. *Journal of Social Service Research, 38*(4), 468–483.

Burby, R. J. (2003). Making plans that matter: Citizen involvement and government action. *Journal of the American Planning Association, 69*(1), 33–49.

Busseri, M. A., Rose-Krasnor, L., Pancer, S. M., Adams, G., Birnie-Lefcovitch, S., Polivy, J., Pratt, M. W., & Wintre, M. (2011). A longitudinal study of breadth and intensity of activity involvement and the transition to university. *Journal of Research on Adolescence, 21*(2), 512–518.

Busseri, M. A., Rose-Krasnor, L., Willoughby, T., & Chalmers, H. (2006). A longitudinal examination of breadth and intensity of youth activity involvement and successful development. *Developmental Psychology, 42*(6), 1313–1326.

Cameron, G., Peirson, L., & Pancer, S. M. (1994). Resident participation in the Better Beginnings, Better Futures prevention project: Part 2—factors that facilitate and hinder involvement. *Canadian Journal of Community Mental Health, 13*, 213–227.

Campbell, D. E. (2004). Acts of faith: Churches and political engagement. *Political Behavior, 26*(2), 155–180.

Campbell, D. E. (2006). *Why we vote: How schools and communities shape our civic life.* Princeton, NJ: Princeton University Press.

Campbell, D. E. (2008). Voice in the classroom: How an open classroom climate fosters political engagement among adolescents. *Political Behavior, 30*(4), 437–454.

Carballo, M. (2000). *Religion in the world at the end of the millennium (Gallup International Millenium Survey).* Washington, DC: Gallup International.

Carlo, G., Hardy, S., & Alberts, M. (2006). Moral exemplars. In L. Sherrod, C. FLanadan & R. Kassimir (Eds.), *Youth activism: An international encyclopedia, Vol. 2* (pp. 412–419). Westport, CN: Greenwood Publishing Company.

Catalano, R. F., & Hawkins, J. D. (1996). The social development model: A theory of antisocial behavior. In J. D. Hawkins (Ed.), *Delinquency and crime: Current theories* (pp. 149–197). Cambridge, U.K.: Cambridge University Press.

Centers for Disease Control and Prevention (2008). *Nationally representative CDC study finds 1 in 4 teenage girls has a sexually transmitted disease.* Atlanta, GA: Centers for Disease Control and Prevention. http://www.cdc.gov/stdconference/2008/press/release-11march2008.pdf

Centers for Disease Control and Prevention (2014). *2009 HIV among youth.* Atlanta, GA: Centers for Disease Control and Prevention. http://www.cdc.gov/hiv/risk/age/youth/

Chavis, D. M., & Wandersman, A. (1990). Sense of community in the urban-environment—A catalyst for participation and community-development. *American Journal of Community Psychology, 18*(1), 55–77.

Checkoway, B. (1982). Public-participation in health-planning agencies: Promise and practice. *Journal of Health Politics Policy and Law, 7*(3), 723–733.

Checkoway, B., O'Rourke, T. W., & Bull, D. (1984). Correlates of consumer participation in health planning agencies: Findings and implications from a national survey. *Policy Studies Review, 3*, 296–310.

Cialdini, R. B., Reno, R. R., & Kallgren, C. A. (1990). A focus theory of normative conduct—Recycling the concept of norms to reduce littering in public places. *Journal of Personality and Social Psychology, 58*(6), 1015–1026.

Cohen, S., & Wills, T. A. (1985). Stress, social support, and the buffering hypothesis. *Psychological Bulletin, 98*(2), 310–357.

Colby, A., & Damon, W. (1992). *Some do care: Contemporary lives of moral commitment.* New York: Free Press.

Conover, P. J., & Searing, D. D. (2000). A political socialization perspective. In L. M. McDonnell, P. M. Timpane & R. Benjamin (Eds.), *Rediscovering the democratic purposes of education* (pp. 91–124). Lawrence, Kansas: University Press of Kansas.

Corporation for National and Community Service, (2008). *Long-distance volunteering in the United States, 2007.* Washington, DC: Office of Research and Policy Development, Corporation for National and Community Service. http://www.volunteeringinamerica.gov/assets/resources/Long-Distance_Volunteering.pdf

Conway, J. M., Amel, E. L., & Gerwien, D. P. (2009). Teaching and learning in the social context: A meta-analysis of service learning's effects on academic, personal, social, and citizenship outcomes. *Teaching of Psychology, 36*(4), 233–245.

Crawford, M. J., Rutter, D., Manley, C., Weaver, T., Bhui, K., Fulop, N., & Tyrer, P. (2002). Systematic review of involving patients in the planning and development of health care. *British Medical Journal, 325*(7375), 1263–1265.

Crean, H. F. (2012). Youth activity involvement, neighborhood adult support, individual decision making skills, and early adolescent delinquent behaviors: Testing a conceptual model. *Journal of Applied Developmental Psychology, 33*(4), 175–188.

Crosby, R. A., DiClemente, R. J., Wingood, G. M., Harrington, K., Davies, S., & Oh, M. K. (2002). Activity of African-American female teenagers in black organisations is associated with STD/HIV protective behaviours: A prospective analysis. *Journal of Epidemiology and Community Health, 56*(7), 549–550.

Cutlip, A. C., Bankston, W. B., & Lee, M. R. (2010). Civic community and nonmetropolitan white suicide. *Archives of Suicide Research, 14*(3), 261–265.

Cutrona, C. E., & Russell, D. W. (1990). Type of social support and specific stress: Toward a theory of optimal matching. In B. R. Sarason, I. G. Sarason & G. R. Pierce (Eds.), *Social support: An interactional view* (pp. 319–367). New York: John Wiley & Sons.

da Silva, L., Sanson, A., Smart, D., & Toumbourou, J. (2004). Civic responsibility among Australian adolescents: Testing two competing models. *Journal of Community Psychology, 32*(3), 229–255.

Davies, H. T. O., & Powell, A. E. (2012). Communicating social research findings more effectively: What can we learn from other fields? *Evidence & Policy, 8*(2), 213–233.

Deci, E. L., & Ryan, R. M. (1987). The support of autonomy and the control of behavior. *Journal of Personality and Social Psychology, 53*(6), 1024–1037.

Delli Carpini, M. X., & Keeter, S. (1996). *What Americans know about politics and why it matters.* New Haven, CT: Yale University Press.

Denault, A. S., Poulin, F., & Pedersen, S. (2009). Intensity of participation in organized youth activities during the high school years: Longitudinal associations with adjustment. *Applied Developmental Science, 13*(2), 74–87.

Dewey, J. (1910). *How we think*. Lexington, MA: Heath (reprinted 1991, Buffalo, NY: Prometheus Books).

Diener, E., Emmons, R. A., Larsen, R. J., & Griffin, S. (1985). The satisfaction with life scale. *Journal of Personality Assessment, 49*(1), 71–75.

Driskell, R. L., Lyon, L., & Embry, E. (2008). Civic engagement and religious activities: Examining the influence of religious tradition and participation. *Sociological Spectrum, 28*(5), 578–601.

Duke, N. N., Skay, C. L., Pettingell, S. L., & Borowsky, I. W. (2009). From adolescent connections to social capital: Predictors of civic engagement in young adulthood. *Journal of Adolescent Health, 44*(2), 161–168.

Duncan, L. E., & Stewart, A. J. (1995). Still bringing the vietnam-war home: Sources of contemporary student-activism. *Personality and Social Psychology Bulletin, 21*(9), 914–924.

Dworkin, J. B., Larson, R., & Hansen, D. (2003). Adolescents' accounts of growth experiences in youth activities. *Journal of Youth and Adolescence, 32*(1), 17–26.

Eccles, J. S., & Barber, B. L. (1999). Student council, volunteering, basketball, or marching band: What kind of extracurricular involvement matters? *Journal of Adolescent Research, 14*(1), 10–43.

Eccles, J. S., Barber, B. L., Stone, M., & Hunt, J. (2003). Extracurricular activities and adolescent development. *Journal of Social Issues, 59*(4), 865–889.

Ehrlich, T. (Ed.). (2000). *Civic responsibility and higher education*. Westport, CT: The American Council on Education and the Onyx Press.

Elder, C., Leaver-Dunn, D., Wang, M. Q., Nagy, S., & Green, L. (2000). Organized group activity as a protective factor against adolescent substance use. *American Journal of Health Behavior, 24*(2), 108–113.

Erikson, E. H. (1968). *Childhood and society (2nd edition)*. New York: Norton.

Erikson, E. H. (1974). *Dimensions of a new identity*. New York: Norton.

Eyler, J. (2002). Reflection: Linking service and learning—Linking students and communities. *Journal of Social Issues, 58*(3), 517–534.

Feldman, A. F., & Matjasko, J. L. (2005). The role of school-based extracurricular activities in adolescent development: A comprehensive review and future directions. *Review of Educational Research, 75*(2), 159–210.

Fergus, S., & Zimmerman, M. A. (2005). Adolescent resilience: A framework for understanding healthy development in the face of risk. *Annual Review of Public Health, 26*, 399–419.

Fieldhouse, E., Tranmer, M., & Russell, A. (2007). Something about young people or something about elections? Electoral participation of young people in Europe: Evidence from a multilevel analysis of the European Social Survey. *European Journal of Political Research, 46*(6), 797–822.

Flanagan, C. A., Cumsille, P., Gill, S., & Gallay, L. S. (2007). School and community climates and civic commitments: Patterns for ethnic minority and majority students. *Journal of Educational Psychology, 99*(2), 421–431.

Flanagan, C. A., & Faison, N. (2001). Youth civic development: Implications of research for social policy and programs. *Social policy Report, 15*(1), 3–14.

Flanagan, C. A., Jonsson, B., Botcheva, L., Csapo, B., Bowes, J., Macek, P., Averina, I., & Sheblanova, E. (1999). Adolescents and the "Social Contract": Developmental roots of citizenship in seven countries. In M. Yates & J. Youniss (Eds.), *International perspectives on community service and activism in youth* (pp. 135–155). Cambridge, UK: Cambridge University Press.

Fletcher, A. C., Elder, G. H., & Mekos, D. (2000). Parental influences on adolescent involvement in community activities. *Journal of Research on Adolescence, 10*(1), 29–48.

Fredricks, J. A., & Eccles, J. S. (2006). Is extracurricular participation associated with beneficial outcomes? Concurrent and longitudinal relations. *Developmental Psychology, 42*(4), 698–713.

Fredricks, J. A., & Eccles, J. S. (2008). Participation in extracurricular activities in the middle school years: Are there developmental benefits for African American and European American youth? *Journal of Youth and Adolescence, 37*(9), 1029–1043.

Freeman, R. B. (1997). Working for nothing: The supply of volunteer labor. *Journal of Labor Economics, 15*(1), S140–S166.

Galston, W. A. (2001). Political knowledge, political engagement, and civic education. *Annual Review of Political Science, 4*, 217–234.

Ger, G., & Belk, R. W. (1996). Cross-cultural differences in materialism. *Journal of Economic Psychology, 17*(1), 55–77.

Giamartino, G. A., & Wandersman, A. (1983). Organizational-climate correlates of viable urban block organizations. *American Journal of Community Psychology, 11*(5), 529–541.

Ginwright, S. A. (2007). Black youth activism and the role of critical social capital in Black community organizations. *American Behavioral Scientist, 51*(3), 403–418.

Glanville, J. L. (1999). Political socialization or selection? Adolescent extracurricular participation and political activity in early adulthood. *Social Science Quarterly, 80*(2), 279–290.

Greenberg, A. (2000). The church and the revitalization of politics and community. *Political Science Quarterly, 115*(3), 377–394.

Greenberg, E. S., Grunberg, L., & Daniel, K. (1996). Industrial work and political participation: Beyond "simple spillover." *Political Research Quarterly, 49*(2), 305–330.

Greenberger, E. & Bond, L., (1984). *Psychosocial maturity inventory.* Irvine, CA: Department of Social Ecology, University of California, Irvine.

Gross, M. L. (1994). Jewish rescue in Holland and France during the World-War-II—Moral cognition and collective action. *Social Forces, 73*(2), 463–496.

Grusec, J. E., & Goodnow, J. J. (1994). Impact of parental discipline methods on the child's internalization of values—A reconceptualization of current points-of-view. *Developmental Psychology, 30*(1), 4–19.

Grusec, J. E., & Skubiski, S. L. (1970). Model nurturance, demand characteristics of the modeling experiment, and altruism. *Journal of Personality and Social Psychology, 14*(4), 352–359.

Hacker, J. S., & Pierson, P. (2010). *Winner-take-all politics: How Washington made the rich richer—and turned its back on the middle class.* New York: Simon & Shuster.

Hall, M., McKeown, L., & Roberts, K. (2001). *Caring Canadians, involved Canadians: Highlights from the 2000 National Survey of Giving, Volunteering and Participating.* Ottawa, ON: Statistics, Canada. http://sectorsource.ca/sites/default/files/rp_2000_nsgvp_highlights.pdf

Hamilton, B. E., & Ventura, S. J. (2012). *Birth rates for U.S. teenagers reach historic lows for all age and ethnic groups.* NCHS data brief, no. 89. Hyattsville, MD: U.S. National Center for Health

Hamilton, S. F., & Fenzel, L. M. (1988). The impact of volunteer experience on adolescent social development: Evidence of program effects. *Journal of Adolescent Research, 3*(1), 65–80.

Hanks, M., & Eckland, B. K. (1978). Adult voluntary-associations and adolescent socialization. *Sociological Quarterly, 19*(3), 481–490.

Hansen, D. M., Larson, R. W., & Dworkin, J. B. (2003). What adolescents learn in organized youth activities: A survey of self-reported developmental experiences. *Journal of Research on Adolescence, 13*(1), 25–55.

Hardy, S. A., Pratt, M. W., Pancer, S. M., Olsen, J. A., & Lawford, H. L. (2011). Community and religious involvement as contexts of identity change across late adolescence and emerging adulthood. *International Journal of Behavioral Development, 35*(2), 125–135.

Harris, A. H. S., & Thoresen, C. E. (2005). Volunteering is associated with delayed mortality in older people: Analysis of the longitudinal study of aging. *Journal of Health Psychology, 10*(6), 739–752.

Harrison, P. A., & Narayan, G. (2003). Differences in behavior, psychological factors, and environmental factors associated with participation in school sports and other activities in adolescence. *Journal of School Health, 73*(3), 113–120.

Hart, D. (2011). *Relations with institutions matter too: Neighborhood organizations influence civic participation in American youth.* Paper presented at the Society for Research on Child Development, Montreal, Quebec, Canada.
Hart, D., & Atkins, R. (2002). Civic competence in urban youth. *Applied Developmental Science, 6*(4), 227–236.
Hart, D., Atkins, R., & Ford, D. (1999). Family influences on the formation of moral identity in adolescence: Longitudinal analyses. *Journal of Moral Education, 28*(3), 375–386.
Hart, D., Donnelly, T. M., Youniss, J., & Atkins, R. (2007). High school community service as a predictor of adult voting and volunteering. *American Educational Research Journal, 44*(1), 197–219.
Hayward, K., Loomis, C., Nelson, G., Pancer, S. M., & Peters, R. D. (2011). *A toolkit for building better beginnings and better futures.* Kingston, Ontario, Canada: Better Beginnings, Better Futures. http://bbbf.ca/Home/tabid/520/language/en-US/Default.aspx
Helliwell, J. F. (2007). Well-being and social capital: Does suicide pose a puzzle? *Social Indicators Research, 81*(3), 455–496.
Helliwell, J. F., & Putnam, R. D. (2000). *Economic growth and social capital in Italy.* Washington: World Bank Inst.
Helliwell, J. F., & Putnam, R. D. (2004). The social context of well-being. *Philosophical Transactions of the Royal Society of London Series B-Biological Sciences, 359*(1449), 1435–1446.
Henderson, A., Brown, S. D., & Pancer, S. M. (2012). Political and social dimensions of civic engagement: The impact of compulsory community service. *Politics and Policy, 40*(1), 93–130.
Henderson, A., Brown, S. D., Pancer, S. M., & Ellis-Hale, K. (2007). Mandated community service in high school and subsequent civic engagement: The case of the "Double cohort" in Ontario, Canada. *Journal of Youth and Adolescence, 36*(7), 849–860.
Henderson, A., Pancer, S. M., & Brown, S. D. (2014). Creating effective civic engagement policy for adolescents: Quantitative and qualitative evaluations of compulsory community service. *Journal of Adolescent Research, 29*(1), 120–154.
Hodgkinson, V. A. (2003). Volunteering in global perspective. In P. Dekker & L. Hallman (Eds.). *The values of volunteering: Cross-cultural perspectives* (pp. 35–53). New York: Kluwer Academic/Plenum Publishers.
Hodgkinson, V. A., & Weitzman, M. S. (1997). *Volunteering and giving among American teenagers 14 to 17 years of age: 1996 edition.* Washington, DC: Independent Sector.
Holtgrave, D. R., & Crosby, R. A. (2003). Social capital, poverty, and income inequality as predictors of gonorrhoea, syphilis, chlamydia and AIDS case rates in the United States. *Sexually Transmitted Infections, 79*(1), 62–64.
Hooghe, M., & Claes, E. (2001). Civic education in Europe: Comparative policy perspectives from the Netherlands, Belgium, and France. In J. Youniss & P. Levine (Eds.), *Engaging young people in civic life* (pp. 219–234). Nashville, TN: Vanderbilt University Press.
Horn, A. S. (2012). The cultivation of a pro-social value orientation though community service: An examination of organizational context, social facilitation, and duration. *Journal of Youth and Adolescence, 41*, 948–968.
Hoskins, B., & Mascherini, M. (2009). Measuring active citizenship through the development of a composite indicator. *Social Indicators Research, 90*(3), 459–488.
Inter Press Service News Agency (2005). Tsunami impact: EU Pledges Ongoing Support. http://www.ipsnews.net/2005/12/tsunami-impact-eu-pledges-ongoing-support/
Jackman, R. W. (1987). Political-institutions and voter turnout in the industrial democracies. *American Political Science Review, 81*(2), 405–423.
Jacobs, J. (2004). *Dark age ahead.* New York: Random House.
Janoski, T., & Wilson, J. (1995). Pathways to voluntarism: Family socialization and status transmission models. *Social Forces, 74*(1), 271–292.
Jennings, M. K. (2002). Generation units and the student protest movement in the United States: An intra- and intergenerational analysis. *Political Psychology, 23*(2), 303–324.

Jennings, M. K., & Niemi, R. G. (1968). Transmission of political values from parent to child. *American Political Science Review, 62*(1), 169–184.

Jennings, M. K., & Niemi, R. G. (1974). *The political character of adolescence.* Princeton, NJ: Princeton University Press.

Jennings, M. K., Stoker, L., & Bowers, J. (2009). Politics across generations: Family transmission reexamined. *Journal of Politics, 71*(3), 782–799.

Jimenez, T. I., Musitu, G., Ramos, M. J., & Murgui, S. (2009). Community involvement and victimization at school: an analysis through family, personal and social adjustment. *Journal of Community Psychology, 37*(8), 959–974.

Johnson, M. K., Beebe, T., Mortimer, J. T., & Snyder, M. (1998). Volunteerism in adolescence: A process perspective. *Journal of Research on Adolescence, 8*(3), 309–332.

Jones, M. B., & Offord, D. R. (1989). Reduction of antisocial-behavior in poor children by non-school skill-development. *Journal of Child Psychology and Psychiatry and Allied Disciplines, 30*(5), 737–750.

Jones-Correa, M. A., & Leal, D. L. (2001). Political participation: Does religion matter? *Political Research Quarterly, 54*(4), 751–770.

Kahn, K. F., & Kenney, P. J. (1999). Do negative campaigns mobilize or suppress turnout? Clarifying the relationship between negativity and participation. *American Political Science Review, 93*(4), 877–889.

Kahne, J., Chi, B., & Middaugh, E. (2006). Building social capital for civic and political engagement: The potential of high-school civics courses. *Canadian Journal of Education, 29*(2), 387–409.

Karp, J. A., & Banducci, S. A. (2008). Political efficacy and participation in twenty-seven democracies: How electoral systems shape political behaviour. *British Journal of Political Science, 38*, 311–334.

Kasser, T. (2002). *The high price of materialism.* Cambridge, MA: MIT Press.

Kasser, T. (2011). Cultural values and the well-being of future generations: A cross-national study. *Journal of Cross-Cultural Psychology, 42*(2), 206–215.

Kasser, T., Cohn, S., Kanner, A. D., & Ryan, R. M. (2007). Some costs of American corporate capitalism: A psychological exploration of value and goal conflicts. *Psychological Inquiry, 18*(1), 1–22.

Kawachi, I., Kennedy, B. P., & Glass, R. (1999). Social capital and self-rated health: A contextual analysis. *American Journal of Public Health, 89*(8), 1187–1193.

Kawachi, I., Kennedy, B. P., Lochner, K., & Prothrow-Stith, D. (1997). Social capital, income inequality, and mortality. *American Journal of Public Health, 87*(9), 1491–1498.

Keeter, S., Zukin, C., Andolina, M. W., & Jenkins, J. (2002). *The civic and political health of the nation: A generational portrait.* Medford, MA: The Center for Information and Research on Civic Learning and Engagement (CIRCLE). http://www.civicyouth.org/research/products/Civic_Political_Health.pdf

Kegler, M. C., Painter, J. E., Twiss, J. M., Aronson, R., & Norton, B. L. (2009). Evaluation findings on community participation in the California Healthy Cities and Communities program. *Health Promotion International, 24*(4), 300–310.

Kelly, D. C. (2006). Parents' influence on youths' civic behaviors: The civic context of the caregiving environment. *Families in Society-the Journal of Contemporary Social Services, 87*(3), 447–455.

Kennedy, B. P., Kawachi, I., Prothrow-Stith, D., Lochner, K., & Gupta, V. (1998). Social capital, income inequality, and firearm violent crime. *Social Science & Medicine, 47*(1), 7–17.

Kenny, C. B. (1992). Political participation and effects from the social environment. *American Journal of Political Science, 36* (1), 259–267.

Kerrisey, J. & Schofer, E. (2013). Union membership and political participation in the United States. *Social Forces, 91*, 825–928.

Kim, D., & Kawachi, I. (2006). A multilevel analysis of key forms of community- and individual-level social capital as predictors of self-rated health in the United States. *Journal of Urban Health-Bulletin of the New York Academy of Medicine, 83*(5), 813–826.

Kim, D., Subramanian, S. V., Gortmaker, S. L., & Kawachi, I. (2006). US state- and county-level social capital in relation to obesity and physical inactivity: A multilevel, multivariable analysis. *Social Science & Medicine, 63*(4), 1045–1059.

Kinney, D. A. (1993). From nerds to normals: The recovery of identity among adolescents from middle school to high school. *Sociology of Education, 66*(1), 21–40.

Klandermans, B., & Oegema, D. (1987). Potentials, networks, motivations, and barriers: Steps towards participation in social-movements. *American Sociological Review, 52*(4), 519–531.

Klar, M., & Kasser, T. (2009). Some benefits of being an activist: Measuring activism and its role in psychological well-being. *Political Psychology, 30*(5), 755–777.

Knack, S. (2002). Social capital and the quality of government: Evidence from the states. *American Journal of Political Science, 46*(4), 772–785.

Knafo, A., & Schwartz, S. H. (2008). Accounting for parent-child value congruence: Theoretical considerations and empirical evidence. In U. Schonpflug (Ed.), *Perspectives on cultural transmission* (pp. 240–268). Oxford, UK: Oxford University Press.

Kosterman, R., & Feshbach, S. (1989). Toward a measure of patriotic and nationalistic attitudes. *Political Psychology, 10*(2), 257–274.

Krampen, G. (2000). Transition of adolescent political action orientations to voting behavior in early adulthood in view of a social-cognitive action theory model of personality. *Political Psychology, 21*(2), 277–297.

Kraut, R., Patterson, M., Lundmark, V., Kiesler, S., Mukopadhyay, T., & Scherlis, W. (1998). Internet paradox: A social technology that reduces social involvement and psychological well-being? *American Psychologist, 53*, 1017–1031.

Krugman, P. (2007). *The conscience of a liberal.* New York: W.W. Norton & Company.

Ladewig, H., & Thomas, J. K. (1987). *Assessing the impact of 4-H on former members: The 4-H alumni study.* College Station, TX: Texas A & M University.

Lam, P. Y. (2002). As the flocks gather: How religion affects voluntary association participation. *Journal for the Scientific Study of Religion, 41*(3), 405–422.

Lamborn, S. D., Mounts, N. S., Steinberg, L., & Dornbusch, S. M. (1991). Patterns of competence and adjustment among adolescents from authoritative, authoritarian, indulgent, and neglectful families. *Child Development, 62*(5), 1049–1065.

Lancee, B., & ter Hoeven, C. L. (2010). Self-rated health and sickness-related absence: The modifying role of civic participation. *Social Science & Medicine, 70*(4), 570–574.

Landau, S. (2004). *The business of America: How consumers have replaced citizens and how we can reverse the trend.* New York: Routledge.

Langton, K. P., & Jennings, M. K. (1968). Political socialization and high school civics curriculum in United States. *American Political Science Review, 62*(3), 852–867.

Larson, R. W., Hansen, D. M., & Moneta, G. (2006). Differing profiles of developmental experiences across types of organized youth activities. *Developmental Psychology, 42*(5), 849–863.

Larson, R. W., & Walker, K. C. (2010). Dilemmas of practice: Challenges to program quality encountered by youth program leaders. *American Journal of Community Psychology, 45*(3–4), 338–349.

Latane, B., & Darley, J. (1970). *The unresponsive bystander: Why doesn't he help?* New York: Appleton-Century-Crofts.

Lau, R. R., Sigelman, L., & Rovner, I. B. (2007). The effects of negative political campaigns: A meta-analytic reassessment. *Journal of Politics, 69*(4), 1176–1209.

Layte, R. (2012). The association between income inequality and mental health: Testing status anxiety, social capital, and neo-materialist explanations. *European Sociological Review, 28*(4), 498–511.

Lee, M. R. (2008). Civic community in the hinterland: Toward a theory of rural social structure and violence. *Criminology, 46*(2), 447–478.

Lerner, R. M., Lerner, J. V., Almerigi, J. B., Theokas, C., Phelps, E., Gestsdottir, S., et al. (2005). Positive youth development, participation in community youth development programs, and community contributions of fifth-grade adolescents: Findings from the first wave of the 4-H study of positive youth development. *Journal of Early Adolescence, 25*(1), 17–71.

Lerner, R. M., Lerner, J. V., Phelps, E., et al. (2009). *Waves of the future: The first five years of the 4-H study of positive youth development.* Boston, MA: Institute for Applied Research in Youth Development, Tufts University.

Levinson, M. (2007). *The civic achievement gap.* CIRCLE Working Paper 51. Medford, MA: The Center for Information and Research on Civic Learning and Engagement (CIRCLE).

Lewis, M. A., & Noguchi, E. (2008). My neighbors made me do it: An exploration of a neighborhood network model of activism. *Journal of Statistical Mechanics-Theory and Experiment,* no. 8 (August).

Lochner, K. A., Kawachi, I., Brennan, R. T., & Buka, S. L. (2003). Social capital and neighborhood mortality rates in Chicago. *Social Science & Medicine, 56*(8), 1797–1805.

London, P. (1970). The rescuers: Motivational hypotheses about Christians who saved Jews from the Nazis (pp. 241–250). In J. Macaulay & L. Berkowitz (Eds.), *Altruism and helping behavior.* New York: Academic Press.

Lopez, M. H., Levine, P., Both, D., Kiesa, A., Kirby, E., & Marcelo, K. (2006). *The 2006 civic and political health of the nation: A detailed look at how youth participate in politics and communities.* College Park, MD: The Center for Information and Research on Civic Learning and Engagement (CIRCLE).

Losito, B., & Mintrop, R. (2001). The teaching of civic education. In J. Torney-Purta, R. Lehmann, H. Oswald & W. Schulz (Eds.), *Citizenship and education in twenty-eight countries: Civic knowledge and engagement at age fourteen* (pp. 157–173). Amsterdam: IEA.

Magen, Z., Birenbaum, M., & Ilovich, T. (1992). Adolescents from disadvantaged neighborhoods—Personal characteristics as related to volunteer involvement. *International Journal for the Advancement of Counselling, 15*(1), 47–59.

Mahatmya, D., & Lohman, B. (2011). Predictors of late adolescent delinquency: The protective role of after-school activities in low-income families. *Children and Youth Services Review, 33*(7), 1309–1317.

Mahoney, J. L. (2000). School extracurricular activity participation as a moderator in the development of antisocial patterns. *Child Development, 71*(2), 502–516.

Mahoney, J. L., Cairns, B. D., & Farmer, T. W. (2003). Promoting interpersonal competence and educational success through extracurricular activity participation. *Journal of Educational Psychology, 95*(2), 409–418.

Mahoney, J. L., & Cairns, R. B. (1997). Do extracurricular activities protect against early school dropout? *Developmental Psychology, 33*(2), 241–253.

Mahoney, J. L., & Magnusson, D. (2001). Parent participation in community activities and the persistence of criminality. *Development and Psychopathology, 13*(1), 125–141.

Mahoney, J. L., Schweder, A. E., & Stattin, H. (2002). Structured after-school activities as a moderator of depressed mood for adolescents with detached relations to their parents. *Journal of Community Psychology, 30*(1), 69–86.

Mahoney, J. L., & Stattin, H. (2000). Leisure activities and adolescent antisocial behavior: The role of structure and social context. *Journal of Adolescence, 23*(2), 113–127.

Marcia, J. E. (1966). Development and validation of ego-identity status. *Journal of Personality and Social Psychology, 3*(5), 551–558.

Marjanovic, Z., Greenglass, E. R., Struthers, C. W., & Faye, C. (2009). Helping following natural disasters: A social-motivational analysis. *Journal of Applied Social Psychology, 39*(11), 2604–2625.

Marsh, H. W. (1992). Extracurricular activities: Beneficial extension of the traditional curriculum or subversion of academic goals? *Journal of Educational Psychology, 84*(4), 553–562.

Marsh, H. W., & Kleitman, S. (2002). Extracurricular school activities: The good, the bad, and the nonlinear. *Harvard Educational Review,* 72(4), 464–514.

Marsh, H. W., & Kleitman, S. (2003). School athletic participation: Mostly gain with little pain. *Journal of Sport & Exercise Psychology,* 25(2), 205–228.

Masten, A. S. (2011). Resilience in children threatened by extreme adversity: Frameworks for research, practice, and translational synergy. *Development and Psychopathology,* 23(2), 493–506.

Matsuba, M. K., & Walker, L. J. (2004). Extraordinary moral commitment: Young adults involved in social organizations. *Journal of Personality, 72*(2), 413–436.

McAdam, D. (1988). *Freedom summer*. New York: Oxford University Press.

McAdam, D. (1989). The biographical consequences of activism. *American Sociological Review, 54*(5), 744–760.

McAdams, D. P., Bauer, J. J., Sakaeda, A. R., Anyidoho, N. A., Machado, M. A., Magrino-Failla, K., White, K. W., & Pals, J. L. (2006). Continuity and change in the life story: A longitudinal study of autobiographical memories in emerging adulthood. *Journal of Personality, 74*(5), 1371–1400.

McClurg, S. D. (2003). Social networks and political participation: The role of social interaction in explaining political participation. *Political Research Quarterly, 56*(4), 449–464.

McClurg, S. D. (2006). Political disagreement in context: The conditional effect of neighborhood context, disagreement and political talk on electoral participation. *Political Behavior, 28*(4), 349–366.

McDevitt, M., & Chaffee, S. (2000). Closing gaps in political communication and knowledge: Effects of a school intervention. *Communication Research, 27*(3), 259–292.

McDevitt, M., & Kiousis, S. (2007). The red and blue of adolescence: Origins of the compliant voter and the defiant activist. *American Behavioral Scientist, 50*(9), 1214–1230.

McFarland, D. A., & Thomas, R. J. (2006). Bowling young: How youth voluntary associations influence adult political participation. *American Sociological Review, 71*(3), 401–425.

McHoskey, J. W. (1999). Machiavellianism, intrinsic versus extrinsic goals, and social interest: A self-determination theory analysis. *Motivation and Emotion, 23*(4), 267–283.

McIntosh, H., Hart, D., & Youniss, J. (2007). The influence of family political discussion on youth civic development: Which parent qualities matter? *PS-Political Science & Politics, 40*(3), 495–499.

McKenzie, B. D. (2004). Religious social networks, indirect mobilization, and African-American political participation. *Political Research Quarterly, 57*(4), 621–632.

McLellan, J. A., & Youniss, J. (2003). Two systems of youth service: Determinants of voluntary and required youth community service. *Journal of Youth and Adolescence, 32*(1), 47–58.

McLeod, J. M. (2000). Media and civic socialization of youth. *Journal of Adolescent Health, 27*(2), 45–51.

McNeal, R. B. (1999). Participation in high school extracurricular activities: Investigating school effects. *Social Science Quarterly, 80*(2), 291–309.

Meier, S., & Stutzer, A. (2008). Is volunteering rewarding in itself? *Economica, 75*, 39–59.

Melchior, A. (1999). *Summary report: National evaluation of Learn and Serve America*. Waltham, MA: Center for Human Resources, Brandeis University.

Merriam-Webster On-Line Dictionary (no date). *Definition of "citizenship."* http://www.merriam-webster.com/dictionary/citizenship

Metz, E., McLellan, J., & Youniss, J. (2003). Types of voluntary service and adolescents' civic development. *Journal of Adolescent Research, 18*(2), 188–203.

Metz, E., & Youniss, J. (2003). A demonstration that school-based required service does not deter—but heightens—volunteerism. *PS-Political Science & Politics, 36*(2), 281–286.

Metz, E. C., & Youniss, J. (2005). Longitudinal gains in civic development through school-based required service. *Political Psychology, 26*(3), 413–437.

Metzger, A., Dawes, N., Mermelstein, R., & Wakschlag, L. (2011). Longitudinal modeling of adolescents' activity involvement, problem peer associations, and youth smoking. *Journal of Applied Developmental Psychology, 32*(1), 1–9.

Metzger, A., & Smetana, J. G. (2009). Adolescent civic and political engagement: Associations between domain-specific judgments and behavior. *Child Development, 80*(2), 433–441.

Miller, D. L., Scheffler, R., Lam, S., Rosenberg, R., & Rupp, A. (2006). Social capital and health in Indonesia. *World Development, 34*(6), 1084–1098.

Miller, J. M., & Krosnick, J. A. (2004). Threat as a motivator of political activism: A field experiment. *Political Psychology, 25*(4), 507–523.

Mino, M., Deren, S., Kang, S. Y., & Guarino, H. (2011). Associations between political/civic participation and HIV drug injection risk. *American Journal of Drug and Alcohol Abuse, 37*(6), 520–524.

Mishel, L., Bernstein, J., & Allegretto, S. (2007). *The state of working America, 2006/2007*. Ithaca, NY: Cornell University Press.

Moen, P., Dempster-McClain, D., & Williams, R. M. (1989). Social integration and longevity: An event history analysis of women's roles and resilience. *American Sociological Review, 54*(4), 635–647.

Moen, P., Dempster-McClain, D., & Williams, R. M. (1992). Successful aging: A life-course perspective on women's multiple roles and health. *American Journal of Sociology, 97*(6), 1612–1638.

Moos, R. H., & Humphrey, B. (1973). *Group environment scale: Technical report*. Palo Alto, CA: Consulting Psychologists Press.

Morrell, M. E. (2003). Survey and experimental evidence for a reliable and valid measure of internal political efficacy. *Public Opinion Quarterly, 67*(4), 589–602.

Moyers, R. L., & Enright, K. P. (1997). *A snapshot of America's nonprofit boards: Results of the NCNB nonprofit governance survey*. Washington, DC: National Center for Nonprofit Boards.

Musick, M. A., Herzog, A. R., & House, J. S. (1999). Volunteering and mortality among older adults: Findings from a national sample. *Journals of Gerontology Series B-Psychological Sciences and Social Sciences, 54*(3), S173–S180.

Musick, M. A., & Wilson, J. (2003). Volunteering and depression: the role of psychological and social resources in different age groups. *Social Science & Medicine, 56*(2), 259–269.

Musick, M. A., Wilson, J., & Bynum, W. B. (2000). Race and formal volunteering: The differential effects of class and religion. *Social Forces, 78*(4), 1539–1570.

Mussen, P., & Eisenberg-Berg, N. (1977). *Roots of caring, sharing and helping*. San Francisco, CA: Freeman & Company.

Mustillo, S., Wilson, J., & Lynch, S. M. (2004). Legacy volunteering: A test of two theories of intergenerational transmission. *Journal of Marriage and the Family, 66*(2), 530–541.

Mutz, D. C. (2002). The consequences of cross-cutting networks for political participation. *American Journal of Political Science, 46*(4), 838–855.

Narayan, D., & Pritchett, L. (1999). Cents and sociability: Household income and social capital in rural Tanzania. *Economic Development and Cultural Change, 47*(4), 871–897.

National Drug Intelligence Center (2011). *The economic impact of illicit drug use on American society*. Washington, DC: United States Department of Justice. http://www.justice.gov/archive/ndic/pubs44/44731/44731p.pdf

National Institute on Alcohol Abuse and Alcoholism (2005). *Epidemiology of alcohol problems in the United States*. Rockville, MD: U.S. Department of Health and Human Services. http://pubs.niaaa.nih.gov/publications/Social/Module1Epidemiology/Module1.html

Nelson, G., Pancer, S. M., Hayward, K., & Peters, R. D. (2005). *Partnerships for prevention: The story of the Highfield Community Enrichment Project*. Toronto, ON: University of Toronto Press.

Nelson, G. & I. Prilleltensky, I. (Eds.). (2010). *Community psychology: In pursuit of liberation and well-being (2nd edition)*. Hampshire, UK: Palgrave Macmillan.

Newport, F. (2007). *Questions and answers about Americans' religion*. Washington, DC: Gallup. http://www.gallup.com/poll/103459/questions-answers-about-americans-religion.aspx

Niemi, R. G., & Junn, J. (1998). *Civic education: What makes students learn*. New Haven, CT: Yale University Press.

Obradovic, J., & Masten, A. S. (2007). Developmental antecedents of young adult civic engagement. *Applied Developmental Science, 11*(1), 2–19.

Ohmer, M. L. (2007). Organizations and its relationship to volunteers' self- and collective efficacy and sense of community. *Social Work Research, 31*(2), 109–120.

Oliner, S. P., & Oliner, P. M. (1988). *The altruistic personality: Rescuers of Jews in Nazi Europe*. New York: The Free Press.

Oman, D., Thoresen, C. E., & McMahon, K. (1999). Volunteerism and mortality among the community-dwelling elderly. *Journal of Health Psychology, 4*(3), 301–316.

Omoto, A. M., & Snyder, M. (1995). Sustained helping without obligation—motivation, longevity of service, and perceived attitude-change among aids volunteers. *Journal of Personality and Social Psychology, 68*(4), 671–686.

Organization for Economic Cooperation and Development (OECD) (2014). *Trade union density*. Paris, France: OECD Stat.extracts. http://stats.oecd.org/Index.aspx?DataSetCode=UN_DEN

Pancer, S. M. (1997). Program evaluation. In S. W. Sadava & D. R. McCreary (Eds.), *Applied social psychology* (pp. 47–67). Englewood Cliffs, NJ: Prentice Hall.

Pancer, S. M. (2004). *Personal values and youth involvement*. Paper presented at the Biennial Meeting of the Society for Research on Adolescence, Baltimore, MD.

Pancer, S. M. (2005). *Young people a powerful force for good*. Kitchener-Waterloo, ON: *The Record*.

Pancer, S. M., Baetz, M. C., & Rog, E. J. (2002). *Developing an effective corporate volunteer program: Lessons from the Ford Motor Company of Canada*. Toronto, ON: Imagine, Canada.

Pancer, S. M., Brown, S. D., Henderson, A., & Ellis-Hale, K. (2007). *The impact of high school mandatory community service programs on subsequent volunteering and civic engagement*. Toronto, ON: Imagine, Canada.

Pancer, S. M., Brown, S. D., & Barr, C. W. (1999). Forming impressions of political leaders: A cross-national comparison. *Political Psychology, 20*(2), 345–368.

Pancer, S. M., & Cameron, G. (1993). *Better Beginnings, Better Futures resident participation report*. Kingston, ON, Canada: Better Beginnings, Better Futures. http://bbbf.ca/ReportsPublications/tabid/547/language/en-US/Default.aspx

Pancer, S. M., & Cameron, G. (1994). Resident participation in the Better Beginnings, Better Futures prevention project: Part 1—The impacts of involvement. *Canadian Journal of Community Mental Health, 13*, 197–211.

Pancer, S. M., & Eckerle Curwood, S. (2009). *Making a difference: Factors that sustain civic participation of emerging adults*. Paper presented at the Biennial Meeting of the Society for Research in Child Development, Denver, CO.

Pancer, S. M., & Foxall, K. (1998). Our journey from Better Beginnings to Better Futures. Kingston, ON, Canada: Better Beginnings, Better Futures. http://bbbf.ca/ReportsPublications/tabid/547/language/en-US/Default.aspx

Pancer, S. M., Hayward, K., & Heise Bennett, D. (2013). *inREACH: Final process and monitoring evaluation report*. Waterloo, ON, Canada: Crime Prevention Council, Waterloo Region.

Pancer, S. M., & Landau, E. S. (2009). Politics, democracy and the psychology of persuasion. *Journal of Parliamentary and Political Law, 3*(1), 55–80.

Pancer, S. M., & Pratt, M. (1999). Social and family determinants of community service involvement in Canadian youth. In M. Yates & J. Youniss (Eds.), *International perspectives on community service and activism in youth* (pp. 32–55). Cambridge, UK: Cambridge University Press.

Pancer, S. M., Pratt, M., Hunsberger, B., & Alisat, S. (2007). Community and political involvement in adolescence: What distinguishes the activists from the uninvolved? *Journal of Community Psychology, 35*(6), 741–759.

Pancer, S. M., Rose-Krasnor, L., & Loiselle, L. (2002). Youth conferences as a context for engagement. In B. Kirshner, J. L. O'Donoghue, & M. McLaughlin (Eds.). *Youth participation: Improving institutions and communities* (pp. 47–64). New Directions for Youth Development, No. 96. San Francisco, CA: Jossey Bass.

Pancer, S. M., & Westhues, A. (1989). A developmental stage approach to program-planning and evaluation. *Evaluation Review, 13*(1), 56–77.

Parboteeah, K. P., Cullen, J. B., & Lim, L. (2004). Formal volunteering: a cross-national test. *Journal of World Business, 39*(4), 431–441.

Pasek, J., Feldman, L., Romer, D., & Jamieson, K. H. (2008). Schools as incubators of democratic participation: Building long-term political efficacy with civic education. *Applied Developmental Science, 12*(1), 26–37.

Pattie, C., & Johnston, R. (1998). Voter turnout at the British general election of 1992: Rational choice, social standing or political efficacy? *European Journal of Political Research, 33*(2), 263–283.

Pattie, C. J., & Johnston, R. J. (2009). Conversation, disagreement and political participation. *Political Behavior, 31*(2), 261–285.

Patton, M. Q. (2002). *Qualitative research and evaluation methods* (3rd edition). Thousand Oaks, CA: Sage.

Penner, L. A., Brannick, M., Connell, P., & Webb, S. (2005). The effects of the September 11 attacks on volunteering: An archival analysis. *Journal of Applied Social Psychology, 35*, 1333–1360.

Perkins, D. D., Florin, P., Rich, R. C., Wandersman, A., & Chavis, D. M. (1990). Participation and the social and physical-environment of residential blocks: Crime and community context. *American Journal of Community Psychology, 18*(1), 83–115.

Peters, R. D., Bradshaw, A. J., Petrunka, K., Nelson, G., Herry, Y., Craig, W., et al. (2010). *The Better Beginnings, Better Futures Project: An ecological, community-based prevention approach: Findings from Grade 3 to Grade 9*: Monographs of the Society for Research on Child Development.

Piliavin, J. A., & Callero, P. L. (1991). *Giving blood: The development of an altruistic identity.* Baltimore, MD: Johns Hopkins University Press.

Piliavin, J. A., & Siegl, E. (2007). Health benefits of volunteering in the Wisconsin longitudinal study. *Journal of Health and Social Behavior, 48*(4), 450–464.

Points of Light Foundation (2000). *The corporate volunteer program as a strategic resource: The link grows stronger.* Washington, DC: Points of Light Foundation.

Poortinga, W. (2006). Do health behaviors mediate the association between social capital and health? *Preventive Medicine, 43*(6), 488–493.

Pratt, M. W., Hunsberger, B., Pancer, S. M., & Alisat, S. (2003). A longitudinal analysis of personal values socialization: Correlates of a moral self-ideal in late adolescence. *Social Development, 12*(4), 563–585.

Prestby, J. E., Wandersman, A., Florin, P., Rich, R., & Chavis, D. (1990). Benefits, costs, incentive management and participation in voluntary organizations: A means to understanding and promoting empowerment. *American Journal of Community Psychology, 18*(1), 117–149.

Putnam, R. D. (1993). *Making democracy work.* Princeton, N.J.: Princeton University Press.

Putnam, R. D. (2000). *Bowling alone: The collapse and revival of American community.* New York: Simon & Schuster.

Rahn, W. M., & Transue, J. E. (1998). Social trust and value change: The decline of social capital in American youth, 1976-1995. *Political Psychology, 19*(3), 545–565.

Ranson, S., Arnott, M., McKeown, P., Martin, J., & Smith, P. (2005). The participation of volunteer citizens in school governance. *Educational Review, 57*(3), 357–371.

Rappaport, J. (1987). Terms of empowerment exemplars of prevention: Toward a theory for community psychology. *American Journal of Community Psychology, 15*(2), 121–148.

Rappaport, J. (1995). Empowerment meets narrative: Listening to stories and creating settings. *American Journal of Community Psychology, 23*(5), 795–807.

Rappaport, J. (1998). *The art of social change: Community narratives as resources for individual and collective identity.* Newbury Park, CA: Sage Publications Inc.

Rappaport, J. (2000). Community narratives: Tales of terror and joy. *American Journal of Community Psychology, 28*(1), 1–24.

Reinders, H., & Youniss, J. (2006). School-based required community service and civic development in adolescents. *Applied Developmental Science, 10*(1), 2–12.

Reno, R. R., Cialdini, R. B., & Kallgren, C. A. (1993). The transsituational influence of social norms. *Journal of Personality and Social Psychology, 64*(1), 104–112.

Rhodes, J. E. (2004). The critical ingredient: Caring youth-staff relationships in after-school settings *New Directions for Youth Development, 101*, 145–161.

Rice, M. E., & Grusec, J. E. (1975). Saying and doing: Effects on observer performance. *Journal of Personality and Social Psychology, 32*(4), 584–593.

Roese, N. J., & Sande, G. N. (1993). Backlash effects in attack politics. *Journal of Applied Social Psychology, 23*(8), 632–653.
Rog, E. J., Pancer, S. M., & Baetz, M. C. (2004). *Community and corporate perspectives on corporate volunteer programs: A win-win approach to community betterment.* Toronto. Toronto, ON: Imagine, Canada.
Rohan, M. J., & Zanna, M. P. (1996). Value transmission in families. In C. Seligman, J. M. Olson & M. P. Zanna (Eds.), *The psychology of values: The Ontario symposium* (vol. 8, pp. 253–276). Hillsdale, NJ: Erlbaum.
Roker, D., Player, K., & Coleman, J. (1999). Young people's voluntary and campaigning activities as sources of political education. *Oxford Review of Education, 25*(1–2), 185–198.
Rook, K. S., & Sorkin, D. H. (2003). Fostering social ties through a volunteer role: Implications for older-adults' psychological health. *International Journal of Aging & Human Development, 57*(4), 313–337.
Rooney, B. L., & Murray, D. M. (1996). A meta-analysis of smoking prevention programs after adjustment for errors in the unit of analysis. *Health Education Quarterly, 23*(1), 48–64.
Rose-Krasnor, L. (2008). Future directions in youth involvement research. *Social Development, 18*(2), 497–509.
Rose-Krasnor, L., Busseri, M. A., Willoughby, T., & Chalmers, H. (2006). Breadth and intensity of youth activity involvement as contexts for positive development. *Journal of Youth and Adolescence, 35*(3), 385–399.
Rosenberg, M. (1965). *Society and the adolescent self-image.* Princeton, NJ: Princeton University Press.
Rosenfeld, R., Messner, S. F., & Baumer, E. P. (2001). Social capital and homicide. *Social Forces, 80*(1), 283–310.
Rosenthal, S., Feiring, C., & Lewis, M. (1998). Political volunteering from late adolescence to young adulthood: Patterns and predictors. *Journal of Social Issues, 54*(3), 477–493.
Ruiter, S., & De Graaf, N. D. (2006). National context, religiosity, and volunteering: Results from 53 countries. *American Sociological Review, 71*(2), 191–210.
Saphir, M. N., & Chaffee, S. H. (2002). Adolescents' contributions to family communication patterns. *Human Communication Research, 28*(1), 86–108.
Saxon-Harrold, S. K. E., Weiner, S. J., McCormack, M. T., & Weber, M. A. (2000). *America's religious congregations: Measuring their contributions to society.* Washington, DC: Independent Sector.
Scales, P. C., Benson, P. L., & Roehlkepartain, E. C. (2011). Adolescent thriving: The role of sparks, relationships, and empowerment. *Journal of Youth and Adolescence, 40*(3), 263–277.
Scales, P. C., & Roehlkepartain, E. C. (2004). *Community service and service-learning in U.S. public schools, 2004: Findings from a national survey.* St. Paul, MN: National Youth Leadership Council.
Scheffler, R. M., Brown, T. T., Syme, L., Kawachi, I., Tolstykh, I., & Iribarren, C. (2008). Community-level social capital and recurrence of acute coronary syndrome. *Social Science & Medicine, 66*(7), 1603–1613.
Scheufele, D. A., Nisbet, M. C., & Brossard, D. (2003). Pathways to political participation? Religion, communication contexts, and mass media. *International Journal of Public Opinion Research, 15*(3), 300–324.
Scheufele, D. A., Nisbet, M. C., Brossard, D., & Nisbet, E. C. (2004). Social structure and citizenship: Examining the impacts of social setting, network heterogeneity, and informational variables on political participation. *Political Communication, 21*(3), 315–338.
Schmidt, J. A., Shumow, L., & Kackar, H. (2007). Adolescents' participation in service activities and its impact on academic, behavioral, and civic outcomes. *Journal of Youth and Adolescence, 36*(2), 127–140.
Schussman, A., & Soule, S. A. (2005). Process and protest: Accounting for individual protest participation. *Social Forces, 84*(2), 1083–1108.

Schwadel, P. (2005). Individual, congregational, and denominational effects on church members' civic participation. *Journal for the Scientific Study of Religion, 44*(2), 159–171.

Schwartz, S. H. (1992). Universals in the content of social values: Theoretical advances and empirical tests in 20 countries. In M. P. Zanna (Ed.), *Advances in experimental social psychology, Vol. 25* (pp. 1–65). New York: Academic Press.

Schwartz, S. H. (1994). Are there universal aspects in the structure and contents of human-values. *Journal of Social Issues, 50*(4), 19–45.

Schwartz, S. H. (2010). Basic values: How they motivate and inhibit prosocial behavior. In Mikulincer, M. & Shaver, P. R. (Eds), (2010). *Prosocial motives, emotions, and behavior: The better angels of our nature.* (pp. 221–241). Washington, DC: American Psychological Association.

Semenza, J. C., Rubin, C. H., Falter, K. H., Selanikio, J. D., Flanders, W. D., Howe, H. L., et al. (1996). Heat-related deaths during the July 1995 heat wave in Chicago. *New England Journal of Medicine, 335*(2), 84–90.

Serow, R. C., & Dreyden, J. I. (1990). Community-service among college and university-students—individual and institutional relationships. *Adolescence, 25*(99), 553–566.

Shah, D. V., Kwak, N., & Holbert, R. L. (2001). "Connecting" and "disconnecting" with civic life: Patterns of Internet use and the production of social capital. *Political Communication, 18*(2), 141–162.

Sherkat, D. E., & Blocker, T. J. (1993). Environmental activism in the protest generation: Differentiating 1960s activists. *Youth & Society, 25*(1), 140–161.

Sherkat, D. E., & Blocker, T. J. (1997). Explaining the political and personal consequences of protest. *Social Forces, 75*(3), 1049–1070.

Skinner, R., & Chapman, C. (1999). *Service-learning and community service in K-12 public schools* (NCES 1999-043). Washington, DC: U.S. Department of Education, National Center for Education Statistics.

Smetana, J. G., & Metzger, A. (2005). Family and religious antecedents of civic involvement in middle class African American late adolescents. *Journal of Research on Adolescence, 15*(3), 325–352.

Smith, A., Schlozman, K. L., Verba, S., & Brady, H. (2009). *The internet and civic engagement.* Washington, DC: Pew Internet & American Life Project, Pew Research Center. http://www.pewinternet.org/Reports/2009/15--The-Internet-and-Civic-Engagement.aspx

Smith, C., & Faris, R. (2002). *Religion and American adolescent delinquency: Risk behaviors and constructive social activities.* (National Study of Youth and Religion, CB #3057). Chapel Hill, NC: The University of North Carolina.

Smith, E. S. (1999). The effects of investments in the social capital of youth on political and civic behavior in young adulthood: A longitudinal analysis. *Political Psychology, 20*(3), 553–580.

Smith, J. R., & McSweeney, A. (2007). Charitable giving: The effectiveness of a revised theory of planned behaviour model in predicting donating intentions and behaviour. *Journal of Community & Applied Social Psychology, 17*(5), 363–386.

Spring, K., Grimm, R., & Dietz, N. (2008). *Community service learning in America's schools.* Washington, DC: Office of Research & Policy Development, Corporation for National and Community Service.

Staub, E. (1991). Altruistic and moral motivations for helping and their translation into action. *Psychological Inquiry, 2*(2), 150–153.

Stearns, E., & Glennie, E. J. (2010). Opportunities to participate: Extracurricular activities' distribution across and academic correlates in high schools. *Social Science Research, 39*(2), 296–309.

Stiglitz, J. E. (2012). *The price of inequality: How today's divided society endangers our future.* New York: W.W. Norton & Co.

Stukas, A. A., Snyder, M., & Clary, E. G. (1999). The effects of "mandatory volunteerism" on intentions to volunteer. *Psychological Science, 10*(1), 59–64.

Talo, C., Mannarini, T., & Rochira, A. (2014). Sense of community and community participation: A meta-analytic review. *Social Indicators Research, 117*(1), 1–28.

Tashakkori, A., & Teddlie, C. (Eds.). (2003). *Handbook of mixed methods in social and behavioral research*. Thousand Oaks, CA: Sage.

Taylor, T. P., & Pancer, S. M. (2007). Community service experiences and commitment to volunteering. *Journal of Applied Social Psychology, 37*(2), 320–345.

Thoits, P. A., & Hewitt, L. N. (2001). Volunteer work and well-being. *Journal of Health and Social Behavior, 42*(2), 115–131.

Thompson, A. (1993). Rural emergency volunteers and their communities: A demographic comparison. *Journal of Community Health, 18*, 379–393.

Tieu, T. T., & Pancer, S. M. (2009). Youth involvement and first-year students' transition to university. *Journal of the First-Year Experience and Students in Transition, 21*, 43–63.

Tieu, T. T., Pancer, S. M., Pratt, M. W., Wintre, M. G., Birnie-Lefcovitch, S., Polivy, J., & Adams, G. (2010). Helping out or hanging out: the features of involvement and how it relates to university adjustment. *Higher Education, 60*(3), 343–355.

Torney-Purta, J., & Amadeo, J. A. (2003). A cross-national analysis of political and civic involvement among adolescents. *PS-Political Science & Politics, 36*(2), 269–274.

Torney-Purta, J., Lehmann, R., Oswald, H., & Shulz, W. (Eds.). (2001). *Citizenship and education in twenty-eight countries: Civic knowledge and engagement at age fourteen*. Amsterdam: IEA.

Triandis, H. C. (1995). *Individualism and collectivism*. Boulder, CO: Westview Press.

Troll, L. E., Neugarten, B. L., & Kraines, R. J. (1969). Similarities in values and other personality characteristics in college students and their parents. *Merrill-Palmer Quarterly of Behavior and Development, 15*(4), 323–336.

Tufekci, Z., & Wilson, C. (2012). Social media and the decision to participate in political protest: Observations from Tahrir Square. *Journal of Communication, 62*(2), 363–379.

Uggen, C., & Janikula, J. (1999). Volunteerism and arrest in the transition to adulthood. *Social Forces, 78*(1), 331–362.

Unger, D. G., & Wandersman, A. (1985). The importance of neighbors: The social, cognitive, and affective components of neighboring. *American Journal of Community Psychology, 13*(2), 139–169.

U.S. Department of Labor. (2013). *Volunteering in the United States 2012 (USDL-13-0285)*. Washington, DC: U.S. Department of Labor, Bureau of Labor Statistics. http://www.bls.gov/news.release/pdf/volun.pdf

U.S. Department of Labor. (2014). *Union members summary (USDL-14-0095)*. Washington, DC: U.S. Department of Labor, Bureau of Labor Statistics. http://www.bls.gov/news.release/union2.nr0.htm

U.S. Department of Health and Human Services (1999). *Mental health: A report of the Surgeon General*. Rockville, MD: U.S. Department of Health and Human Services. http://profiles.nlm.nih.gov/ps/retrieve/ResourceMetadata/NNBBHS

Uslaner, E. M. (2002). Religion and civic engagement in Canada and the United States. *Journal for the Scientific Study of Religion, 41*(2), 239–254.

Uslaner, E. M., & Brown, M. (2005). Inequality, trust, and civic engagement. *American Politics Research, 33*(6), 868–894.

Verba, S., Schlozman, K. L., & Brady, H. E. (1995). *Voice and equality: Civic voluntarism in American politics*. Cambridge, MA: Harvard University Press.

Vezina, M., & Crompton, S. (2012). *Volunteering in Canada*. Ottawa, ON, Canada: Statistics Canada. http://www.statcan.gc.ca/pub/11-008-x/2012001/article/11638-eng.pdf

Wandersman, A., & Giamartino, G. A. (1980). Community and individual difference characteristics as influences on initial participation. *American Journal of Community Psychology, 8*(2), 217–228.

Warburton, J., & Smith, J. (2003). Out of the generosity of your heart: Are we creating active citizens through compulsory volunteer programmes for young people in Australia? *Social Policy & Administration, 37*(7), 772–786.

Ware, J. E., Snow, K. K., Kosinski, M. A., & Gandek, M. S. (1993). *SF-36 health survey manual and interpretation guide*. Boston, MA: The Health Institute, New England Medical Centre.

Watts, R. J., & Flanagan, C. (2007). Pushing the envelope on youth civic engagement: A developmental and liberation psychology perspective. *Journal of Community Psychology, 35*(6), 779–792.

Weitzman, E. R., & Kawachi, I. (2000). Giving means receiving: The protective effect of social capital on binge drinking on college campuses. *American Journal of Public Health, 90*(12), 1936–1939.

West, D. M. (2009). *2008 campaign ads hit an all-time low*. Washington, DC: Brookings. http://www.brookings.edu/opinions/2008/0916_campaignads_west.aspx

Westheimer, J., & Kahne, J. (2004). What kind of citizen? The politics of educating for democracy. *American Educational Research Journal, 41*(2), 237–269.

Westholm, A. (1999). The perceptual pathway: Tracing the mechanisms of political value transfer across generations. *Political Psychology, 20*(3), 525–551.

Wilkinson, R. G., & Pickett, K. (2009). *The spirit level: Why more equal societies almost always do better*. London: Allen Lane.

Wilson, J. (2000). Volunteering. *Annual Review of Sociology, 26*, 215–240.

Wilson, J., & Musick, M. (1997). Who cares? Toward an integrated theory of volunteer work. *American Sociological Review, 62*(5), 694–713.

Wintre, M. G., Yaffe, M., & Crowley, J. (1995). Perception of parental reciprocity scale (POPRS): Development and validation with adolescents and young adults. *Social Development, 4*(2), 129–148.

Wood, D., Larson, R. W., & Brown, J. R. (2009). How adolescents come to see themselves as more responsible through participation in youth programs. *Child Development, 80*(1), 295–309.

Wood, R. L., & Warren, M. R. (2002). A different face of faith-based politics: Social capital and community organizing in the public arena. *International Journal of Sociology and Social Policy, 22*(9/10), 6–54.

Wyatt, R. O., Katz, E., & Kim, J. (2000). Bridging the spheres: Political and personal conversation in public and private spaces. *Journal of Communication, 50*(1), 71–92.

Xu, Q. W., Perkins, D. D., & Chow, J. C. C. (2010). Sense of community, neighboring, and social capital as predictors of local political participation in China. *American Journal of Community Psychology, 45*(3–4), 259–271.

Yagmurlu, B., & Sanson, A. (2009). Parenting and temperament as predictors of prosocial behaviour in Australian and Turkish Australian children. *Australian Journal of Psychology, 61*(2), 77–88.

Yates, M., & Youniss, J. (1996). Community service and political-moral identity in adolescents. *Journal of Research on Adolescence, 6*(3), 271–284.

Yates, M., & Youniss, J. (1997). *Community service and social responsibility in youth*. Chicago: University of Chicago Press.

Yates, M., & Youniss, J. (1998). Community service and political identity development in adolescence. *Journal of Social Issues, 54*(3), 495–512.

Youniss, J. (2011). Civic education: What schools can do to encourage civic identity and action. *Applied Developmental Science, 15*(2), 98–103.

Youniss, J., McLellan, J. A., & Yates, M. (1997). What we know about engendering civic identity. *American Behavioral Scientist, 40*(5), 620–631.

Youniss, J., McLellan, J. A., & Yates, M. (1999). Religion, community service, and identity in American youth. *Journal of Adolescence, 22*(2), 243–253.

Youniss, J., & Reinders, H. (2010). Youth and community service: A review of U.S. research, a theoretical perspective, and implications for policy in Germany. *Zeitschrift Fur Erziehungswissenschaft, 13*(2), 233–248.

Youniss, J., & Yates, M. (1997). *Community service and social responsibility in youth*. Chicago: University of Chicago Press.

Zaff, J. F., Malanchuk, O., & Eccles, J. S. (2008). Predicting positive citizenship from adolescence to young adulthood: The effects of a civic context. *Applied Developmental Science, 12*(1), 38–53.

Zaff, J. F., Moore, K. A., Papillo, A. R., & Williams, S. (2003). Implications of extracurricular activity participation during adolescence on positive outcomes. *Journal of Adolescent Research, 18*(6), 599–630.

Zeldin, S. (2004). Preventing youth violence through the promotion of community engagement and membership. *Journal of Community Psychology, 32*(5), 623–641.

Zeldin, S., McDaniel, A. K., Topitzes, D., & Calvert, M. (2000). *Youth in decision-making: A study on the impacts of youth on adults and organizations.* Madison, WI: Department of Human Development and Familty Studies, University of Wisconsin Extension.

Zimmerman, M. A., & Rappaport, J. (1988). Citizen participation, perceived control, and psychological empowerment. *American Journal of Community Psychology, 16*(5), 725–750.

Zukin, C., Keeter, S., Andolina, M., Jenkins, K., & Delli Karpini, M. X. (2006). *A new engagement: Political participation, civic life, and the changing American citizen.* New York: Oxford.

ABOUT THE AUTHOR

Dr. Mark Pancer is Professor Emeritus of Psychology at Wilfrid Laurier University in Waterloo, Ontario, Canada. His research on civic participation has been published in a wide range of journals, both within and outside his home discipline of psychology. He has contributed chapters to several books, and is coauthor of the book *Partnerships for Prevention: The Story of the Highfield Community Enrichment Project.* Professor Pancer was elected Fellow of the Canadian Psychological Association in 1993 in recognition of his contributions to the science and profession of psychology in Canada.

INDEX

Page numbers for boxes are followed by b, figures by f, and tables by t.

CPSIA information can be obtained
at www.ICGtesting.com
Printed in the USA
BVHW040055040820
585262BV00010B/274

9 780199 752126